# THE CHURCH, SOCIETY, AND HEGEMONY

# The Church, Society, and Hegemony

## A CRITICAL SOCIOLOGY OF RELIGION IN LATIN AMERICA

Carlos Alberto Torres

TRANSLATED BY
Richard A. Young

Westport, Connecticut
London

**Library of Congress Cataloging-in-Publication Data**

Torres, Carlos Alberto.
 The Church, society, and hegemony : a critical sociology of
religion in Latin America / Carlos Alberto Torres ; translated by
Richard A. Young.
  p.   cm.
 Includes bibliographical references and index.
 ISBN 0-275-93773-9 (alk. paper)
  1. Sociology, Christian—Latin America.  2. Religion and
sociology—History.  3. Catholic Church—Argentina.  4. Church and
state—Argentina.  5. Argentina—Church history.   I. Title.
 BR600. T67     1992
 306.6′098—dc20           92-9118

British Library Cataloguing in Publication Data is available.

Library of Congress Catalog Card Number: 92-9118
ISBN: 0-275-93773-9

First published in 1992

Praeger Publishers, 88 Post Road West, Westport, CT 06881
An imprint of Greenwood Publishing Group, Inc.

Printed in the United States of America

The paper used in this book complies with the Permanent
Paper Standard issued by the National Information Standards
Organization (Z39.48-1984).

10  9  8  7  6  5  4  3  2  1

To my father,
Domingo Roberto Torres,
*in memoriam*

# Contents

# Foreword

*The Church, Society and Hegemony: A Critical Sociology of Religion in Latin America*, by the noted Latin American sociologist Carlos Alberto Torres, is a welcome addition to the specialized literature. This book may be seen as composed of three parts. The first section, from Chapter 1 to Chapter 5—in which a number of classical writers are re-interpreted—provides a sociological framework for the study of religion. In the second section, Chapters 6 to 8, the author delves into the general theme of his work: the question of the "Popular Church" in Latin America. Finally, Chapter 9 is concerned with the Church in Argentina, from the colonization until the generation of 1880, through the period of military repression between 1976 and 1983, to the emergence of Argentine democracy after 1983.

Marx's view of the religious question is placed within the context of Marx's reception in Latin American theological and religious circles, especially in relation to the position of Hugo Assmann. The review of Durkheim and Weber highlights categories that Torres will later use in his concrete interpretation of the Latin American and the Argentinean Church. But it is especially in his study of Antonio Gramsci that Torres establishes the horizons of his analysis. Gramsci's concept of hegemony in reference to the state and his concept of "intellectuals" with respect to the church is not surprising given that, at the beginning of this century the situation in Italy, like in no other European country, including Spain, had much in common with that of Latin America and particularly Argentina. Gramsci is therefore a theorist whose ideas may be very usefully applied to the study of religion and the Church in Latin America. In Chapter 5, focusing primarily on the contribution of the Chilean sociologist J. Joaquín Brunner, but using other writers as well, Torres begins to develop his hypothesis of the Church as a fundamental institution in the reproduction of social life, as a "disciplinary order," both in its internal structure and its relation to society at large.

As is argued in the second part of the book, the Popular Church (or church of the poor) implies a contradiction with respect to the traditional functions assigned to religious institutions of social mediation. Torres skillfully shows how Christian communities assume a critical function, both from the perspective of theological interpretations and from a praxis of contestation. The concept of the "popular" becomes central, on account of its political implications, and there emerges the figure of a "prophetic (even 'revolutionary') Christian." Among religious experiences of the twentieth century, it is one of the most interesting sociological phenomena.

It is this concept that allows Torres, in Chapter 7, to offer a critique of some of the typologies in vogue (such as Vallier's) that seek to describe the different tendencies (political as well as ideological) within the Catholic Church, and to propose a comprehensive typology that combines a technical-theological criterion, an "internal Church praxis" criterion, a strictly ideological and political criterion, and a "social praxis" criterion. In his typology Torres proposes the categories of "neo-Christianity," "social Christianity," and "socialism." In my own work I have argued that "social-Christianity" could be designated under the heading of "neo-Christendom" because it was inspired by Jacques Maritain, and that "neo-Christianity" might also be read as "traditional conservatism." Torres is aware of these distinctions when he argues, in Chapter 9, that "the Argentine church, as a church of Christendom and a traditional intellectual, has subtly influenced the constitution of common sense of both the popular and hegemonic classes" but concludes that "although the Church was able to exert a certain cultural influence, this was not sufficient to constitute political hegemony." Highlighting some of the most salient ideological features of the radical Christian movements in the region, features which may have contributed to undermining of the Catholic Church's search for political hegemony in the 1960s and 1970s, Torres chooses the term "socialism" to classify them, emphasizing their anti-capitalist character and orientation. Perhaps the term "anticapitalism," rather than "socialism," would be more appropriate if one wishes to include the theologians of liberation and the base church communities of social-democratic origins, many of which have not entirely accepted traditional historical materialist approaches. Torres, in discussing the crisis of the Catholic Church in the last two decades, has developed some of these distinctions.

In view of the above, the chapter on "The Catholic Church in Argentina" provides an excellent concrete case study, because in Argentina we find ourselves in a highly polarized situation, which some of the "types" proposed occur in an almost pure state. The author, who knows the subject at first hand, extends his analysis to the present and offers a fine-tuned theoretical framework. This topic will continue to be relevant throughout the 1990s, given that Protestant churches as well as the Catholic Church are increasingly becoming active institutions in the daily life of Latin America.

Enrique Dussel
Universidad Autónoma Metropolitana-
Iztapalapa (Mexico)
President, Study of History of the Church
of Latin America, CEHILA

# Preface

The purpose of this book is to revive an important part of the philosophical and social tradition associated with analysis of the religious phenomenon and its forms, a tradition that, for many reasons, has not been adopted, systematized, criticized, and reformulated in Latin America.

Virtually all the great philosophers and social scientists have broached the subject of the religious; and for some, it has been a real obsession. It was Hegel, for instance, who decisively touched on the influence of political problems on religious beliefs and practices in his first theological writings, while studying with Schelling and Hölderlin at the Theological University of Tübingen. Herbert Marcuse suggested that his term *Volksgeist* refers to the spirit of a nation, its history, its religion and the degree of political involvement obtained by religion, aspects that may not be separated with respect to either their influence or their quality. In Hegel they are interwoven, forming a single entity. His Volksgeist is therefore closely related to Montesquieu's reference to the *esprit général* of a nation as the foundation of its political and social laws. Thus, at least since Hegel, discussion of the close ties between religion and politics has not been a matter of sudden intellectual interest

The indignation of Marx and Engels was quite genuine when they pointed out in 1845 that subservience to Hegel was the reason why a broad critique of Hegelianism had not been attempted, and they remarked that certain "pure and authentic" categories such as "substance" and "self-consciousness" had been adopted only to be debased subsequently by more vulgar names such as "Species," "the One Being," and "Man" (Marx & Engels, 1970: 17). Marx's critique of this debasement of Hegel's Volksgeist led him to propose an analytical approach to ideology and an entire series of sociocultural, political, and economic phenomena that eventually constituted the true nerve-center for the development of the social sciences and philosophy.

In the light of the preceding comments, the key concern of this book is to inquire into the intellectual production of social scientists who, beginning with the critical milieu of post-Hegelianism, focused their study of the religious phenomenon and its forms within the context of the emerging capitalist mode of production. Thus, Chapters 1–4 are devoted to a critical rereading of the religious question in Karl Marx, Emile Durkheim, Max Weber, and Antonio Gramsci. Without attempting a systematic confrontation among these alternatives, it is intended to retrieve the fundamental theoretical coordinates that have been introduced in one form or another and reappear time and again in the few critical studies of religion in Latin America that exist. Chapter 5, by seeking to demonstrate that these writers share the same fundamental concern in endeavoring to show the connections between religion and the reproduction of the social order, is intended to indicate how this concern identifies and defines the principal areas of an agenda for a critical inquiry into the sociology of religion.

The next chapters refer to recent historical processes and analyze the connections among religion, the churches, and social praxis in Latin America. The central phenomenon and true epicenter of many of the discussions on religion in Latin America is the rise and consolidation of a "Popular Church," a subject dealt with in Chapter 6. The Popular Church and especially Liberation Theology appear today as phenomena that are decidedly Latin American in origin. In the opinion of Catholic orthodoxy, as expressed by Cardinal Joseph Ratzinger, prefect of the Sacred Congregation for the Doctrine of the Faith, they "have contributed like 'evangelical leavening' to the awakening of the consciousness of the oppressed"—recognition indeed from those who deny theological legitimacy to the Theology of Liberation (Sacred Congregation, 1984) at the same time as they seek to silence some of its most stimulating voices, such as that of the Brazilian Franciscan Leonardo Boff.

This new political-religious environment associated with the Popular Church is analyzed in Chapter 7 in the light of a systematization, analysis and critique of the internal tendencies of the Catholic Church in Latin

America—an exercise that will allow us to sketch the broader outlines of the different philosophical, political, and theological positions within the Church in the Continent (i.e., the Americas and particularly, in this book, Latin America). On this basis, Chapter 8 proposes a theoretical framework for religion and Churches in Latin America that is intended to contribute to empirical research on the subject. Like all the chapters of the book hitherto, its central concern is eminently theoretical and therefore analytical. For this reason, reference to concrete processes is for the purpose of illustration only and is not intended to provide historical or political analyses of recent phenomena. Such an approach is reserved for our final chapter, Chapter 9, which is an extended commentary on the State, the Catholic Church, and hegemony in Argentina.

Any discussion of religion always has a high emotional tone, a polemical air, and irreconcilable theoretical and ethical positions. This is inevitable. The first condition for any analysis is a complete empirical docility with respect to the reality that is to be studied, described, and explained in a particular theoretical context; thus, in order to undertake a detailed inquiry into such an emotional and contentious subject, we have opted for a certain "methodological atheism." It is for the reader to judge the originality and analytical rigor of our results.

## TRANSLATOR'S NOTE

Most of the citations of Dr. Torres's manuscript are in Spanish, many from original sources in that language, but many are from translations into Spanish from other languages. Although I have given all his citations in English, I have used published English sources whenever possible, and I am grateful to Ana López San Miguel for her assistance in locating them. (R.A.Y.)

# 1

## The Critique of Religion in Marx

The literature on the subject of Marx's critique of religion is vast, and it would be naive to attempt a summary of the major lines of discussion in the limited space allowed in the present study. However, it seems useful to give a brief presentation of the central problems and to organize them in terms of a discussion undertaken from a general theoretical and, in some respects, comparative perspective.

Whenever the Marxist critique of religion is reviewed it is customary to point out that Karl Marx was the recipient of the thought of Ludwig Feuerbach, taking from him the concept of religion as self-alienating.

Theologians and speculative philosophers, allow me to give you this advice: free yourselves of your metaphysical preconceptions and prejudices if you want to reach things as they really are, that is to say, the truth. And there is no other way to reach truth and freedom than that which goes through Feuerbach. This river of fire is the Purgatory of the present. (Marx, [1843] 1927: 175)

Although he recognized his debt, Marx objected that Feuerbach, even after he unmasked the illusory character of the claims of religion—that is to say, after he located the "essence" of religion in humanity—was wrong to treat the human being as an abstract entity. Feuerbach forgot that human beings, as a result of their own reality, were the sum of social relations, from which it followed that their "religious conscience" had to be considered as an eminently social product. As Joaquin Matthes states, the abstract individual analyzed by Feuerbach belongs to a concrete social form.

Taking note of the historical reality of Christianity, Marx energetically opposes the reification to which religion is submitted in Feuerbach's theory. For Marx, religion is a radically historical category. It is just that, according to him, the historicity of (the Christian) religion is *concrete* and *definite*; religion arose in particular historical circumstances; as a form of social consciousness it responds to a specific period of history in human society and will disappear when this period reaches its end. And since the history of human society is made by humans the transcending of that period and its corresponding social consciousness is the responsibility of human action. The critique of religion is no more than a first step towards the revolutionary transformation of social relations that nurture religion. (Matthes, 1971, vol. 1: 72)

However, Feuerbach is not the only source of Marx's inspiration. Some authors even dispute the hypothesis that Feuerbach's influence was the basic one that dominated the direction he took on religion. According to Charles Wackenheim,

Hegelianism is not the only source of the thought of the young Marx. The complex character of the theory of religion in Marx is testimony to the variety of influences. Epicurus, Spinoza and the French Encyclopaedists stand alongside Bauer and Feuerbach. The philosophy of Enlightenment and Romanticism provide Marx with themes and arguments. It even occurs that currents of thought repudiated in other respects, nurture his critique of religion. But, after Hegel, the influence of Feuerbach appears to be the decisive one—at least at the level of expression. Marx owes much to Feuerbach in relation to his critique of Hegelianism, but we believe that we have demonstrated sufficiently that the central intuition of Marxist theory is prior to and outside the influence of Feuerbach. (Wackenheim, 1973: 352)

When discussing the critique of religion in Marx, it is less common to point out that it reclaims and is nurtured by the entire critical tradition of the eighteenth and nineteenth centuries, particularly French Materialism, the Encyclopedists, and the philosophy of the German Enlightenment before G.W.F. Hegel. It is therefore important to locate the cultural environment in which Marx's critique takes shape and to know many of its basic assumptions. In what follows the most important tenets of the "classical" critique of religion are stated.

First, the claims of religion are the products of human beings. They project their fears, desires, and ideals into a hypothetical world, separate from the material, concrete one in which they exist, and endow this "supernatural" world with extraordinary and unusual powers the balance of which hinges basically on the person of a Superior Being with the dual function of serving as creator of the universe (the prime cause of all things) as well as its regulator (its arbitrator and judge).

Second, this projection has important psychological functions to the extent that it compensates for the experience of frustrations on this earth and projects the complexes of desires, plans, and sensations unrealizable in a human world onto another beyond it.[1]

Third, even when religion has subjective equilibratory functions it hinders self-realization, because its institutionalization as the mediation between natural and cultural processes prevents self-objectification. It keeps humans submerged in a naive awareness of their reality, preventing them from developing a scientific attitude toward it.

Fourth and finally, as a result of the institutionalization of religion as a social phenomenon, it is used by those who hold power (whether the nobility under feudalism or the bourgeoisie under capitalism) as an institution of social control, and, above all, as a factor in the creation of an anthropological schizophrenia. A temporal dualism[2] is thereby established which, by projecting a here and a beyond in the form of a corporeal and a transcendental entity, grants the latter the possibility of the ultimate and true fulfillment of Humanity and leaves to the former only a transitory stage of ephemeral value and potential.[3] Thus the manipulation of the present is facilitated by the disorganization of the classes and subordinate sectors of society, who are steeped in a pietist and, above all, a "metaphysical" outlook, which, more strictly speaking, is an eschatological and cosmological point of view.

Given the origins of the materialist critique of religion, where, then, is the originality of the Marxist approach? It lies fundamentally in the association of the religious phenomenon with the theory of false consciousness. In other words, in the categorical affirmation that all religion is an ideology. For historical materialism, as Leo Kofler has pointed out, all history that has elapsed to date is the history of the antinomy between being and consciousness, so that every ideology, placed beyond the fundamental axes and the laws of development of the social being, therefore constitutes a false consciousness of reality (Kofler, 1968).

The reasoning is relatively simple. According to Marx, the capitalist production of commodities by means of other commodities reifies the human being. But human beings are reified (*Verdinglichung*) not only with respect to their real relation to the objective, which is, at the same time, a negation of the necessary process of objectification (*Versachlichung*) referred to by Hegel, but also with respect to their own mind, where the rational process corresponding anthropologically to the development of self-consciousness—Hegel's externalization (*Entausserung*)—reverts into the basic process of alienation (*Entfremdung*), or loss of self-consciousness in the world of the objective (Marcuse, 1955; Raurich, 1976).

On account of this process of alienation, human beings, whose lives are determined within the frame of the capitalist division of labor in society, become—from a gnoseological perspective—a deceptive and even false consciousness because they take their relation with the thing to be true and no longer recognize the relation with the person that lies behind it; they are unable to recognize the social relations that underlie things.

Through this process, the social being as such, and as it is in reality, cannot be captured by awareness and thought and is reflected in reverse in human consciousness. The complication with ideology in classic Marxism is its double gnoseological condition: to be a false consciousness of reality and, at the same time, express objective ideas about that same reality. In other words, society cannot conceive of its being except in reified form, while, at the same time, the moment of reification represents the broadest ideological point from which the bourgeois social being is conceivable. This was characterized by Marx, when referring to the material world, as the fetishism of commodities. Kofler points out,

Consequently, the fact that ideology and being are recognized as correlative elements of one and the same process does not in any way contradict the statement that the original concept of ideology, taken in a way that is full of the meaning of the entire context of the theory of the superstructure-infrastructure, really contains two moments: the tendency towards objective knowledge and the tendency towards deception. (Kofler, 1968: 166)

This is not the place to develop an exhaustive argument on the problem of ideology within Marxism (see Lenk, 1974; 9–46; Méznaros, 1978; de

Ipola, 1982; Roueanet, 1978; Rositi, 1979). However, it is valid to state that, as an expression of common sense, ideology for Marxism is made up of a relatively coherent ensemble of claims, values, or essences that reflect how the agents of social formation live the conditions of their own existence.[4]

From the original perspective of Marx, religion—as one of the mechanisms of legitimation of social praxis and concealment of the social relations of exploitation—is an ideology with beliefs and stereotypes that permeate common sense. Its social role is assimilated to the conventional functions of any ideology.[5]

Just to illustrate the point, it could be said that, from the original Marxist point of view, religion—by corresponding to a collective claim concerning the activities and ambitions of social groups and classes, or even the State itself—would justify the kind of stratification that prevails and the mechanisms of hegemony in society. As a representative for the prevailing norms, values, and actions of the social structure and as a form of validation of the State as a normalizing and coercive agent, it would contribute to the rationalization of the established principles of social, political, and economic organization. As the factor determining the ordering of social incentives for the purpose of directing duly constituted social activities, it would contribute to the organization of public support for state initiatives. Finally, it would provide a means of discriminating between legitimate and nonlegitimate social forms and actions within the social framework. In this manner, religion as an ideology would contribute to the institutionalization of society's needs at a global level, framing them at the same time within the perspective of the State.[6] Thus, from a Christian perspective based on a Marxist approach, Raúl Vidales remarks,

For Marx, Christ, Money, the State, Capital are, in the first place, forms of mediation, that is to say, realities whose meaning is to give expression to man and therefore means by which man recognizes himself and, by recognizing himself, accedes to being for himself. But, in the second place, to the extent that they become autonomous objects dominating man, these are forms of mediation that carry the alienation of man, the loss of self respect, within them. (Vidales, 1978: 32)

Religion, therefore, as an ideology that results from social praxis at the same time as it operates within it, is a way of knowing. As such, it is part of the objective constitution of that reality and may function as the source of understanding of a process, even when as a general rule it is a significant factor contributing to the false consciousness of social agents.[7]

By way of a brief digression, it could be pointed out with respect to the implications of religious factors and processes for political praxis that one of the most vigorous currents of Marxist thought adopts a political definition of religion and, in general terms, makes it an enemy of the proletariat. This Leninist observation has serious consequences for certain Christian-Marxist tendencies, as Reyes Mate and Hugo Assmann conclude:

It has been said that the political definition of the essence of religion was a stroke of genius by Lenin. What is certainly true is that this position has two serious consequences: the first leads to a negation of all religious understanding of religion, since such an understanding would essentially compromise the class struggle. . . . The second consequence consists in rejecting the idea that the class struggle enters the church, since this makes implicit the idea of a religion . . . of the proletariat. (Mate & Assmann, 1974: 15)

In this sense, Lenin's affirmation insists that there should be coherence between proletarian consciousness and atheistic militancy, between revolution and atheism (Milhau, 1974). This is obviously not the prevailing criterion of different Marxist trends,[8] and many examples could be cited, such as the declaration by the Central Committee of the Unified Socialist Party of Cataluña in Spain, which stated in September 1976,

We declare that Christians who join the Party are aware, along with broad sectors of the Christian masses, that political compromise is autonomous and lay in character. This is to say that it is neither atheistic nor believing. Independently of the reasons why each one opts for socialism, the Christians who come into the Party do so as a class option and do not deduce their militancy from their faith. (Central Committee, 1977: 64)

Returning, then, to the premises of Marxist analysis, the entire group of assumptions already mentioned, derived from the traditions of the French and German Enlightenment and post-Hegelian criticism, may be summarized in the following statement: religion is human. This thesis, to the extent that it is closely bound to Feuerbach's proposal, was also superseded by Marx. Let us restate what has already been said. Marx observed that, although Feuerbach correctly criticized Hegel's idealist stance, he also fell into a metaphysical trap by characterizing human beings as an essence and understanding them from a speculative, abstract perspective. Marx sought to deepen the criticism, which depended till then on the classical materialist tradition, and stated that the human person is simply a complex of social relations and religion is therefore an eminently social phenomenon.

Various fundamental coordinates of Marxist thought in its original form are covered by this argument. First, religion is the product of the kind of social and material relations that exist. Second, it is a projection of the human consciousness that reflects those social relations in a distorted form and has the disguising of the causes of true misery as its goal by providing a solution in a future life, heaven and paradise, as opposed to the conflict of the present, earth and sin. Nevertheless, it is possible to detect a certain conviction in Marx that a "religious" reading of reality may, paradoxically, become a way of understanding a material process. Third, the causes of religion should not be sought in the mental, intentional, conscience, or psychological structures of individuals, or in the possible existence of certain metaphysical phenomena motivating individuals to design and reinforce part of their feelings and their religious conscience. The causes are to be found strictly in the network of social relations in which humanity is immersed. As a result, every religion is always an ideology. However, there remains to be asked what kind of religious phenomenon Marx considered as the basis of his theory, and this has provided the theme for many polemics among critics and students of Marxist thought.[9]

Unlike Durkheim, Marx was not concerned with the religious phenomenon in general, since for him preoccupation with the religious question does not derive from merely academic interest, but from a practical consideration. For Marx, "The critique of religion is the assumption underlying every critique" (cited by Mate & Assmann, 1974: 12). In this sense, although Marx was concerned with the forms taken by religious institutions in his day—that is to say, although Christianity is in some way the focus of his analysis—it is not Christianity in general, but its Protestant version and particularly the forms of religious institutionalization that occurred in Germany, France, and England at the beginning of the nineteenth century. Indeed a broader analytical reduction is possible. Greatly influenced by the German intellectual environment, Marx criticized the perspective of Hegel in particular as a concrete theodicy with philosophical but also social implications. Marx objected to Hegel's schema as a particular interpretation of Christianity as a historical phenomenon and its association at a theoretical level with the construction of an Absolute Being who, in the final recourse, constitutes the religious foundation of the State.

For this reason, Roger Garaudy affirms in a well-documented study (1973) that, generally speaking, it may be said that Marx had Hegel's interpretation of religion before him (Mate & Assmann, 1974). However, religion was not a primary concern for Marx because he considered that, having been the principal concern of the young Hegelians, its critique—both in general terms and in its essential lines—had reached a conclusion in German philosophical circles (Miranda, 1978: 257–72; Mate & Assmann, 1974: 11).

In summary, thus far we have argued that the theory of religion in the young Marx was identifiable with his theory of false consciousness: religion is a distorted projection of reality, the expression of real misery, but at the same time a protest against it, as Marx affirmed in his critique of the philosophy of the State in Hegel: "Religious misery is, on the one hand, the expression (*Ausdruck*) of real misery and, on the other, a protest (*Protestation*) against real misery. . . . The abolition of religion as an illusory (*illusorischen*) happiness of the people is necessary for their real happiness (*Wirklichen*)" (cited by Dussel, 1977b: 20).

However, Marx does not see anything positive in the "protest" against real life of which religion is the vehicle and does not consider the possibilities of religion as a factor opening new opportunities. That is to say that, in theory, Marx does not look at religion as an ideological phenomenon capable of producing a split, but, on the contrary, as a phenomenon that contributes to the consolidation of social relations of exploitation. His point of view has profoundly historical origins. On the one hand, when he was writing, the polemic between science and faith was still active with all its cultural implications, especially for the strengthening of the evolutionist cause in opposition to creationism or a materalist outlook on nature.[10] On the other, in addition to the markedly secular atmosphere of the nineteenth century, the concrete reality of the world of religion was that of a Church allied to political power and often subordinated to it under the emergence of competitive capitalism. One important aspect of this question was the absence of a radical wing or a significant critical outlook within the Catholic or Protestant Churches capable of entering into a dialogue with socialist and communist groups who were beginning to evolve a political and philosophical identity. Nor were there the popular urban or rural movements, connected to religious organizations, that could question capitalism at its birth, as occurs in our times in so many Latin American countries. Obviously, we are referring to movements that are progressive in nature—not to those with a restorative or counterrevolutionary character that, from millenarian perspectives, questioned capitalism from a religious point of view, but for the purpose of a return to a feudal or medieval past. Finally, it is relevant to point out here the distrust felt among socialists toward internal reform movements within the Church hierarchies. In this context it is worth mentioning the reservations expressed by Marx in his correspondence with Friedrich Engels about Monsignor Wilhelm Emmanuel von Ketteler, the bishop of Mainz, whom Marx, (with proverbial irascibility) dubbed a "bourgeois dog," although the monsignor was considered a "social bishop" in his day and wrote on the condition of the working class, Liberalism, Christianity, and Socialism (Ketteler, 1981).

Returning to the critique of religion in Marx, there is, as a general rule, one aspect that is overlooked. For Marx, religion—as a process of thought—is an ideology fundamentally because it is not scientific thought. From a cognoscitive approach to reality, Marx accepts that in humanity's primitive stages religion was valid as a way of thought, as a form of speculative practice among individuals. An example will help clarify the point. When humans first saw a lightning bolt set the woods alight, they probably felt fear for the unknown and the destructive potential of fire. This fear led them, in their ignorance of the cause of the fire and, above all, in their unfamiliarity with its social usefulness, to worship it by keeping it burning in their dwellings as the abode of the sacred. With the passage of time, they discovered its usefulness as a source of heat or in the cooking of food; and in some fashion, from this magical or religious projection on nature, humans began to incorporate new knowledge through experimentation. Marx does not deny the propaedeutic value of religion in human knowledge, but he also declares that its cognoscitive function ended in the light of the superiority of experimental science, which was gaining an increasing following in his time.

Thus it may be gathered that, in Marx's thought, the perpetuation of religious institutions and religion itself under capitalism is an ideology insofar as they represent a false consciousness of reality (that is, a lack of understanding of the real causes of things) and the "opium of the masses," insofar as they are a mystification of the relations of exploitation and the mechanisms of perpetuation of the capitalist conditions of production. Thus, the circularity of his critical schema allows Marx to state that religion is, in substance, part of a more general process of legitimation of social reification under capitalism.

The projection of Marxist theory onto religious phenomena has multiple effects. It would be incorrect to speak of a Marxist theory of religion in any strict sense of the term, although it is possible to speak of materialist hypotheses about such a theory. The first conclusion that may be drawn is that Marx undertakes a radical critique of religion. As phenomena contributing to human knowledge, religion and theology appear obsolete. As a phenomenon of individual piety, it is alienating and contrary to a scientific understanding of reality. The evident corollary of this thought is the observation that religion will tend to disappear. It will persist while a mode of production such as capitalism persists and will disappear when the latter disappears. Its fate is tied to that of capitalism and to presocialist modes of production.[11]

The second conclusion is that, although the Marxist critique of religion was originally derived from an earlier critique (as the assumption underlying it), it is subordinated in its elaboration to the critique of ideologies. Since religious thought (and theology) is no less than an ideology, then all the established notions that regard the dominant ideas of an age as being the ideas of the dominating class (Marx & Engels: 1974: 11–90) are valid in this context. Marx would not in any way subscribe to the stance of the young post-Hegelians who made the critique of religion their central theme—although—notwithstanding this conclusion—interpretations do exist that emphasize the critique of religion in the thought of Karl Marx as the undercurrent and basis assumption of his entire critique (Calvez, 1966).

In the third possible conclusion, the Marxist critique encompasses all institutions that relate to religion within the social matrix. As a result, it must be seen as a critique of the practice and theory of Churches and sects, as well as all organized and even nonorganic forms of religious practice in society.

The fourth possible conclusion is that it is a critique with a clear prediction: since the Church and religion were dominant facts in feudalism and were a fundamental support for the development of capitalism in society, they will tend to disappear as a constituted social activity within the socialist mode of production. The implied assumption is that, in a system where social and individual needs may be satisfied outside relations of domination and subordination, humans will no longer find it necessary to engage in interior speculation about the existence of a God who will transport them beyond a finite material universe, particularly when this universe is no longer alienating. Clearly this assumption has been developed in nineteenth-century Marxism in a way that seems to go further than Marx's theoretical speculations. We are referring to the group of theoretical suppositions that visualize the social horizon as the moment when the scientific ideology of historical materialism will have spread to all levels of society so that the State will disappear (or be extinguished), and will it all its ideological machinery (in which religion, and the Church especially, have a dominant role). When this occurs, Humanity will look for transcendency through the exercise of a socialist ethic and, in the context of a dialectical search, will form the "new social socialist being." From this point of view, it will be an age in which all forms of obscurantism will disappear and all magical rites and practices will therefore be meaningless.[12] In any event, Marx has no doubt at all about the possible intrinsic legitimacy of religion, which will always appear as an obstacle from a precapitalist past and will inevitably tend to be less important for human life in a socialist society.

The complexities and the very history of social struggles in Latin America have led to a reevaluation of Marxist analysis and some of the premises of Marxism on religion among those who claim a socialist perspective based on Christian ethical convictions. For example, Reyes Mate and Hugo Assmann categorize the Marxist critique from the outlook of Christians on the left.

The Marxist critique of religion is a challenge thrown, in the first place, to Christians. On the one hand, the Marxist critique is a critique of the church. It is a critique of the Church as an established, historical, empirical institution. It is not an exclusively Marxist critique and belongs to Christian history itself (the heresies did no less). On the other, it is a critique of Christianity. Christianity is taken as an historical concretion of religion in general. Thirdly, it is a critique of magical religion. Here, not only are the functionality of the church or the bourgeois identification of religion criticized, but also the supra-naturalist construction of Christianity. Finally, it is a critique of religion in its entirety, not of just a part, but of all of it. (Mate & Assmann, 1974: 36)

Perhaps the determination of these different levels of criticism has made it possible now to distinguish the different levels of what came to be called the "Marxist-Christian dialogue," one of the most interesting sociological and political phenomena of the decades since the sixties. This dialogue has been carried out on a political and academic theoretical plane in Europe and in Latin America on a plane that is perhaps essentially practical and political (Betto, 1989; Castro & Betto, 1987).

Marx was not a theoretician of religion, but, on the other hand, he was a critic. What is important is that his analytical view has, within the sociological tradition, made it possible to confront countless specific polemics and discussions. Without having been a theoretician of religion, the imprint of his thought is very much present in academic and political discussions on the religious phenomenon in Latin America—discussions that have followed a path quite different from the assumptions that animated the Marxist critique in its beginnings. Nevertheless, the situations of many nations in Latin America show us that important segments of the agenda of Marx's critique of religion continue to be valid for sociological theory as will be demonstrated later in this study.

## NOTES

1. On this point, see Sigmund Freud (1950, 1965), from which it may be appreciated that he was a recipient of the same currents of thought, particularly French Materialism. See also José Díaz Murugarren's critique of religion as an obsessive neurosis (1977).

2. Dussel (1974b) provides one of the most thorough studies of anthropological dualism in Christian thought, demonstrating the radical tension present within a doctrinal tradition such as Christianity.

3. This thesis evidently departs from the analysis proposed by Max Weber on the ethical projections of Protestantism concerning secular reality, as will be seen in Chapter 3.

4. Adam Schaff (1980: 13) identifies three types of definitions of ideology—genetic, structural, and functional—although his own is functional.

5. Attention should be given to the importance of this point. It seems evident that Louis Althusser's perspective has most influenced the interpretation of the problem of ideology in Marx for an entire generation of Marxists in Latin America. In brief, given the necessarily "opaque" character of the social structure, Althusser proposed the interpretation of ideology as a system of deforming claims (Althusser, 1970). This deformation is systematic, directed, and determined (de Ipola, 1982: 2). From Althusser's point of view, the social function of ideology consists in assuring social cohesion in general by regulating the link that connects individuals to their tasks (Althusser, 1971). That is to say, as Emilio de Ipola correctly points out, Althusser's reading of the problem of ideology in Marxism leads to the following conclusions: (1) every ideology invokes/constitutes individuals as subjects; (2) it guarantees the subjection of these subjects to a central Single Subject; (3) it ensures reciprocal acknowledgment between the subjects and the Subject, among the subjects themselves, and of the subjects by themselves through the relationship based on reflection inscribed in its structure; and finally (4) it provides the absolute guarantee that if the subjects recognize what they are and behave accordingly, all will be well (de Ipola, 1982: 34–35). Althusser applies this analysis, taking

Christian ideology as an example (Althusser, 1970: 33–35). It should be stressed, therefore, that a reading of the original Marxist perspective on religion as an ideology is generally cast in Latin America in the language of Althusser. A more appropriate and fruitful reading may be found in the work of Antonio Gramsci (Portelli, 1977), whose contribution to Marxism will be discussed in our Chapter 4.

6. In this reading of the original Marxist vision, religion as an ideology is the factor that assures the integration of individual subjectivity to the social structure. However, to return the discussion to contemporary interpretations, and to follow de Ipola, at least two different sides to the question of religion as an ideology must be acknowledged. On the one hand, the "ideological" does not designate a collection of empirically separable social facts, but a dimension in the analysis of every social fact (de Ipola, 1982). In this sense, the "religious" as a constituent of the ideological could be a fundamental dimension of analysis needed to understand a particular social process (postrevolutionary Nicaragua, for example, see Vilas, 1984: Harris & Vilas, 1985). On the other hand, the "forms of existence and exercise of the social struggles within the domain of the social processes of the production of meanings" (de Ipola, 1982: 73) should be understood as ideologies. As de Ipola points out, the class struggle stands first among social struggles under capitalism, but not all antagonisms and ideological conflicts may be reduced to class differences: certain forms of ethnic, gender, or territorial and regional oppression have roots and an ideological dynamic different from determinations of class. A number of analyses have given an account of this further problematic with respect to the question of religion (Ezcurra, 1983; de Lella, 1984).

7. We are evidently referring to conventional Marxist analysis of religion. The first People's Commissar in Education of the Russian Revolution, Anatoly V. Lunacharski, pointed out that "no revolution or profound reform is achieved in a religious society unless they are also revolutionary in the area of relations with God. The prophet, therefore, has the duty to speak in the name of God" (1976: 83, cited by Dussel, 1977b).

8. Jacques Milhau ends his work on religion with the observation that "real, true atheism is the general profile of the activity of human society when it becomes theoretically and practically able to take its own destiny in its hands" (Milhau, 1974: 118). This reductionism to a true atheism as the only ethical and theoretical basis for confronting reality cannot be accepted, for example, by the Christian revolutionaries of Nicaragua who preach, by contrast, that "between Christianity and Revolution there is no contradiction." It is evidently clear that this latter kind of suprahistorical observation contradicts the very spirit of Marx's reasoning. In a letter he wrote but never sent to the editors of *Otechestvennye Zapiski* (a periodical published in Saint Petersburg)— a letter that Engels found among Marx's papers in 1884 and made available for publication in Geneva—Marx stated with reference to the misinterpretations

of his own theories concerning the possibilities of revolution in Russia that "events that are strikingly analogous, but taking place in different historical milieus, lead to totally disparate results. By studying each of these developments separately, one can easily discover the key to this phenomenon, but one will never arrive there with the master key of a historico-philosophical theory whose supreme virtue consists in being suprahistorical" (cited by Alavi & Shanin, 1982: 110).

9. Georges Cottier's study (1959) is an excellent text, which reflects, from a non-Marxist perspective, many of the concerns that arose in postwar Europe as a result of the expansion of Marxism; pp. 145–239 are especially enlightening.

10. It is hardly surprising that Bertrand Russell in 1935—still imbued with the atmosphere of affirmation of scientific humanism—should state, "We have seen that when practical consequences were at stake, as in witchcraft and medicine, science has sided with the reduction of suffering, while theology has stimulated the natural savagery of man. The spread of the scientific view, in opposition to theology, has worked indisputably until now in favour of happiness" (Russell, 1973: 167).

11. However, it often seems to be emphasized in certain Marxist currents in particular that religion will disappear not only due to the process of cultural proletarianization, but also due to the development of the means of industrial production—which, even in socialist societies, will leave no place for rural culture where religious convictions are especially deeply rooted. In this regard, Antoine Casanova points out that "industrialization and atheism are inseparable" (cited by Milhau, 1974: 110). Paradoxically, the increasing importance of neoconservative thought in a highly industrialized society like the United States—expressed in movements like the Moral Majority or the outlook of so many fundamentalist sects and churches, or even the growing influence of Oriental and agrarian religions in this society—would tend to belie the association between industrialization and atheism.

12. It should be pointed out, however, that the influences on this idea are curiously closer to anarchism, with its belief in mutual support and the destruction of the State, and to French Encyclopedism than to the thought of Karl Marx, who debated many of these questions with Mikhail Bakunin. Along with Encyclopedic materialism, there is also a train of thought that gives pride of place to the inevitability of the advance of the social world (following the same laws as the natural world) toward a horizon of human fulfillment inherent in the organic structure of all individuals. Consider, for example, the following observation by Prince Peter Kropotkin: "*Mutual Aid—Justice—Morality* are thus the consecutive steps of an ascending series, revealed to us by the study of the animal world and man. They constitute an *organic necessity* which carries in itself its own justification, confirmed by the whole of the evolution of the animal kingdom. . . . Mutual Assistance, Justice and Morality are rooted in man's mind with all the force of an inborn instinct" (Kropotkin, 1924: 30–31).

# 2

# Religion as a Primitive Phenomenon: Emile Durkheim

Emile Durkheim's sociology of religion was inspired by that well-known phrase in Marx according to which the social existence of humanity determines its social consciousness. Nevertheless, in one of the final paragraphs of *The Elementary Forms of Religious Life*, Durkheim endeavors to distance himself from Marxism.

Therefore it is necessary to avoid seeing in this theory of religion a simple restatement of historical materialism: that would be misunderstanding our thought to an extreme degree. In showing that religion is something essentially social, we do not mean to say that it confines itself to translating into another language the material forms of society and its immediate vital necessities. It is true that we take it as evident that social life depends upon its material foundation and bears its mark, just as the mental life of an individual depends upon his nervous system and in fact his whole organism. But collective consciousness is something more than a mere epiphenomenon of its morphological basis, just as individual consciousness is something more than a simple efflorescence of the nervous system. In order that the former may appear, a synthesis *sui generis* of particular consciousness is required. Now this synthesis has the effect of disengaging a whole world of sentiments, ideas, and images which, once born, obey laws all their own. They attract each other, repel each other, unite, divide themselves, and multiply, though these combinations are not commended and necessitated by the condition of the underlying reality. The life thus brought into being even enjoys so great an independence that it sometimes indulges in manifestations with no purpose or utility of any sort, for the mere pleasure of affirming itself. (Durkheim, 1915: 423–24)

As one commentator states, however, Durkheim's debt to Marx is undeniable (Zeitlin, 1968: 258ff). Durkheim was right to say that his theory was not a simple restatement of Marxist theses, but he was mistaken in believing that Marx had considered consciousness as a mere epiphenomenon of material reality. His ideas on the problem of the autonomy of superstructures, including where they touch on the religious question, were closely studied by Antonio Gramsci under another optic and from the opposite direction.[1] The real divergence is twofold. On the one hand, Durkheim endeavors to generalize Marx's statement beyond the economic to include other social relations. For Durkheim, "social consciousness" was an essentially conservative force, while in Marx the whole area of consciousness was a fundamental element in the revolutionary transformation of social relations, even if, for him, religion generally expressed a false consciousness of reality. For Durkheim, however, religion gives expression to social reality in a positive, functional manner, and herein lies his antithetical ideological inversion. For Durkheim, society becomes the true creator of the individual and, in his theory of religion, the divine is the symbolic expression of social forces.[2]

For Durkheim, religion is a group phenomenon, since it is the group that gives it its character and specific unity. On the other hand, religion has the retroactive effect of uniting the group, bringing people together with bonds of solidarity. "In this way Durkheim gives a conservative emphasis to his general thesis that religious ideas are derived from society and serve to bind the members of a society together. This essential and positive function of religion—solidifying a society—explains why it is a ubiquitous and permanent institution" (Zeitlin, 1968: 277–78).

Let us consider Durkheim's theory of religious phenomena systematically. First of all, it is a classic representative of the position that for gnoseological and methodological reasons refuses to define the essence of religion and asks instead about the structural and functional meaning that phenomena appearing to be religious have for a society. In some ways, the initial question is not about the essence, but about the origins of religion and its function in different social systems (Matthes, 1971).[3] The complement of this sociological question is the analysis of the social conduct of religion as a factor in the integration, cohesion, and preservation of social reality—as the instrument for the articulation of its organic solidarity over its mechanical solidarity.[4]

Thus, Durkheim differs greatly from the critique of religion during the French Enlightenment as represented by figures such as the Baron de Montesquieu, Voltaire, the Baron Holbach, and Michel de Montaigne. He also has little in common with the post-Hegelian critique of religion produced in nineteenth-century Germany, especially in the work of Ludwig Feuerbach, J. Joachim Spalding, Christian Wolff, Max Stirner, and Bruno Bauer; and of course, there is a considerable distance between him and Marx.

Durkheim does not undertake the analysis and critique of one religion in particular (e.g., Christianity, as in the earlier cases), but refers in a general way to its analysis as a socially prevalent phenomenon in the majority of societies he knows—independent of its expression as a sect, Church, or religion. As Joachin Matthes points out, Durkheim "considers that the origin of religion is to be found in the regulating character of social action and conduct, and understands that sacred conduct is, from this point of view, no more than an especially effective form of social conduct" (Matthes, 1971: 21).

In summary, then, the two distinctive characteristics of Durkheim's theory of religion are to investigate its origin and not its essence, and to focus his study not on a specific religion (e.g., Christianity) but on the phenomenon of religion in general and its presence in the social context. His point of departure is an empirical observation: "But that which is necessary and possible, is to indicate a certain number of external and easily recognizable signs, which will enable us to recognize religious phenomena wherever they are met with, and which will deter us from confounding them with others" (Durkheim, 1915: 23). Hence he undertakes a search for an empirically verifiable definition of the religious. For this reason, his methodological procedure is to rule out, progressively, all possible analogies of the religious phenomenon with others like it. Next, he reexamines the usual preconceptions about religion in order, finally, to unify the central elements of the concept in a coherent proposition.

He begins by reviewing some of the commonest definitions, which seem prejudicial to him and which associate religion with the supernatural, the mysterious, the extraordinary, or the unforeseen. "It is far from being true, then, that the notion of the religious coincides with that of the extraordinary or the unforeseen. . . . *In fact, we shall see that, even with the most simple religions we know, their essential task is to maintain, in a positive manner, the normal course of life"* (Durkheim, 1915: 28–29; emphasis added).

Then he sets aside the belief that religion is derived from or has its center in gods or spirits endowed with powers superior to those possessed by common humanity. By contrast, he states that there are rites without gods and even rites from which gods derive. "Religion is more than the idea of gods or spirits, and consequently cannot be defined exclusively in relation to these latter" (Durkheim, 1915: 35). Taking this statement as his point of departure, he endeavors to break with analogies. The difficulties of defining religion in these terms arise from proceeding as if it were a kind of indivisible entity,[5] when for Durkheim it is a whole made up of parts, a more or less complex system of myths, dogmas, rites, and ceremonies.

He therefore reaches an important conclusion for the development of his theory: every religious phenomenon possesses a heteroclitic collection of beliefs, understood as states of opinion or speculative representations, and rites, understood as particular forms of action. At the same time, these two elements, essential to all religions, divide the world into two major areas—the sacred and the profane—which are profoundly heterogeneous with respect to each other:

But the real characteristic of religious phenomena is that they always suppose a bipartite division of the whole universe, known and knowable, into two classes that embrace all that exists but which radically exclude each other. . . .
When a certain number of sacred things sustain relations of coordination or subordination with each other in such a way as to form a system having a certain unity, but which is not comprised within any other system of the same sort, the totality of these beliefs and their corresponding rites constitutes a religion. (Durkheim, 1915: 40–41)

Thus, Durkheim poses an additional problem. The nature of sacred things is different from the profane; and if they are different in essence, they present an altogether different problem. As a result, one must now ask what has led humanity to see the world as two heterogeneous and incompatible worlds, since nothing experienced through the senses seems to suggest so radical a division. Answering this question involves, for Durkheim, confronting a much wider but very significant problem for his inquiry: how to distinguish religion from a similar phenomenon such as magic.

He starts with what he considers a basic premise: magic and religion

**Table 2.1**
**Durkheim's Comparison of Religious and Magic Beliefs**

| RELIGIOUS BELIEFS | MAGIC BELIEFS |
|---|---|
| 1.      particular collectivity or social group, which declares its adherence to them and practices the rites that accompany them. | 1. They never lack a certain generality and, very often, are even spread through extensive levels of the population. |
| 2. Individuals feel themselves bound to each other by the sole fact that they have a common faith. | 2. However, individuals do not feel themselves bound to each other by these beliefs. |
| 3. They suppose the existence of a Church. | 3. There is no Church of Magic. The magician has a clientele, not a Church, and associations of magicians are rare, almost exceptional. Moreover, a Church is not necessary for the practice of magic. |
| 4. There exists a moral community among the faithful and the priests. | 4. There is no moral group to unite the magician to clients or the latter among themselves. Moreover, associations of magicians, if they exist (even for sharing "discoveries"), do not include the laity. |

are two very different social phenomena, so that it would be difficult to sustain the hypothesis of a certain identity between them, especially "because of the marked repugnance of religion for magic, and in return, the hostility of the second towards the first" (Durkheim, 1915: 43). To confirm these differences, Durkheim proposes a typology of religious and magic beliefs compared, as shown in Table 2.1.

Evidently, the notion of Church is the key in the analysis undertaken by Durkheim to define religion (Matthes, 1971; Goddijn, 1973). He is beset by doubts concerning the possible contradiction between individual and Church "cults" or worship practices, but concludes that

individual cults are not distinct and autonomous religious systems, but merely aspects of the common religion of the whole Church, of which the individuals are part. . . . In a word, it is the Church of which he is a member which teaches the individual what these personal gods are, what their function is, how he should enter into relations with them and how he should honour them. (Durkheim, 1915: 46)

Accordingly, he is then able to propose a definition of the religious phenomenon and of religion per se:

*A religion is a unified system of beliefs and practices relative to sacred things, that is to say, things set apart and forbidden—beliefs and practices that unite into one single moral community called a Church, all those who adhere to them.* (Durkheim, 1915: 47)

This definition allows us to distinguish several important facets of the phenomenon and, at the same time, undertake a general review of what has been concluded:

1. The idea of religion is inseparable from the idea of Church or sect, which indicates that religion is an essentially collective phenomenon.
2. Moreover, religion has two clear and distinct dimensions, being constituted, on the one hand, on the basis of a system of commonly shared beliefs and, on the other, by a system of commonly shared practices.
3. The unification of all believers into "one single moral community" implies a particular process of primary socialization,[6] originating with the family in the first instance, but continued in confessional educational institutions and even in strictly "cultural" institutions (parishes, etc.), given, at the same time, a certain sense of belonging to a group (generally a stable one, in which either primary or secondary relations may predominate). There exists a peculiar process of social control that the religious institution in general and the cultural group in particular exert on individuals, with consequent implications for their social conduct. The vitality of this process depends on various factors: the degree of adequacy and/or distance of "moral norms" in relation to social norms and values; the historical realization of religion in each society in particular; the kind of religion in question and its insertion in the various social classes and groups; the urban and/or rural area of the dominant group in the religious community; the size of the area inhabited; and other characteristics of the population and locale.

Thus, in Durkheim's view of things, "religious beliefs" have distinctive characteristics: (1) they are always common to a particular collectivity that declares its adherence to them and the practice of its rites; (2) they bind individuals to each other—to a greater or lesser degree according to cases—by the simple fact of their common faith; (3) they suppose the existence of a Church or sect (which constitutes a specific difference with respect to "magic beliefs" and also "natural beliefs"); and finally (4), they suppose a certain division of cultural tasks between the faithful, or the laity, and the priests, who are the executive functionaries of worship— but assume a "moral community" that includes both.

Following Durkheim's own itinerary, we have therefore reached the conclusion anticipated at the beginning of his text on the sociology of religion.

The general conclusion of the book which the reader has before him is that religion is something eminently social. Religious representations are collective representations which express collective realities; the rites are a manner of acting which take rise in the midst of the assembled groups and which are destined to excite, maintain or recreate certain mental states in these groups. (Durkheim, 1915: 10)

Durkheim takes the analysis of totemism as his point of departure, supposing it to be the most ancient form of religion, given that, according to the anthropological discoveries of his time, it had been found among peoples that could be called primitive, such as the Australian aborigines he studied. He understood that the social structure of these societies is simple and homogeneous, their culture unified and limited, the basic social personality very similar, and the prevailing social cohesion of a mechanical type (in that all elements are part of a culture and the collectivity dominates the individual) as opposed to an organic social cohesion, as found in more developed societies with a broader interdependence among individuals resulting from a more complex division of social work. It is religion that explains and sustains, according to Durkheim, the mechanical solidarity of primitive peoples (Milanessi, 1974: 80–85; Desroche, 1965; Ferrarotti, 1966; Goldenweiser, 1977; Le Bras, 1960: 45–46). Moreover, Durkheim points out that religion derives from the feelings of solidarity that bind each individual to a group, tribe, or clan. The expression of this feeling is the totem, which has the double dimension of naming the group (it is a collective designator) and representing it symbolically. As the clan or group tends to perpetuate itself and endeavors to overcome the difficulties that threaten its existence, totemic awareness is strengthened until the sacredness (taboo) of the totem is proclaimed. Thus clan, totem, and taboo form the basic trilogy of the religious reality. Rituals arise as a result of a mythic devotion to the totem—expressing the radical separation between the mundane, which will appear aggressive or banal, and the sacred, which will be represented in the taboo and the spirituality of the group.

For Durkheim, all historically known religions develop from a primitive totemic experience, of which they still preserve the meaning and essential function. Hence the validity of J. Milanessi's observation in which he points out that the essentially social function of religion clearly appears when it is nothing less than "the symbolic projection of the social 'ethos' having as its object the creation of feelings of dependence on the group, of confidence in society, of willingness to cooperate, of altruism" (Milanessi, 1974: 83). Thus, in this early sociology of religion, Durkheim emphasizes the meaning of religion as a positive phenomenon promoting the cohesion of individuals in a social formation, which again reflects the positivist perspective of Saint-Simon.

It is important to note that, given the age in which Durkheim was writing and the proximity of the positivist environment in science, it would seem obvious for his analysis to be infected by scientism and anticlericalism; however, it was not. Concerning the links between science and religion, Durkheim states, "Having left religion, science tends to substitute itself for this latter in all that which concerns the cognitive and intellectual functions" (Durkheim, 1915: 429). However, for Durkheim, this substitution does not imply that science should deny religion. How can science, he wonders, deny a system of given facts, a reality? Since for him science does not create the facts of daily life but interprets and expresses them, he concludes by affirming the existence of something "eternal" that science cannot replace and for which science has not provided a substitute for the modern era.

Thus there is something eternal in religion which is destined to survive all the particular symbols in which religious thought has successively enveloped itself. There can be no society which does not feel the need of upholding and reaffirming at regular intervals the collective sentiments and the collective ideas which make its unity and its personality. (Durkheim, 1915: 427)

Perplexed by the durability of the religious phenomenon in modern societies—not just in primitive societies—Durkheim admits the existence of an eternal substratum in every organized human grouping, an eternal entity to which he does not want to give metaphysical status. However, the essentially conservative underpinning in Durkheim's thought does not lie in this affirmation, which perhaps contradicts his view of social facts as things, but in his considering every religious phenomenon as an element of social unity and cohesion, an element forever preserved over and above all determination of classes, and, most importantly, a phenomenon beyond social conflict, which is essentially anomic and militates against organic solidarity.[7]

At the end of his study, the importance of the relations between religion and economics does not escape Durkheim, although he declared himself unable at that time to specify the nature and basis of the connection between the two: "Hence it is seen that the ideas of economic value and of religious value are not without connection. But the question of the nature of these connections has not yet been studied" (Durkheim, 1915: 419, n. 1). Seen in historical perspective, this will be one of the principal tasks for the sociology of religion of Max Weber.

## NOTES

1. As an example of the importance attached to superstructures in Durkheim, see the discussion on morbidity in the "German mentality" as a principal cause of World War I (as critiqued in Rodríguez Zúñiga, 1978: 133–39). The parallels with Gramsci's thought may be found in Hugues Portelli's analysis (1977).

2. For Durkheim, the statement "Man is a social being" becomes a clearly conservative statement because it always assigns greatest importance to the adaptation of humanity to circumstances and never to the adaptation of circumstances to the purposes of humanity. In keeping with certain authors, Durkheim develops the conservative tendencies in the thought of Saint-Simon, principally retrieving from him his assertion that "moral ideas are the real cement of society." Hence, the theoretical work of Durkheim—intimately connected with the development of socialism, although in an inverse and antagonistic sense— consists entirely in the elaboration of "an organic consensual model" that is essentially antithetical to the Marxist model because it denies all antagonism between the individual and society. Durkheim was primarily concerned with individual solidarity and the social order and, above all, with adjustment of the social system by bringing the moral code into harmony with the division of social labor. He dedicated practically all his theoretical endeavors to this end, particularly in his works on education, morality, moral education, and religion. He believed that the goal Saint-Simon had set himself of elaborating a new and appropriate set of universally acceptable moral and rational beliefs still remained to be achieved in his time, which was marked by the colonial and imperial politics of the Great Powers. For an excellent commentary on Saint-Simon's thought—a commentary from which his impact on a theoretical framework like Durkheim's can be inferred—see George Gurvitch (1970).

3. It is commonplace to locate Durkheim among the founders of contemporary sociology. Sociology was born in close association with modern social anthropology—or ethnography, to the French—and the origin and evolution of these sciences is closely tied in with the development of imperialism toward the end of the nineteenth and beginning of the twentieth centuries. For this reason, it is not surprising that Durkheim's elaboration of his theory is a lively witness to his disquiet with respect to a society undergoing ceaseless transformation, evolution, and expansion, beginning to capture the "empty" spaces of peripheral countries, to export idle capital from the metropolitan centers to these regions, to create new markets for products and labor, and to control in the short run the periodic crises of the capitalist economy arising from overproduction and achievement. In the context of this period of expansion, there arises a sense of perplexity when confronting internal phenomena of these advanced societies that are not explicable by themselves. Durkheim's question about why individuals commit suicide if their social activities are undertaken in an integrated environment based on the new social division of labor and within the framework of organic solidarity is the question of the social scientist alarmed and perplexed by new social complexities that are the fruit of the development of capitalism itself. From the point of view of social ethnography or anthropology, knowing about the culture of those traditional or primitive societies that were beginning to be incorporated on a large scale into the system of world capitalism was no doubt a legitimate matter of inquiry in the context of the progress of knowledge, and a very functional one in the process of colonization. This is to say that, from this perspective, the central issue was to question not the impacts and repercussions of the colonizing process and its connections with the development of capitalism in the metropolitan countries, but the cultural conditions of the colonized societies, the real and latent points of conflict with respect to the new culture that was being imposed, and the mechanisms for making the process of territorial colonization more effective, especially in its cultural aspects.

4. This is the direction that Talcott Parsons takes from Durkheim's thought and explores systematically. In one of his major works, Parsons points out that it is the consensus among the members of a society about the orientation of its relative values that defines the institutionalization of its basis patterns of achievement. If, for Parsons, consensus is a question of degree, self-sufficiency in this context refers to the degree to which the institutions of a society have legitimized themselves through commitments to values accepted by their members. Parsons thus points out,

Values are related to other components of a cultural system such as empirical knowledge, expressive symbol systems, and the constitutive symbolic structures that compose the core of religious systems. *Ultimately, values are mainly legitimized in religious terms.* In the context of cultural legitimation, then, a society is self-sufficient to the extent that its institutions are legitimized by values that its members hold with relative consensus *and* that are in turn legitimized by their congruence with other components of the cultural system, especially its constitutive symbolism. (Parsons, 1971: 9–10; first emphasis added)

5. Definitions with these god-linked characteristics abound in sociological analyses on the question—especially those based on the standpoint of particular confessions: Rudolf Otto's definition, for example, "Religion is the ultimate source from which all human existence is nourished and on which it depends in all its aspects: the communication of Man with God"; or Gustav Mensching's, "Religion is a living encounter with the sacred and Man's response defined by the sacred" (both cited in Matthes, 1971; vol. 1. 25–26). Perspectives such as these operate on a theoretical and methodological plane of little use to sociological analysis, which, as a point of departure, requires—in Anton Zijderveld's fortunate phrase, retrieved by Peter Berger (1967: 100) and probably acceptable to Durkheim—a certain "methodological atheism." In conclusion, we owe not only to Marx, but also to Durkheim, the indication that religious phenomena be considered from the standpoint of their empirical "materiality" by seeking only the verifiability and/or confirmation of the social datum as such and not its connection with a supposed metaphysical entity or with the existence—accepted a priori—of a particular deity. This helps to explain in part the weaknesses and limitations of a so-called Catholic Sociology, such as that attempted by Aldo Büntig in Latin America toward the ends of the sixties and the beginning of the seventies, or a Protestant Sociology, like that undertaken in the United States in the mid-fifties and early sixties.

6. In the conventional social sciences, the process of socialization has been defined as "the process whereby society transmits its own culture from one generation to another and adapts the individual to accepted and approved models (of social behavior) of organized social life" (Fichter, 1972: 34). It consists of a process of social apprenticeship of which the basic subprocesses may be identified as follows: imitation (the more or less exact reproduction of preexisting models); suggestion (the more or less conscious yielding to the social pressure exercised by the complex of culture and society); and competition (the drive and search for gratification arising from interiorization of the culture). The result will be the inculcation of basic social patterns and norms. The stages of socialization vary according to the orientation or school of social psychology that considers them, while the agents of socialization—the family, the school, advertising, social groups, and especially language—are accepted as fundamental. For some culturalists, the result of the process of basis socialization in a given society is constituted by the basis social personality, insofar as it is a particular psychological configuration belonging to the members of a given society and manifesting itself in a certain way of life on which individuals build their own variations (Kardiner, 1939).

7. It is evident that with a positivist and evolutionist schema as the underpinning of Durkheim's analysis, society appears as an indivisible "corpus,"

homogeneous in its diversity and, above all, self-regulating, and that on analyzing a particular phenomenon, like religion, there is always a globalizing and integrating perception of each aspect within the perspective of an organically constituted society. Hence it is of interest to mention one of the criticisms made by Peter Berger from a consensual perspective: "One of the important weaknesses of Durkheim's sociological theory of religion is the difficulty of interpreting within its framework religious phenomena that are *not* society-wide—in the terms used here, the difficulty of dealing in Durkheimian terms with sub-societal plausibility structures" (1967: 48, n.22). Another point worthy of criticism is that, when he aspires to detailed knowledge of the functional and integrating elements of religion, Durkheim never considers the critical aspects that may result from religious practice—aspects that, if they existed as social action, could be included in his analysis as part of the processes of social anomie. This is to be understood from the fact that, if Durkheim considered religion not only as a constituent element of social reproduction, but also as a factor that could disorganize social order based on organic solidarity, his entire thesis on the integrating character of religion would be constrained and his analysis of the dynamic of the transformation of modern societies would have to be broadened considerably.

# 3

# Religion, Economic Rationality, and Civilization: Max Weber's Theses

Within the framework of the sociology of religion, perhaps few texts have had the popularity that Max Weber's essay *The Protestant Ethic and the Spirit of Capitalism* still enjoys. Although it is not his most basic text on the subject, it is the most polemical, and his work has always been at the heart of discussions on sociology and social philosophy. Thus, Georg Lukács cited his discourse as a fundamental milestone along the path to fascism taken by German irrationalism, and classified it as a conceptual schema that conflicts with historical materialism at the same time as it endeavors to supersede it.

Weber, as we have seen, started out from the interaction between the economic ethics of religions and economic formations, whereby he asserted the effective priority of the religious motive. His problem was to explain why capitalism had come about only in Europe. In contrast to the earlier view of capitalism as any accumulation of wealth, Weber was at pains to grasp the specific character of modern capitalism and to relate its European origin to the difference between ethico-religious development in the East and West. To achieve this, his principal step was to de-economize and "spiritualize" the nature of capitalism. This he presented as a rationalizing of socio-economic life, the rational calculability of all phenomena. Weber now devised a universal history of religion in order to show that oriental and ancient religions produced economic codes constituting inhibiting factors in the rationalization of everyday life. Only Protestantism (and within Protestantism, chiefly the dissident sects) possessed an ideology agreeable to this rationalization and encouraging it. Time and again Weber declined to see in the economic codes a consequence of the economic structures. . . . And in consequence of his identification of technology and economics—a vulgarizing simplification that acknowledged only mechanized capitalism as the authentic variety—Weber then arrived at the "decisive" historical "argument" that the Protestant economic ethos which speeded up and fostered capitalist development was already there "*before* the 'capitalist development.' " In this he saw a refutation of historical materialism. (Lukács, 1980: 606–7)

This lengthy paragraph from Lukács has the merit of summarizing the most important topics of Weber's sociology of religion while, at the same time, showing that this kind of theoretical and historical discussion is not entirely outside the polemics generated among the historico-social sciences about the logic of scientific argumentation. In this regard, we would therefore like to identify the following different aspects in Weber's work: (1) the relation between economic rationality and religious ethics, that is, in its more general sense, the earlier statement by Emile Durkheim that Weber would take up in various works: the need to study the connections between economics and religion; (2) the conflict in approaches between a "comprehensive" sociology and that of historical materialism in the analysis of a concrete and circumscribed phenomenon such as religion; (3) the meaning of the religious phenomenon in civilization or, in other words, the study of the conduct and consciousness of religion as a specific social action with ends, means, and meaning; and (4) as a consequence of the preceding point, the question of classes and social strata and their relation to religion.

In our opinion, any analysis that might seek to study the sociology of religion in Weber without locating it in the extensive and multifaceted context of his entire work would be mistaken.[1] Its first important aspect is his methodological approach, which is of a historicist and antipositivist stamp—a derivative of the philosophical solution of Wilhelm Dilthey. Wilhelm Windelband, and Heinrich Rickert, but with touches of originality. It is a method that hinges on the distinction between ideal and normative knowledge, that analyzes society as a social system and establishes methodological requirements according to which the elaboration of "ideal types" makes it possible to sidestep the problem of social law and social significance and even prevents Weber's entire approach, based on the "comprehension" of the social fact, from being submerged in an irrevocable relativist perspective (Weber, 1973).

Attempting to define the central element of his entire theory, we find that three aspects combine and complement each other, even chronologically, to form the nucleus of his vast sociological undertaking: (1) the analysis of German society and the Protestant ethic; (2) the comparative study of civilizations on the basis of the threefold concept of society, religion, and secular ethics; and (3) Weber's political sociology, hinging on the notions of domination, organization, and legitimacy.

In the first aspect, Weber studies the change from an agrarian to an industrial capitalist society and the implications and correlations existing between what he calls the spirit of capitalism (economic rationalism) and the Protestant ethic (puritanism). In the second, he pursues the study of the relations among social groups and classes, religious leadership and the religiosity of the masses, seeking to provide a comparative analysis of society and religion in China, India, and Ancient Palestine. Finally, in the third—in some ways, his attempt at a great theoretical synthesis— he looks at the problem of domination[2] (in its legal, traditional, and charismatic modalities) as the crux of the theory and at its relation to leadership, the modern State, and the struggle for power.

It is within this framework that the theoretical discourse on religion is inscribed. To try to see it as a marginal concern without substantive character, as a serendipitous product of Weber's enlightened mind, is a serious error. His integrated perspective allows him to grasp the arsenal of theoretical concepts and notions connected with the religious phenomenon to the extent, for example, that one of the fundamental concepts in the domain of his political sociology—charismatic leadership—refers to the "sacred gift" received by the individual who exercises this type of leadership in a community. This concept, as is evident in etymological terms, originates in Weber's analysis of religion.

As Reinhard Bendix points out (1962), Weber analyzed the reciprocal effects of society and religion, but within a comprehensive attempt to analyze the evolution of what we might call "Western civilization." The principal objectives of his sociology of religion were to examine the effect of religious ideas on economic activities, to analyze the relation between social stratification and religious ideas, and to identify and explain the distinctive processes of Western civilization. His analysis centers therefore on the interrelation of religious ideas with the structure of "status" and power of the groups and classes that make up society.[3] As Bendix observes, "Weber approached the study of religious ideas in terms of their relevance for collective actions, and specifically in terms of the social processes whereby the inspirations of the few become the convictions of the many" (Bendix, 1962: 259).

At this point, then, moving along toward a systematic presentation of Weber's fundamental theses concerning the sociology of religion, we should broach the question of Protestant ethics and the spirit of capitalism. The most general aspect of his analysis concerns, as we stated, the influence of religious values on economic conduct; or speaking more strictly, he seeks to understand the possible correlation and causal influence between ascetic Protestantism and the spirit of capitalism. As a preliminary step, it is therefore appropriate to point out what Weber understands by the capitalist system. For him, it is "a very complex system of institutions, highly rational in character, and the product of a number of developments peculiar to Western civilization" (Zeitlin, 1968: 123–24). Among all the factors that, in his opinion, were conducive to the birth and development of capitalism,[4] he seeks to investigate in particular the "elective affinity" of the ethical precepts of ascetic Protestantism and the spirit of capitalism. He maintains that Luther's reading of the Biblical term *calling* (*Beruf* in German) alludes, with particular force, to the realization of a task that is morally binding and set by God—a task that has its real bases in the construction of the everyday life of society from an eschatological perspective, but with a distinctly civilizing residue in comparison with Christianity before the Reformation. According to Zeitlin,

[Weber] is asserting on the basis of half completed research that there was a mutually reinforcing convergence of the Protestant ethic and the capitalist ethos; and he is *examining* in this instance the degree to which the latter was derived from the former. . . . On the theoretical level, then, Weber is *suggesting* that these were relatively autonomous developments which intersected at a given historical point to contribute to the formation of the modern rational temperament: There was a great "elective affinity" between the norms of the new religious movement and the psychological requirements of the new economic system. (Zeitlin, 1968: 129–30)

It was not necessary to wait long before a critique of this thesis of the elective affinity between Protestantism and capitalism was advanced. Although he figured them into his plan of work,[5] Weber never did examine the influences that acted in the opposite direction, namely, the effects of economic change on the formation of ascetic Protestantism. Hence his focus, although provisional, was never more than a unilateral point of view on the question, as extensive literature has shown (Samuelson, 1957; Fischoff, 1944; Lavalli, 1968; Eisenstandt, 1968; Parsons, 1958).

While it would be inappropriate to claim that Weber finally abandoned his thesis on the role of ascetic Protestantism (as some analysts have concluded), the impression remains, on re-reading his texts on religion in China, India, and Ancient Palestine, that he was more and more inclined to view capitalism as part of a much broader, general, and complex historical process in the West—a process that did not take place in the same manner in the East: the rationalization of daily life. This conviction is reaffirmed when Weber analyzes the makeup of government bureaucracy in imperial China and how it differs from its Western counterpart.

But where does Weber direct his attention when he endeavors to theorize on religion as a human phenomenon? In response to this question, we should refer to an innovative and important aspect of his work. Like Durkheim, he avoids concerning himself with the "essence" of religion, but, unlike Durkheim, he considers it unnecessary to elaborate a definition a priori. Such a definition would have to result from his entire theory (although, in the end, it is not to be found in his researches).

To define "religion," to say what it *is*, is not possible at the start of a presentation such as this. Definition can be attempted, if at all, only at the conclusion of the study. The essence of religion is not even our concern, as we make it our task to study the conditions and effects of a particular type of social action.

The external courses of religious behavior are so diverse that an understanding of this behavior can only be achieved from the viewpoint of the subjective experiences, ideas, and purposes of the individuals concerned—in short, from the viewpoint of the religious behavior's "meaning" (*Sinn*). (Weber, 1968, vol. 2: 399)

Not only does Weber refuse to propose a definition of the religious phenomenon—even an operational one—but he advances two important aspects of his thought in his treatment of the theme, namely, a subjective focus and a basic outline for understanding a social reality made up of human meanings that obtain material form through social action. Carried to its extreme, Weber's phrasing is conclusive. In short, understanding the social act in "religious" terms may only be undertaken on the basis of the lived experiences, claims, and subjective purposes of the individual. This proposition discards the methodology of Durkheim, who inclines toward the objective analysis of social reality by understanding all social facts as "things." In the same way, Weber's proposal avoids the Marxist suggestion of enclosing the analysis of the religious phenomenon within the dialectic of the infrastructure and superstructure and, in particular, within the theory of false consciousness. The interpretive material arising from the polemic on this point is very extensive.

The second aspect of Weber's thought—namely, that religion is a datum of social reality—is equally relevant, and is the basic point on which Marx, Durkheim, Weber and Gramsci coincide, that is the starting point for the existence of a sociology of religious phenomena. In Weber, however, religious phenomena remain within the realizable field of determination of the social act in the sense that all religious social action has a basically "intrahuman" content and contributes to the development of everyday life, which, for Weber, is to say that it contributes to the development of society itself and the social in general. Thus, in the course of his inquiry into religion, he asserts that "religious or magical behavior or thinking must not be set apart from the range of everyday purposive conduct, particularly since even the ends of the religious and magical actions are predominantly economic" (Weber, 1968, vol. 2: 400)

Here again, Weber reinforces his thesis on the interrelation between economics and religion, especially if we connect this comment with his earlier analysis of the development of capitalism, or with what could, from a different theoretical outlook, be called the origin of the accumulation of capital. In this earlier analysis Weber had emphasized, with regard to various types of community and society, the process of dissolution of the domestic community and the constitution of the *oikos*, defined as the organized meeting of needs even if for this purpose it is necessary to incorporate exploitation of a lucrative nature. Thus, he is able to state that "religiously or magically motivated behavior is relatively rational behavior, especially in its earliest manifestations. It follows rules of experience, though it is not necessarily action in accordance with a means-end schema" (Weber, 1968, vol. 2: 400).

Weber's contribution, oriented toward a "subjective" interpretation of actions imbued with subjectivity, is therefore important. He contributes to removing the myths about religious action in the social setting by studying it as a "sacred" activity in secular contexts and granting it a respectable degree of impact on society. Perhaps without wanting to, we may find a Weber who, though he does not consider religion in ideological terms, nevertheless discovers relevant and constituent aspects of it in the fabric of social relations. These aspects, in a reading taken after the fact, may be very important to any analysis of the mystifying effects of religious consciousness (particularly at the level of popular religiosity), as well as the conflictive effects of religious practices with respect to social power itself. Thus we find, for example, the emergence of popular movements within religious practices, such as the Popular Churches in Latin America, that are led and directed from the perspective of the class struggle and are essentially opposed to the dominant classes. Perhaps it would not be far-fetched to say that an analysis of the religious determinations of these social and political practices may not be foreign to the approach taken by Weber.

In contrast with Durkheim, Weber points out that the determination of the religious act has its origin (and corresponding meaning) in the "belief in spirits" (Weber, 1968, vol. 2: 401). The human being identified alien powers—on the one hand, the "soul"; on the other, the "gods," "demons," and/or "supernatural powers" (Weber, 1968, vol. 2: 403)— and the ordering of them constitutes the realm of religious action. In this respect, Weber's taxonomy of societal reality identifies a specific social order to which religious action is connected, even if—without being entirely irrational—religious action may not, in light of its purposes, be defined as rational. In the course of his studies, Weber defines three specific and basic problems that the sociology of religion as an academic subject will inherit as indispensable topics: (1) the connections among religious institutions, religion itself, and other social institutions; (2) the forms of institutionalization of religion; (3) the types of religious leadership. Even in his comparative studies on religion in China, India, and Palestine, Weber indicated basic aspects of the relation between the legitimation of religion and social structure, and his work has clearly inspired various sociologists. Peter Berger, for example, writes as follows:

Religious legitimations arise from human activity, but once crystallized into complexes of meaning that become part of a religious tradition they can attain a measure of autonomy as against this activity. Indeed, they may then act back upon actions in everyday life, transforming the latter, sometimes radically. . . .

Religion thus serves to maintain the reality of that socially constructed world within which men exist in their everyday lives. Its legitimating power, however, has another important dimension—the integration into a comprehensive nomos of precisely those marginal situations in which the reality of everyday life is put in question. (Berger, 1967: 41–42)

This dual dimension of the religious phenomenon—its contribution to the stabilization of the status quo through social mystification by making a fetish of social relations, while at the same time contributing to the contradictory modification of those relations—was not perceived by

Weber with the same clarity as Berger; Weber only insinuated the theme. However, we should recall that the function of the prophet according to Weber—whether as an instrument of ethical or of exemplary prophecy in his analyses of Ancient Palestine—has the character of a double negation: a negation of the crystallization of the salvatory message in questionable social and religious forms, as well as a negation of the prevailing social structure, which is generally reinforced by the kind of crystallization of Jewish theodicy in effect at the time. In the final analysis, the social action of the prophet—according to Weber—allows him to be considered as both a religious and a social reformer.

Max Weber distances himself from the entire anthropological tradition founded by Marcel Mauss and Claude Lévi-Strauss since he does not see the origin of the priest in the magician. In Weber's opinion, they are two functionaries who, although different, are sociologically related. The priest is the professional functionary who influences the "gods" through worship, in contrast to sorcerer (and magicians) who coerce the "demons" by conjuring them through magic. Nevertheless, for Weber, the magic stage is one of the (perhaps primitive) stages of all religions. At the same time, the magical side (the devil) of the rite is a function of its religious side (the diety). Both are encompassed by the same theodicy and every demon is not a secular entity, but an eminently sacred one, even as a necessary complement to the ineffably sacred or the holy.

Since the functionaries of religion are the center of Weber's sociological observations, studying their role is very important for an understanding of the causes and social impacts of religion on culture. Referring to Christianity in particular, Reinhard Bendix very accurately summarizes one of Weber's principal hypotheses about religious leaders that has influenced many of the sociological and even exegetical and Biblical analyses of our times:

On the basis of comparative evidence Weber concluded that the great religious leaders had been active in urban areas but not in the great culture centers of the world. He linked this generalization to the idea that men in these culture centers believed or assumed they knew the answers and were no longer able to ask questions of profound religious significance because they had become enmeshed in the techniques of civilization. (Bendix, 1962: 269)

Hypotheses like this one must be related to new circumstances such as the impact of certain "millenarian" and "salvationist" sects in a society like North America. In this context, it is appropriate to remember the People's

Temple and the circumstances and factors that led to the collective suicide of 923 of its members in Georgetown, Guyana, on November 26, 1978, or the importance, in the suburban perimeters of Latin America and in relatively less developed areas, of Churches and sects that, as in the case of the Jehovah's Witnesses, were very influential in the political conduct of the people during the sixties in Chile (Pin, n.d.). Particularly remarkable is the activity of North American Churches and sects, with consequences that may be of considerable scope in the long term, among the indigenous populations of the Mexican states of Oaxaca and Chiapas or the Sumo and Miskita populations along the Atlantic coast of Nicaragua.

In summary, among the various materials on religion developed by Weber, there are several levels of analysis that collectively shape the basic analytical structure of religious phenomena:

1. the interpretation of inductive generalizations about specific religious processes;

2. the interpretive explanation of the social origin of religious doctrines;

3. the elaboration of a method for conceptualizing historical materials, centered, as a general rule, on a three-pronged analysis including the religious leader, doctrine, and the social and historical conditions of the time;

4. the application of this method, on a comparative basis, in order to reveal the distinctive features of different religions compared geographically and historically with other similar or analogous phenomena; and

5. the analysis of the causes of religion and, especially in the Western world, the connections between Protestant thought and ethics and the emergence of capitalism, taking the rationalism characteristic of Western civilization as the crux of interpretation.

In conclusion, it is not possible to understand the sociology of religion in Weber outside the context of his work as a whole. Only in the thematic interrelations of his own intellectual journey does his discussion of the religious phenomenon acquire meaning as a civilizing phenomenon closely connected with the process of rationalization of the Western world, that is, with the rise and consolidation of capitalism as a mode of production. In this light, religion appears as intersubjective social action—as the connection among subjectivities—with the attributes of social control and motivation for action. The material dynamic of the religious underlies the impacts of religion on culture, but the individual conduct of the religious person (especially the religious leader and the prophet) was, for Weber, much more important as his starting point than the connections either between norm and rite, as in Durkheim's theory, or between religious practice and ideology (false consciousness), as in the Marxist view.

The comparative and historical analysis undertaken by Weber on a wide range of materials from China, India, and Ancient Palestine, as well as from the Protestant Reformation, also offers a view different from that of Durkheim and Marx. Durkheim focused his study on the anthropological aspects of totemic practices (as a primordial form of religion) and their impact on social solidarity. Seen in perspective, his was a synchronic focus based on inferential techniques. Marx undertook a detailed study, from the perspective of political philosophy, of the gnoseological condition of the religious mentality, its association with class interest and with the fetishizing of social relations. In Marx there is a very concrete interest in knowing the ideological rationality of religion, its impact on individuals and world views as part of a more general and broader process of making a fetish of social relations. However, he undertook no historical or diachronic studies of religion, notwithstanding the fact that his critique of religion was considered to be the assumption underlying his critique overall.

## NOTES

1. One of the best commentaries on the complexity and scope of Weber's thought is by Reinhard Bendix (1962). Weber himself, in the original outline of his great work *Economy and Society*, had already anticipated the topics on his research agenda, namely, economics and social orders and powers, identified as follows:

1. Categories of social orders. The basic relation between economics and law. The economic relations of associations in general.

2. The domestic community, the home, and business.

3. The association of neighborhood, kinship, and community.

4. The ethnic relations of the community.

5. Religious communities. The dependence of religions on classes; advanced religions and economic ideology.

6. The collectivization of the marketplace.

7. Political associations. Conditions in the development of law. Professions, classes, parties. The nation.

8. Power: (i) the three types of legitimate power; (ii) political and hierocratic power; (iii) illegal power, a typology of the cities; (iv) the development of the modern State, and (v) the modern political parties. (Weber, 1968)

2. The fact that, like Marx, Weber (but in historico-cultural rather than structural-historical terms) based much of his theory on the theme of domination has made many researchers—Irving Zeitlin (1968) and Alvin Gouldner (1970) among others—note that the analyses of Weber (occasionally characterized as the "bourgeois" Marx) are not unrelated to those of Marx himself. Indeed, they appear to be connected to him, and it has been suggested that the direction they take contributes to Marx's exegesis. Zeitlin, for example—far from concurring with Lukács that Weber endeavors to refute historical materialism—points out that Weber is amicably debating Marx's ghost in the sense that he seizes upon and goes deeper into aspects insufficiently developed by Marx. This may serve as a warning not to judge Weber exclusively on the basis of the version of his thought translated and popularized in the social sciences in North America by Talcott Parsons. Digressing briefly, in contemporary political analysis the works of Jürgen Habermas and Claus Offe—especially those focused on the crisis of capitalism and the politics of social welfare—show that the analysis of Marx and Weber are not necessarily opposites or mutually exclusive. Some association between the two theoretical directions poses very stimulating developments. See Habermas (1975) and Offe (1974: 31–55). Finally, a very persuasive argument on this point, concerning the thesis on religion, may be found in the already classic work of Joseph Gabel, "Elements for a Marxist Reading of the Sociology of Religion of Max Weber" (in Gabel, 1970: 173–80).

3. It is enlightening to connect the study of religious ideas as an autonomous theme with developments in the sociology of knowledge. See the two volumes edited by Irving Horowitz (1969), especially the fourth part of volume 1 on the social determination of religious ideas (pp. 211–76).

4. These factors were a permanent rational industry, rational accountancy, rational technology, the rational mind, rational law, the rationalization of conduct in life in general, and the rationalist economic ethic (see Weber, 1964: vol. 1: 46–170).

5. See point 5 in note 1 above on Weber's topics, in which he proposed to study the dependence of religion on classes and the connections between advanced religions and economic ideology.

# 4

# Religion as Historical Bloc: The Perspective of Antonio Gramsci

The objective of Antonio Gramsci's intellectual endeavor—undertaken in less than favorable conditions, in a fascist jail between 1929 and 1937 while affected by ill health and the censorship imposed by the regime of Benito Mussolini[1]—was to explain the failure of the proletarian revolution in the West. On confronting a task of this size, Gramsci opted for new conceptual and explanatory strategies with respect to economic and political production and reproduction of the established social and cultural order by basing himself on a broad reinterpretation of the philosophy of praxis.

His work was and continues to be the object of many and varied readings. Among the tendencies imputed to him are that he was a historicist, Hegelian, Crocian, or heterodox to the point of ceasing to be Marxist and becoming the theoretician of anti-Leninism. Referring to the imputations about Gramsci's work and attempts to confront him with Marx or Lenin by forcing him through an orthodox filter, Massimo Salvadori makes a very pertinent comment: "This method must be decidedly rejected because it is essentially clerical, even when it hides behind the ideology of 'Marxist science,' and because it would suppose that Marxism was a diamond of astral light deposited once and for all into the hands of an honest clerk" (Salvadori, 1970: preface).

There is no doubt that Gramsci was a Marxist intellectual, a militant member of a revolutionary communist party and profoundly involved in the dynamics of the national and international political struggle of the party in his time.[2] Hence, one of the central concerns in Gramsci is the question of the party as an organic intellectual in the constitution of a new historical bloc.[3] However, Gramsci's intellectual output far exceeded the theoretical and political demands of the hour or intra- and interparty polemics, and emerges as one of the great theoretical contributions to political science in this century—perhaps equal to the genius of Max Weber, the conceptual clarity of the Canadian C. Brough MacPherson, or the rigorous conceptual undertaking of the great German critical theoretician Jürgen Habermas. Given the facts, one might apply to Gramsci what George Lichtheim suggested of Habermas two decades ago: "It is not altogether easy to assess the work of a scholar whose professional competence extends from the logic of science to the sociology of knowledge, by way of Marx, Hegel, and the more recondite sources of the European metaphysical tradition" (cited in Bernstein, 1985: 1). Gramsci was a scholar without an institution, without financial support or access to the opinion of his peers. Moreover, he was a political activist. Adjusting Lichtheim's conclusion about Habermas, we might say that Gramsci "seems to have been born with a faculty for digesting the toughest kind of material and then refashioning it into [dis]orderly wholes" (cited in Bernstein, 1985: 1).

The seminal analysis provided by the *Prison Notebooks*, which have the rigor of scientific introspection combined with the literary freshness of a post-Renaissance and, at times, a postmodern intellectual as refined as Gramsci, poses philological and theoretical challenges far beyond the interests and limits of this chapter. Moreover, the fragmentary nature of his reflections, the conceptual paraphernalia to which Gramsci had to resort in order to elude the sharp eye of prison censorship, and the disordered and fragmented—although programmatic—style of his writing invite every interpretation of his work to be considered as essentially provisional and open to conceptual and political argument. In this chapter, we have tried to retain some of the central themes presented in the satisfactory English version (Gramsci, 1980) and the excellent Spanish translation (Gramsci, 1975–77) of Gramsci's works, and, by concentrating on these themes, have traced the main lines of his analysis of religion and the Catholic Church.

## GRAMSCI AND SUPERSTRUCTURES: PARALLELS IN HIS ANALYSIS OF RELIGION AND EDUCATION

J. Jacques Texier (1966) defined Gramsci as the theoretician of superstructures. Along the same lines, Henry Giroux characterized the Marxist theory of education influenced by Gramsci as the "Hegemonic-State Reproductive Model" (Giroux, 1983: 274).

Notwithstanding the importance of the theme of pedagogy in Gramsci, the several analyses based on discussion of education in the *Prison Notebooks* do not reach similar conclusions, but, in the realm of interpretation, reproduce the conceptual and analytical alternatives that may emerge from the ambiguities, silences, and lack of systematization—and development, on occasions—of Gramsci's thought.[4] In Gramsci, every relationship of hegemony is a pedagogical relationship (Torres, 1985). As he points out,

the educational relationship should not be restricted to the field of the strictly "scholastic" relationship. . . . This form of relationship exists throughout society as a whole. . . . It exists between intellectual and non-intellectual sections of the population, between the rulers and the rules, *élites* and their followers, leaders (*dirigenti*) and led, the vanguard and the body of the army. Every relationship of "hegemony" is necessarily an educational relationship. (Gramsci, 1980: 350)

In this sense, Gramsci's contribution to education can be summarized by five main hypotheses: (1) insofar as hegemony is founded on coercion and consensus, it is an educative relationship; (2) despite the fact that hegemony is exerted by the ruling class, it is organized in capitalist society by a particular social category: the intellectuals; (3) education in the process of formation of "social conformism"; (4) the State, as an "ethical State" or, indeed, as an educator, assumes the function of building a new "type" or "level" of civilization; thus, it constitutes an instrument of rationalization; and (5) the establishment of a classless society and the building of a collective will must be achieved through intellectual and moral reform (Gramsci, 1975–77, vol. 1).[5]

To a great extent, as Hugues Portelli showed in his studies on Gramsci (Portelli, 1973, 1977), the study of the specificity of the religious phenomenon is based on the fact that religion, like education, may acquire a relative autonomy. After all, for Portelli, "the true problem posed by Gramsci consists in investigating the reason why the religious *Weltanschauung* has not succeeded in forming a norm of religious life, has not developed into a praxis" (Portelli, 1977: 17). In this sense, a Marxist sociology of religion inspired by Gramsci, Portelli will argue, is to be found in the context of the links between ideology and common sense, religion as a specific ideology—which leads Gramsci from political analysis to a sociological study of the Catholic religion in Italy—and, of course, the links among the State, religion, intellectuals, and hegemony. Since the State, ideology, common sense, hegemony, and intellectuals are central themes in any work intending to claim Gramsci's analysis for the study of education[6]—a fact that shows the analytical parallels in his work on education, religion, and superstructures in general—it is imperative to present a synthesis of his categories for the study of religion.

## THE STATE, HEGEMONY, INTELLECTUALS, AND RELIGION

The notion of hegemony, so important for the analyses of politics, education, culture, or religion, does not have a univocal signal in Gramsci, but fluctuates between two clearly differentiated positions.[7] This ultimately has to do with his antinomies, as expressed in the celebrated essay in which Perry Anderson (1978) suggests that there are at least three views of the State in Gramsci and two positions on hegemony. In the first place, the State is presented in opposition to civil society: the State as political society, as a political administrative apparatus that submits civil society as a whole to a complex process of domination; the State as force. In the second place, the State encompasses civil society—in other words, "hegemony armoured with coercion" (Anderson, 1978: 43–44). Finally in the third place, the State appears to be identical to civil society; the State as consensus. In this instance, for Gramsci, the unity between civil society and political society is organic, so that any distinction is essentially methodological.

There appear to be two clearly differentiated positions on hegemony. On the one hand, hegemony refers to a process of social and political domination in which the ruling classes establish their control over the classes allied to them through moral and intellectual leadership. In this sense, as indicated earlier, hegemony acquires a pedagogical character and both the school and the Church are fundamental instruments or institutions in the process of teaching and learning. On the other hand, hegemony refers to the dual use of force and ideology to reproduce social relations between the ruling and subaltern classes.[8]

One way of reconciling this conflict in Gramsci is to accept that no State may govern based entirely on force, but needs a social basis for control, with clear ideological supports. At the same time, to the extent that hegemony is established as a consensus shared on the basis of common sense, it is part of a complex ideological-political process of persuasion supported in the last resort by the repressive apparatuses of the State. This process of persuasion amounts to a continual confrontation undertaken for the definition of individual subjectivities, the definition of the rational elements that determine the materiality of a culture, and the definition of the ethical-moral premises that guide the practices and conduct of individuals. This is to say that hegemony, as a unity of opposites, is not a static concept, but emerges from a struggle or confrontation.

Hegemony is produced by the organic intellectuals of the ruling classes and is also transmitted by traditional intellectuals. For Gramsci (as interpreted also by Hugues Portelli and Louis Althusser), the Catholic Church is constituted as the organic intellectual of the governing class, especially under feudalism. According to Portelli, the Catholic Church experienced four definite periods as an organic intellectual, namely, "that of the appearance of Catholicism as a revolutionary movement, its alliance with the Low Empire, its mutation as the organic intellectual of the feudal class, and the crisis of hegemony that erupts with the heresies" (Portelli, 1977: 45).

In the *Prison Notebooks*, Gramsci begins his study of intellectuals and the organization of culture by wondering if intellectuals are an autonomous and independent social group or if, by contrast, each social group has its own specialized categories of intellectuals (Gramsci, 1975–77, vol. 2: 11). For him, everyone is an intellectual, but not everyone has an intellectual function in society (Gramsci, 1975–77, vol. 2: 14). Each social group creates an awareness of its own function. In this way, the organic intellectuals that each new class "creates for itself and forms in its progressive development are generally specializations of partial aspects of the primitive activity of the new social type to which the new class has given birth" (Gramsci, 1975–77, vol. 2: 12). However, each economic group that arises finds preexisting categories of intellectuals in history. The most typical category of these intellectuals are the clergy, "for a long time monopolizers (during the entire stage of history that is in part characterized by this monopoly) of some important services: religious ideology, that is to say the philosophy and science of the age, schools, instruction, morality, justice, welfare. . . . The category of the clergy may be considered as the intellectual category organically tied to the landed aristocracy" (Gramsci, 1975–77, vol. 2: 12–13).

There are organic and traditional intellectuals, just as there are superior intellectuals and those who may be considered as being of an intermediate rank and who provide the link that binds the superior level (whether organic or traditional intellectuals) and the masses. Schoolteachers and priests who exercise parochial functions constitute this class of intermediate intellectuals (Gramsci, 1980: 342).[9]

Thus far, it is possible to affirm that there is considerable unity—practically mutual indispensability—between the notion of the State as consensus-coercion and the production of hegemony by a ruling group that, as a function of its economic predominance and its intellectual and moral leadership, is able to impose its principles of social organization on the rest of the classes allied to it and on the subaltern classes as a whole.

The intellectuals are indispensable for the production of hegemony and the articulation of hegemonic relationships between the higher intellectual strata of society and the people-nation. Religion, like education, is a perfect element for generating acquiescence and solidifying beliefs in an established historical bloc. Gramsci analyzes how the Catholic Church—after the crisis in the Catholic-feudal bloc caused by heresy, the Reformation, and the Renaissance (which would culminate in the blow for freedom struck by the French Revolution)—is transformed into a traditional intellectual once the Restoration fails. As Portelli concludes from his analysis of Gramsci's texts, "the Church, then, is falling back: from organic intellectual of the feudal system, it has been reduced to a caste of traditional intellectuals" (Portelli, 1977: 102).

Parallels between the analysis of education and institutionalized religion crop up once more. Although public education continues to be a disputed territory in the democratic State where there is both contradiction and correspondence,[10] the separation between religion and State—from the moment when Christianity ceased to be the religion of the State, especially through the contradictions brought to light by the Protestant Reformation—causes the role of religion in the production and reproduction of hegemonic relations and the social order in general to be, for Gramsci, much more subtle and possibly provisional than perhaps other superstructural activities more closely tied to the State, such as public education or the administration of law. For Gramsci, there are elements of theocracy "in all States where there is no clear and radical separation between Church and State, where the clergy exercises public functions of any kind, and the teaching of religion is obligatory or there are concordats. It is the the inversion of Macchiavelli's maxim: *regnum instrumentum religionis*" (Gramsci, 1975–77, vol. 5: 191).

One element that Gramsci proposed to look into was whether "there is a link, and what it consists of, between the religious unity of a country and the multiplicity of parties and, vice versa, between the relative unity of the parties and the multiplicity of churches and sects" (Gramsci, 1975–77; vol. 5: 202). This sociological hypothesis on the connections between religion and politics arises from Gramsci's appreciation of the situation in the United States, where there were two efficient political parties and hundreds of churches and religious sects, in contrast with France, where there was an enormous number of political parties but a notable religious unity. Gramsci thinks the explanation for this situation could reside in the fact that

both the party and religion are forms of conception of the world and that religious unity is apparent, as is political unity: religious unity hides a real multiplicity of conceptions of the world that find expression in the parties because there is a religious "indifferentism," just as political unity hides a multiplicity of tendencies that find expression in religious sects, etc. Each man tends to have a unique, organic and systematic conception of the world, but since cultural differences are multiple and profound, society presents a strange variegation of currents that show religious or political similarity, according to the historical tradition. (Gramsci, 1975–77; vol. 5: 202)

There are marginal cases where this hypothesis of religious unity and political multiplicity is applicable in a limited way, the case of Argentina as analyzed in Chapter 9 being one of them. When there was a strong integralist Church[11] there in the first three decades of this century, political plurality was very restricted. However, as we argue in Chapter 9, when the Argentinean Church evolved toward more liberal positions, this did not affect its unity, at least not until the sixties, nor did it modify religious unity substantially. With religious unity relatively stable, the number of parties that were formed after the so-called Decade of Infamy (1930–40)—with the predominance of the Conservative Party, the birth of Peronism, the strengthening of the Unión Cívica Radical, and its subsequent fragmentation into the Unión Cívica Radical Intransigente, the Unión Cívica Radical del Pueblo, and the Partido Desarrollista,[12] as well as the continued presence of the Communist Party, the Socialist Party, and a great variety of provincial parties with a small but nevertheless effective representation in the National Congress—shows that Gramsci's hypothesis of religious unity and political diversity is too one-sided and should be qualified according to historical periods and the kind of State that predominates in each social formation.

Although in the United States and particularly in France, the State is a fundamental factor in the reproduction of capital and the political legitimation of the system overall, Guillermo O'Donnell and a number of political scientists argue that the Argentinean State has been colonized by civil society in Argentina and finds itself continually confronting serious crises of democratic stability[13] in which, paradoxically, the prevailing kind of religious unity reinforces the presence of an authoritarian trend of thought in the major institutions, undermining the elements of consensus and political negotiation that constituted the basis of the democratic pact.[14] But let us leave this specific analysis of Gramsci's hypothesis (which he would never investigate empirically, given the conditions of its intellectual production) and return to the theme of the ambivalent role of religion as a contributor to the constitution of common sense and therefore to hegemony.

## RELIGION AS COMMON SENSE: THE AMBIVALENCE OF PRACTICE AND POPULAR KNOWLEDGE

For Gramsci, there are clear parallels between the notion of common sense (as ideology) and religion. Neither of them constitutes an intellectual order, since they may not be reduced to unity and coherence either in the individual or the collective consciousness (Gramsci, 1980: 326). There are practical differences between the philosophy elaborated by intellectuals and the philosophy practiced by the common man and woman—an important distinction for showing the passage from one moment, the philosophy of high culture, to that of the common sense of the people-nation: "In philosophy the features of individual elaboration of thought are the most salient: in common sense on the other hand it is the diffuse, unco-ordinated features of a generic form of thought to a particular period and a particular popular environment" (Gramsci, 1980: 330).

Following the footsteps of Durkheim, Gramsci even offers a secular definition of religion: "a unity of faith between a conception of the world and a corresponding norm of conduct" (Gramsci, 1980: 326).[15] Thought, ethics, and conduct are indissolubly united in Gramsci's analysis. For him, religion is ideology understood not merely as false consciousness, but as politics, as praxis, as conscious action in the search for a common object— a praxis that involves (historically) progressive as well as regressive, that mixes conservative and traditional elements together in a complex amalgam.

Gramsci is very clear about the risks of a popular and mechanistic Marxism that disdains religion by reducing it to the dimensions of the theory of false consciousness.[16] This approach to the subject implies a negative a priori value judgment about religion itself, and excludes the possibility of accepting praxis as partly nonrational and based on sensations (a criticism of positivist Marxism); more important still, it does not allow for the treatment of religion as superstructure, the central theme of Gramsci's theoretical reconstruction.

After involving himself in a careful discussion of what an ideology is (Gramsci, 1980: 376ff), Gramsci concludes that it may be either a necessary superstructure of a specific structure, or simply the arbitrary lucubrations of particular individuals. He rejects the notion of ideology as arbitrary lucubration and endeavors to study ideologies as historically organic, having the following characteristics: they appear to be historically necessary; they have psychological validity; they contribute to organizing the masses; and they create the necessary ground on which people move, acquire consciousness of their respective positions, and even develop social struggles.

At this point, Gramsci evokes Marx's emphasis on the "solidity of popular beliefs" in any specific situation (Gramsci, 1980: 377). He also concludes, "Another proposition of Marx is that a popular conviction often has the same energy as a material force or something of the kind, which is extremely significant" (Gramsci, 1980: 377); and his conclusion reinforces his belief in the dialectic between structure and superstructure in the processes of social transition and the constitution of historical blocs. Accordingly, he argues for a conception of historical bloc "in which precisely material forces are the content and ideologies are the form, though this distinction between form and content has purely didactic value, since the material forces would be inconceivable historically without form and the ideologies would be individual fancies without the material forces" (Gramsci, 1980: 377).

Every historical bloc is based on real conceptions of the world; and thus we even find Gramsci paraphrasing Hegel's *Philosophy of Right*, pointing out that the rational is real and the real is rational—which has provoked a great polemic among militants and academics with a view to defining in particular whether Gramsci makes this statement as a general principle or to describe the unity between superstructure and structure or between thought and action (Gramsci, 1980: 366, n. 57). His statement is the following: "the 'rational' is actively and actually real" (Gramsci, 1980: 366). In any case, conceptions of the world develop from two processes that are occasionally parallel, but mostly intersect in the constitution of an historical bloc, that is, conceptions of the world that logically assert themselves as intellectual constructions and conceptions of the world that emerge from the real activity of the masses, of the people-nation (Gramsci, 1980: 418).

The articulation of this link between intellectuals and the people-nation, insofar as it amounts to a connection at the level of rationalities and sentiments, is indispensable for the constitution of new historical bloc in political praxis. Without passion and the connection of sentiment to new rationalities, it is impossible, in Gramsci's philosophical-political vision, to undertake politics (Gramsci, 1980: 418).

To the extent that for Gramsci the constitution of the individual as people-nation, or of the individual as humanity, takes place in political praxis, every social action is political, even when it does not totally contain within it the "real" philosophy of all people (which is rational). This is to say that, in Gramsci, there exists the notion of common sense, which is traditionally defined as a conception of the world (Gramsci, 1980: 197) but is presented in him as a conception borrowed or imposed on the people-nation to the extent that

for reasons of submission and intellectual subordination, [the people, subaltern classes] adopted a conception which is not its own but is borrowed from another group; and it affirms this conception verbally and believes itself to be following it, because this is the conception which it follows in "normal times"—that is when its conduct is not independent and autonomous, but submissive and subordinate. (Gramsci, 1980: 327)

Defined in these terms, the question of common sense is apparently not unlike the classic Marxist conception of the alienation of the workforce that has been submitted to the dynamics of exploitation, the separation of the immediate producer from the means of production, the exacerbation of the extraction of absolute and relative surplus value, in addition to the legal restrictions imposed by the administrative and judicial apparatuses of the State.[17] However, there is a significant change of direction in Gramsci's interpretation. In every system of thought and collection of norms of conduct that may be expressed as "common sense," there is a "good sense"—a salutary nucleus that is basically rational. Given the circumstances in which the life of the people-nation unfolds, this good sense cannot be objectively externalized and used reflexively. However, it is the only alternative for transforming common sense into a force acting in a direction opposed to the hegemonic direction of society. This is possible because good sense "deserves to be made more unitary and coherent" (Gramsci, 1980: 328). In this manner, as Gramsci points out, "The active man-in-the-mass has a practical activity, but has no clear theoretical consciousness of his practical activity, which nonetheless involves understanding the world insofar as it transforms it. His theoretical consciousness can indeed be historically in opposition to his activity" (Gramsci, 1980: 333).

This text may clearly be read in tandem with Hegel's *Phenomenology of Spirit*, especially in its reference to the slave who, in the conflict of opposing consciousnesses, affirms the lordship of his master through his work, by dominating nature and offering him its fruits—but his fear and submission are, precisely, the origin both of cultural formation and the possibilities of freedom from the relationship between master and slave. Once he discovers within his weakness (submission, fear) the possibilities of breaking the bonds of enslaved labor (appropriation of goods), this is the moment of his recognition of self-consciousness, when it becomes known that "the *truth* of the independent consciousness is accordingly the servile consciousness of the bondsman" (Hegel, 1977: 117). When knowledge acquired through practical activity—through the feeling of fear, subjection, and servility, but, above all, through labor—becomes consciousness, it produces awareness in the bondsman that "being-for-self belongs to *him*, that he himself exists essentially and actually in his own right" (Hegel, 1977: 118). Gramsci, however, does not limit himself to recognizing the value of practical activity as a transformer of the world and as the source of independent consciousness (consciousness for its own sake), but proposes that the theoretical consciousness emerging from this activity may, historically, be in opposition to the activity itself (Gramsci, 1980: 333) precisely on account of this good sense, this salutary nucleus that may be made more unified and coherent.

In summary, every conception of the world, every philosophy (or ideology, in the broader sense in which Gramsci uses the term), is to be found in the foundations of any cultural movement, religion, or faith, which may only develop as a form of practical activity when philosophy is an implied theoretical premise—but philosophy in the sense that it constitutes common sense.[18]

Religion is one manifestation of that common sense, then—administered by specific institutions, such as the Catholic Church, which struggles to maintain unity between the higher levels of philosophy (produced by intellectuals) and common sense (of ordinary men and women), a unity that may only be achieved through politics. However, the struggle to prevent the separation between the intellectuals and the people from affecting the Church is, for Gramsci, to be found at the root of the heretical movements of the Middle Ages and in the rise of religious orders that are centered on strong personalities (St. Dominic, St. Francis) who propel the movements of masses, or in the creation of religious orders like the Jesuits, which in Gramsci's opinion is the last of the great religious orders with reactionary and authoritarian origins. These religious orders not only contribute to the creation of an iron discipline to prevent Catholic intellectuals from exceeding certain limits of differentiation from the masses, but they also systematically introduce reformist programs into the culture of the masses or their common sense without modifying the construction of the intellectual-moral bloc on which it is based (Gramsci, 1980: 331–33).

Gramsci's reasoning with regard to the religious orders of the Catholic Church—especially the role of the Society of Jesus and what he calls "Jesuitism"—is undoubtedly marked by his appreciation of the disputes between "modernism" and "integralism" that kept cropping up in the Catholic Church in the first three decades of this century[19] and that Gramsci knew very well as a regular reader of *La Civiltà Cattolica*. However, it should be pointed out that the historical evolution of the Catholic Church, after the Second Vatican Council in particular, has shown dramatic changes in the "diplomacy" that Gramsci attributed to the Society of Jesus, especially after 1976 when the society issued its document on the option for justice that led many Jesuit provinces to modify their educational practices, abandoning the education of elites,[20] as, for example, in the case of the "Patria" college in Mexico. Although documents like those emanating from the Second Vatican Council, the document of the Society of Jesus on justice, and the "Medellín Document" drafted by the Latin American bishops in 1968 (see Chapter 9, note 71 and the connected text) opened the way for religious orders in Latin America to take on "a preferential option for the poor," this did not in any way constitute a change in the institutional practices of all religious orders. Rather, it legitimized preexisting ideological and political differences within them, and these differences became more evident during the rise and consolidation of the Theology of Liberation, which has clearly adopted an analysis inspired by Gramsci,[21] such as the philosophy of praxis. This is something that Gramsci could not have foreseen in his own time, perhaps. On the contrary, his admonition that the Catholic Church must impose an iron discipline on its intellectuals in order not to widen the gap between itself and the people would now have to be modified to accommodate those episodes in which intellectuals are censured for proposing strategies that would possibly generate an increasing distance between Vatican centralism and the local churches founded on base communities. This situation is clearly perceptible when, for instance, the Sacred Congregation for the Faith calls attention to and even imposes sanctions on theologians of Liberation, as in the well-known case of the Brazilian Franciscan theologian Leonardo Boff a few years ago.[22] The historical perspective proposed by Gramsci is taken up critically in the commentaries of the Brazilian Dominican Frei Betto, who points out the importance of social contradictions for understanding Church practice. Referring to the Church in Brazil in comparison with others in Latin America, Frei Betto argues,

The class struggle also occurs within the Church and places the bishops in different spaces. In a Church where the spirit of corporativism, or corporation, was stronger than the practices of class contradiction that the Argentinian clergy put in place, class relations in Brazil seem highly attenuated. Since the spirit of corporation existed in Brazil, but there was no ideological political link, like that of Christian Democracy to the episcopate in Chile, this characteristic, in effect, allowed the Brazilian Church to be permeated by social contradictions. In Brazil, the clergy is from the popular, peasant class. Even Catholic Action was the first revolutionary progressive element of the Brazilian Catholic Church.[23]

An analysis such as this would have surprised Gramsci, who considered that the Jesuits and the specialized religious orders were important in the Counter-Reformation for the development of movements of the masses but that over time this collection of disciplining institutions were insufficient to maintain control of the Catholic masses. The Church had therefore created a system of recruitment and organization permanently entrusted to an authentic body for organization of the masses. Hence the creation of Catholic Action, a true political party of the Church with specialized institutions such as the Young Catholic Workers, the Catholic University Youth, and so on (Portelli, 1977: 151).

According to Portelli, Gramsci concludes his analysis of religion thus: "The *Notebooks* end, then, with a fairly realistic conclusion: the religious phenomenon is a permanent phenomenon, tied to popular culture; it exceeds the strict framework of the confessional religions to permeate the common sense and, more generally, all ideologies disseminated among the subaltern classes" (Portelli, 1977: 228).

## RELIGION: FROM THE FUTILITY OF DETERMINIST MECHANICISM TO THE CONSTRUCTION OF A NEW HISTORICAL BLOC

Gramsci is conscious that positive religions are an inextricable part of social life. In his notes on Machiavelli, he chose a quotation from Plutarch that is very clear in this respect:

When you are travelling, you may come across cities without walls and writing, without kings and houses (!), without wealth, and without the use of coins, deprived of theaters and gymnasia (palestras). But, a city without temples and gods, that formulates no prayers, oaths, or divinations, or does not make sacrifices to see good and to plead against evil, nobody has ever seen such a one, nor will they ever see it. (cited in Gramsci, 1975–77, vol. 1: 277)

Even accepting the relationship of dependence in which religion seems to be established (human dependence on a divinity, on a collection of norms of conduct established by moral canons that are institutionalized once it is determined that the divinity has pronounced them) (Gramsci, 1975–77, vol. 1: 277), Gramsci will continue to assume the duality of meanings of religion as common sense. Religion for him will be part of a comprehensive or totalitarian process, to use his terminology, for bringing the masses closer to the intellectuals in the construction of a social and individual discipline and for using the everyday experience of humans in the construction of a hegemonic consensus. On the other hand, religion may be conceived of as constituting the nucleus of good sense in common sense.

Given the appropriate conditions for intellectual reflection, religion— as an element that may have a unitary and rational nucleus[24]—may evolve into a system of thought and a critical praxis. This is the Gramsci that will be incorporated into contemporary analyses of the meaning and practice of religion in Latin America by those who understand religion as a constituent element of a historical bloc, as part of a process of contradiction and correspondence between material relations and symbolic representations.[25]

For Gramsci, the history of Christianity would seem to show that "over a certain period of history in certain specific historical conditions religion has been and continues to be a 'necessity,' a necessary form taken by the will of the popular masses and a specific way of rationalizing the world and real life, which provided the general framework for real practical activity" (Gramsci, 1980: 337). This is precisely the central conviction that will animate different directions taken by the pastorate and the Popular Church in Latin America: religion as a historical bloc.

In spite of this, two themes resound in Gramsci's voice, treatment of which demands attention. On the one hand we find that, even while postulating the existence of good sense within common sense, Gramsci ends his studies on popular religion by assuming that the popular classes are ideologically conservative and that all intellectual and moral reform will be as difficult to establish in the subaltern classes as it will be to try to persuade the ruling classes.[26] On the other hand we see that, by adapting to the transformations of the modern capitalist world in Latin America, the Catholic Church still retains power. This has occurred even with the independence of the Catholic parties and unions from the directives of the hierarchies, when the transformation of Catholic Action in many countries has politicized the youth and, to a certain extent, secularized politics of Catholic origin, and, finally, when the crisis in structure (and hegemony) has profoundly affected the Catholic Churches of the region, so that the "crisis in vocations" is not an incidental by-product to be lightly dismissed. In spite of these decisive transformation, the Catholic Church continues to be a very important traditional intellectual, deeply rooted in the midst of Latin American politics, with the result that the analyses and intuitions of Gramsci on religion as an historical bloc acquire new and unexpected dimensions.

## NOTES

1. " 'For twenty years we must stop this brain from functioning,' declared the public prosecutor, pointing to Gramsci" (Gramsci, 1980: lxxxix).

2. Maria Antonietta Macciocchi stated unequivocally, "It is due to Gramsci that the Italian workers movement is by far the most powerful and the most politicized in the West" (1975: 37).

3. Gramsci uses the notion of "historical bloc" as a symbol of unity among opposites, as the consolidation of a new historical synthesis, with ethico-moral elements that allow for articulation between rulers and the ruled, between structure and superstructure as a concrete totality, as well as between ideology and praxis on both an individual and a collective level with a minimum of contradictions. A passage that reflects Gramsci's view of the articulation between structure and superstructure provides the simplest definition of historical bloc: "Concept of 'historical bloc,' i.e. unity between nature and spirit (structure and superstructure), unity of opposites and of distincts" (Gramsci, 1980: 137).

More precisely, Gramsci points out that "structures and superstructures form an 'historical bloc.' That is to say the complex, contradictory and discordant ensemble of the superstructure is the reflection of the ensemble of the social relations of production" (Gramsci, 1980: 366). This analysis of the historical bloc as the unity of opposites (one of the prime laws of the dialectic) is elaborated at both the collective and the individual level: "Man is to be conceived as an historical bloc of purely individual elements and of mass and objective or material elements with which the individual is in an active relationship" (Gramsci, 1980: 360). The mutual indispensability between objective and subjective, individual and collective or structural and superstructual is ever present in Gramsci. The relationship between ideologies and material forces is perhaps the best formulation he found to link both the individual–collective and the structural–superstructural levels.

4. Two excellent texts that show how Gramsci's thoughts on education may be analyzed in frankly contradictory directions are Harold Entwhistle's book (1979) and Walter Adamson's analysis of the relations between political education and hegemony (1980).

5. When the cultural level of the masses is raised, their adherence to the project of the new historical bloc becomes more rational. Thus, the relationships between intellectuals and the masses acquire not only a disciplinary but also a consensual perspective in which consciousness prevails in the pedagogical relationship of the party (no longer a Leninist party of an elite of revolutionary professionals with an enlightened theoretical consciousness, but a party of the masses based on the cultural and moral direction of the subaltern classes). This is clearly defined in the study of the links between education and hegemony in Angelo Broccoli's interpretation (1972), and in the excellent commentary by Mario A. Manacorda (1970). Basing himself on Broccoli, Hugues Portelli (1977: 228) accepts the links between education and hegemony from a Maoist perspective.

6. One of the premises of Portelli's work is that Gramsci is the theoretician of revolution in the West, that is the philosopher of revolution in the West within the advanced capitalist countries. This thesis is taken up as a central thread by Maria Antonietta Macciocchi (1975: 15). However, there is an alternative analytical premise that is perhaps more useful for understanding the importance of Gramsci's analysis in Latin America and especially his contribution to the analysis of the religious phenomenon. This is the premise proposed by Juan Carlos Portantiero when he asserts,

It occurs to me that the use of Gramsci's categories of analysis seems absolutely pertinent to us [because his reflections are] much closer to certain kinds of present day Latin American societies than to the social formations of the more advanced and mature contemporary capitalism. The characteristics of this type of society are precisely those that allow him to re-think, in an original manner, the link between society and politics and the form of the political, distinguishing it from what would be the typical ideal form of the political in representative liberalism. (Portantiero, 1980: 37) See Portantiero (1981) also.

7. See Chantal Mouffe (1979: 180ff).

8. See Henry Giroux (1983: 274–78).

9. In his reflections on the Italian clergy—especially the cardinalate—as a class/caste, Gramsci points out that a study of this group would be "indispensable as a condition and orientation to all the remaining study of the function of religion in the historical and intellectual development of humanity" (Gramsci, 1975–77, vol. 2: 49).

10. See Martin Carnoy & Henry Levin (1985).

11. See Fortunato Malimachi (1988).

12. See Marcelo Cavarozzi (1983) and Tulio Halperín Donghi (1975).

13. See Guillermo O'Donnell (1988).

14. See Atilio Boron et al. (1990).

15. Portelli identifies three definitions of religion in Gramsci: (1) a confessional definition; (2) a lay definition in the style proposed by Benedetto Croce; and (3) a Gramscian definition, that is, religion as a particularly complex cultural ensemble (Portelli, 1977: 17–23).

16. In a certain sense, by opposing Marxism in Gramsci's view as the antidote (the new Reformation) to the Catholic Church in its role as traditional intellectual of the popular masses, Portelli's work ignores the "progressive" dimensions of traditional ideologies or similar possible rereadings of Marxism, with the result that every religion finally ends up being false consciousness.

17. The literature on the alienation of labor (resulting also in psychological and cultural alienation) is very large in Marxism and neo-Marxism. As in all complex theoretical bodies, there are very divergent interpretations of the Marxist theory of alienation. For the most important works by Marx on the subject, see Marx (1968a, 1968b) and Marx and Engels (1974). A study by Nicos Poulantzas (1977) has already become a classic study. The different perspective of George Novack (1979) should also be consulted, as well as the work of Herbert Marcuse (1955, 1973).

18. Gramsci asserts that there is no such thing as philosophy in general: "Philosophy in general does not in fact exist. Various philosophies or conceptions of the world exist" (Gramsci, 1980: 326). The task of the philosophy of praxis in understanding, making explicit, and developing the good sense present in common sense should be a "criticism of 'common sense,' basing itself initially, however, on common sense in order to demonstrate that 'everyone' is a philosopher and that it is not a question of introducing from scratch a scientific form of thought into everyone's individual life, but of renovating and making 'critical' an already existing activity" (Gramsci, 1980: 330–31). There are echoes of this proposition evident in the gnoseological perspective of Paulo Freire and other advocates of the pedagogy of liberation as well as in the entire paradigm of popular education (closely connected to the Popular Church). To begin with the

knowledge refined by the common people, to accept this knowledge as a critical theory in a practical state and not just as popular wisdom, and to contribute (through the introduction of civilizing techniques, especially from the social sciences) to a more critical and programmed development connected to the praxis of transformation of the consciousness and the situations of oppression are all central parts of the programs of popular education and consciousness raising. (See Torres, 1990; La Belle, 1986; Freire & Torres, 1990.)

19. Modernism is the fruit of social tensions of the nineteenth century—in particular, an attempt to force the Catholic Church to confront socialist ideas, using the social doctrine of the Church as a weapon in order to bring Catholics into party politics, especially in the Italian State. The result of modernism was the theory of the Christian democracy, with prominent Catholic philosophers (such as Jacques Maritain in his earliest writings) providing the analytical reasoning. The reaction to modernism was integralism, a theological movement that advocated the necessity of reaffirming the authority of the Catholic Church in opposition to the secularization and politicization of the Faith.

20. Perhaps the most recent testimony to the perception by elements of the extreme right of the new critical positions in the Society of Jesus was the murder of six Jesuit priests, their housekeeper, and her teenage daughter on November 16, 1989, in El Salvador—a murder that newspaper reports and sources in the Church, official institutions, and the U.S. Congress did not doubt was connected to the Salvadoran Army and, moreover, to the administration of President Cristiani. (See *Los Angeles Times*, Saturday, January 5, 1991, p. 4A.)

21. See Michel Clévenot (1980) and Fidel Castro and Frei Betto (1987).

22. See Leonardo Boff's declarations in *La Folha de São Paulo*, Monday, October 29, 1990.

23. Frei Betto, in conversation with the author (São Paulo, May 15, 1990).

24. In this sense, it is interesting to note how Gramsci criticizes mechanistic Marxism for the similarity in its analytical logic to the scholastic practice of traditional Christianity and how he anathematizes the futility of mechanistic determinism (Gramsci, 1980: 337); but he also recognizes at the same time that "when you don't have the initiative in the struggle, and the struggle itself comes eventually to be identified with a series of defeats, mechanical determinism becomes a tremendous force of moral resistance, of cohesion and of patient and obstinate perseverance" (Gramsci, 1980: 336). This condemnation—applied specifically to Marxism and crass materialism, where the historical inevitability of the decadence of capitalism is argued—may be applied overall to the fact that "the mechanicist conception has been a religion of the subaltern" (Gramsci, 1980: 337). The parallels in this analysis of religion as a form of resistance among simple people and the fatalistic conception of the philosophy of praxis are very clear in Gramsci when he concludes, "With regard to the historical role played by the fatalistic conception of the philosophy of praxis, one might perhaps prepare its funeral oration, emphasizing its usefulness for a certain

period of history, but precisely for this reason underlining the need to bury it with all due honors" (Gramsci, 1980: 342).

25. Although many works have taken this direction, two good examples of analyses influenced by Gramsci's perspective may be found in Scott Mainwaring's work on Brazil (1986) and Michael Gismondi's study of religion (1988).

26. For Gramsci, "in the masses as such, philosophy can only be experienced as a faith" (Gramsci, 1980: 339). The role of religion and common sense as a popular force in every ideology has been presented by Portelli (1977: 235) in his conclusions on Gramsci's vision of the Church and religion.

# 5

# Religion and Disciplinary Order: On Social Reproduction

## RELIGION AND SOCIETY

Ever since the classic writers on the subject, it has been maintained that, to undertake a study of religion in a society, any attempted definition based on the "essence" of what religion "is" should be rejected in favor of considering only the conditions and effects of a particular type of community action, the understanding of which, in terms of the social sciences, covers many aspects. On the one hand, such a study would include the way of life, claims, and subjective purposes of the individual, which, from the perspective of Weber's theory, could be called the "rational" sense of religious convictions. On the other hand, a sociology of religion should be concerned with the "structural" effects and processes of the religious phenomenon with respect to social activities as a whole.

In connection with this last point, studies have been made of the impact of religious ethics and morals on some processes of social transformation and other related questions, such as the role of the Churches with regard to homosexuality, abortion, birth control and family planning programs, divorce, and prostitution.[1] The role of religion with respect to the basic socialization of children and adults is also considered important in both the rural and urban areas of Latin America, particularly in peripheral regions. Hence the importance of the educational activities of the Churches and their connections with the processes of social change, education, and politics, and the popular urban movements of the Continent (i.e., the Americas, but specifically Latin America in this book). There is an extensive literature on the connections between religious thought and organization (especially of Christianity and the Catholic Church) and the revolutionary movements of Latin America.[2] There has also been considerable inquiry into the "elective affinity" between the ethical precepts of puritan Protestantism and the historical processes of a broad and general character that have occurred in the "Western" world, such as the "rationalization of social action." Attention has even been drawn to the link between certain religious sects and different processes of ethnic transculturation and acculturation, as well as to the link between political ideology and religious conscience. From functionalist perspectives, particular focus has fallen on the study of the psychosocial profile of the "religious being," the connections among religious doctrines, individual conscience, and processes of social control, and, in effect, all those questions that refer to the psychological and motivational problems of individuals. In brief, the field of research into religion is fertile and developing, especially in advanced industrialized societies, where great important is attached to religious phenomena given their "integrating" function—based on organic solidarity among the members of a community—which redounds to the advantage of the processes of overall social integration (Parsons, 1971; Parsons, Bales & Shills, 1970).

In Latin America, by contrast, the processes and structures interrelated with religion are practically lacking analysis. It would be difficult to cite a text originating in Latin America that undertakes the study of these processes rigorously and systematically.[3] With the exception of certain universities, Church colleges, and seminaries in the region, even the academic practice of the sociology of religion is almost nonexistent. However, the discipline has undeniable precursors among the classics of sociology,[4] while religious phenomena are acquiring a growing importance in the political and ideological struggle of the region. As one analysis of the development of the social sciences in the Continent has been pointed out, "Given the increasing importance of religious movements in Latin America, above all on account of their increasingly intense involvement in social matters, the absence of sociological knowledge in this area is all the more lamentable" (Solari, Franco & Jutkowitz, 1976: 282–83).

## RELIGION AS DISCIPLINARY ORDER

Beginning with the classics in the field, we find that Marx, Durkheim, Weber and Gramsci were concerned with the sociological study of religion and sought to understand its connection with the reproduction of social order. One central element unites their four perspectives, which are not necessarily complementary: this is the idea of religion as a disciplinary order, closely linked to the idea of religion as ethics.[5] Religion as a disciplinary order implies that individuals, constituted as a workforce, acquire through the structure of the religious act a systematic moral education that clarifies the connections of humanity with nature and of human beings among themselves as social beings through reference to a specific theodicy free of any intersection with society or nature. This is to say that religion stimulates codes of conduct, values, preconceptions, knowledge, class customs, and differing cultural assets (different with respect to their cultural codes) as much in the socially dominant classes as in those that are socially subordinated.

By seeing the problem of religion as the disciplining of the workforce, we can appreciate that the reproduction of the established order is obtained through the creation of the appropriate social conditions needed for the accumulation of capital (or the continuation of the dominant social production of the time) so that, in a highly hierarchical world, there are selected both those who can and should act to establish norms and those who should in conscience respect them.

In addition to the above, since many religious processes may amount to justifications of the social order whereby the institutionalization of the religious order is a constitutive element of the ordering of society (as is the case of many countries in Southeast Asia and the Arab world), ideological and social differences are legitimized on the basis of distinctions that do no more than generate inequalities arising from differences in class, race, gender, and political preference. In this sense, religious order operates as a differentiating factor in that it reproduces the differentiation derived from external conditions but adds to it the legitimation belonging to the norm and the socially accepted religious conduct.

In Latin America the grand themes of the restoration of order are precisely elaborated in conservative Church circles and theologically sanctioned for pastoral implementation. Thus, the need to promote national unity fosters opposition to the risks inherent in alternative ways of developing. The elimination of dangerous foreign ideologies, the cultivation of national values and—especially in times of intense social struggle—the sermons against pluralism have all been important banners in promoting the fight against communism and proposing the ideologies of national security as identifiable with the status quo (both secular and religious). The internal security of the state, social tranquility, and, in many cases, the freezing of partisan activity are therefore seen as prerequisites for the practice of religion along pre-established lines.

The preaching of religion, especially from the point of view of integrationist and neodevelopmentalist perspectives (see Chapter 7), is presented as the definition of truth refined by the historical praxis of a Church and its pastors. This truth is free of the onus of establishing its own value; it is technically apt, having been debated by experts and publicly sanctioned by the functionary or functionaries of an exemplary profession; it is not ideological, since it is disconnected from the social struggle, social structures, and interests; it is pedagogical, since it directs the conduct of those who submit to its dictates, and is without sociological overtones that might lead to divergent interpretations. The potential of this mechanism for discipline in any community is evidently very high. By placing itself above all material interests and in perfect communion with all, it detaches the immediate problems from the community while inserting the latter into another problematic of much great dimensions and scope. It identifies norms of thought and conduct without identifying the limitations of a critical reflection on reality or an alternative praxis. In a disciplinary world like the religious, alternative thought must be elaborated by those who have the charisma and the mandate (the functionaries of the cult), while the possibility of an alternative praxis is generally confined to certain guidelines to which the individual must adapt under pain of remaining outside the discipline accepted as the governing principle. The idea of the reflexivity of the human being, especially in Catholic doctrines, is only permitted outside the disciplinary order—which considerably limits the possibility of any breach and divides reality Manichaeistically between good and evil conduct, determined in conformity with specific norms and not according to processes of negotiation arising through the connections and interaction of inter subjectivities constituted on the basis of affirmation and confrontation.

There is certainly an implied functionalist meaning underlying this notion of religion as the practice of social discipline. As a "social agent," and in order to constitute it, the human being is reduced to the process by which the values that will subsequently guide social action are internalized. The externalizing of "social facts" (in the style of Durkheim) and the particularities they contribute to actors and their conduct is an attempt to theorize on the relations between social action and the different properties of social collectivities. However, there is an important limitation in a disciplinary order like religion. The notion of social life as actively constituted by the action and interaction of the members of a collectivity is belied by emphasis on the action of the values and ethics of procedure. In this manner, the phenomena of power, interest, conflict, domination, and exploitation remain on a secondary level as epiphenomena of norms and values whose character is based on their being the central feature in the construction of the daily life of society—and hence, it is the imposition of this scale of values at all costs that is the theoretical center of specific theodicies that mold the conduct of individuals. Finally, one aspect defined very clearly by Anthony Giddens with reference to functionalist theory in general is directly applicable to religious disciplinary ideologies, namely, their limitation arising from placing in a central position the essentially negotiated character of norms that are both as divergent and conflictive in interpretation as the social interests that sustain them (Giddens, 1976: 21, 80).

In any event, the two central ideas of the disciplinary order of religion are intimately connected to the processes of social control. The first is a restriction on the exercise of the free will that in theory the human being is granted. This implies a loss of specificity as a social agent, to the extent that the human being lives immersed in a world of norms and values that determine (orient, specify, and judge) social action. The idea was already present in Durkheim when he advanced his basis assumption that God or any sacred object is a symbolic representation of society. Even Durkheim himself, with typically positivist reasoning, sought to know the "reality" underlying religious ideas. If the symbolic manifestation that lies behind the religious idea simply represents society, what function, Durkheim asks, does this symbol fulfill with respect to human beings and their social action? And to this question he gives no conclusive reply.

As José Joaquín Brunner correctly points out, "If social control is understood as an experience of the individual, it is possible to distinguish schematically between the experience of the control exerted directly on the person and the control obtained by the internalized system of symbolic limits, or the system of classification" (Brunner, 1978: 238). Order (or system of classification) and pressure seem to be fundamental components of social control, especially when this is understood as the cluster of classification systems that address the symbolic universe from which the individual constructs frameworks of intelligibility by means of processes of communication. Let us consider in greater detail the

**Table 5.1**
**Forms of Control**

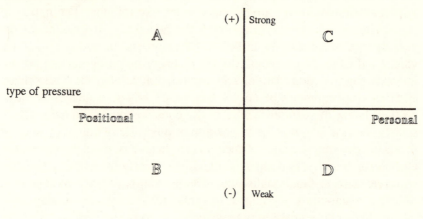

typical-ideal schema proposed by Brunner (See figure 5.1).

According to Brunner's analysis, this schema—although impression-istic in character—has the virtue of interpreting distinct types of social control, its forms of operation and its consequences (Brunner, 1978: 239). The horizontal axis represents forms of control exerted by pressure. On the extreme left, the pressure is strictly positional, exerted through the position of authority of the controller or its insertion in the social structure. On the right is personal pressure, namely, pressure exerted on the basis of a personalized regulation of the one controlled, independent of any appointed role.

In the case of type A, the individual "is socialized in a world of hierarchies and 'truths of authority' within a system of relations structured around clear patterns of domination" (Brunner, 1978: 239–40). Commu-nication is practically unilateral—between a transmitter of messages that constitute irrefutable imperatives about a declared truth and a receiver who is considered distant, submissive, and pervious, who receives and acts strictly according to the tenets of a prescribed role. In this quadrant, Brunner identifies the culmination of authoritarian forms of order, cha-racterized by a strong system of classification, and laying claim to a public monopoly that requires a concentrated power able to keep it in force (Brunner, 1978: 248). In quadrant A, discipline is the concept and the praxis that communication articulates. Although Brunner does not say so explicitly, it seems clear that, in terms of religious communication, the practice and preaching of what we will define in Chapter 7 as the ideological lines of neo-Christianity and the traditional right could clearly function on the basis of this kind of social control.

Social control type B reflects experiences described by Brunner as ambivalent. The underlying system of classification is weak, but the process of transmission maintains the strong structuring of positional hierarchies. Here Brunner identifies the rites of the academic university life as clear examples of the type of communication established. Perhaps the ideological tendency that we describe in Chapter 7 as charismatic spiritualism could be classified as using this kind of social control, particularly since, paraphrasing Brunner, the rites established in this category (which is based on multiple systems of classification and personal control) "celebrate creativity and personality and tend to disguise the tension between a precariously legitimized authority and those personalities that need to exalt themselves and, at the same time, submit to positional hierarchies" (Brunner, 1978: 243).

In type C, positional control has been substituted by forms of personalized control that "do not resort to a hierarchy of roles to express themselves, but appeal to a direct, persuasive, non-disciplinary influence as a means of control. The individual is socialized in a highly and strongly classified world, governed by the rigidity of its categories, through relations that are symmetrical or tend to be symmetrical. This is the case of the educated middle class mother of a family formed under the norms of the 'Protestant ethic' " (Brunner, 1978: 244). According to Brunner himself, the "Protestant ethic" is found in this form of social control. As Weber points out, the specific differences of the Reformation with respect to Catholicism include—in addition to having accentuated ethical distinctions and increased the religious dividend attached to work in the world—its having developed distinct forms of piety in each of the reformed Churches and, above all, its having changed the condition of indifference toward the profession of religion that resulted from the apostolic life of Catholicism (especially with respect to traditionalism) by means of a methodically rationalized ethical conduct (Weber, 1964: 95ff). One of the characteristics of this kind of social control, which could be associated in our classification in Chapter 7 with the ideological lines of social-Christianity and populism, is that, having reached a point where the rites tend to celebrate the dimensions of the order and the forms of participation in it, when disputes or tensions arise they are inclined to be resolved "by abandoning the forms of personal control and asserting a discipline associated with positions of authority that have not manifested themselves explicitly until now" (Brunner, 1978: 245). On this point, Brunner alludes to the importance of theological polemics and discussions in faculties of theology in which these positions of authority are brought out when the debate threatens to remove the symbolic limits of central definitions in doctrine and ideology.

Finally, type D shows experiences of social control structured around weak systems of classification and personal forms of social pressure (Brunner, 1978: 245). These experiences are difficult to institutionalize, according to Brunner, and often appear in the guise of different forms of utopias. In our own classification of the ideological tendencies of the Catholic Church in Latin America, they could well be represented by socialism and perhaps some forms of charismatic spiritualism.

Brunner's argument is a very stimulating way of identifying the different experiences of social control, especially in view of the similarity between types A and C (authoritarian social control of thought and experiences) and certain religious forms and practices.

The hierarchical principles of classification are rules of control and realization. If we follow Basil Berstein's analysis (1982), both the social division of labor (which establishes these principles in the end) and the distribution of power depend basically on class relations. The principles of control, as well as tacit practices, are reflected in the codes that, like mechanisms for determining social positioning, generate the ideology of social subjects. The advantage of religion over other principles and institutions of social control is that it is able to combine order and pressure in the most forceful manner by giving material form to the creation, distribution, reproduction, and legitimation of physical and symbolic values that are founded on the social division of labor but are transmitted by a particular ethic of social conduct.

The second (vertical) axis is derived from the preceding discussion of strong principles of classification and the connection between norms and values. Social control in this context is established through the integration of a world of norms and values incorporated by the process of reproduction of the subjective identities of individuals who belong to different social classes (given the multiclass nature of the religious institution) through the cultural capital, habits, and differential socializing forms of the language of the dominant sectors of society. In religious doctrine there is an implied politicization of knowledge about daily life by means of a hidden agenda that refers the correspondence of emotions, individual struggles, prima facie perceptions, and even class instincts and rationalizations to an antiseptic and distant universal referent framed within a Biblical reading of current social reality.

Like all regulatory and classificatory mechanisms, readings of reality undertaken from theological perspectives may evidently differ according to the social (and knowledge-based) interests that underlie this hidden agenda. But the problem does not reside so much in the process that underlies the discernment of symbols and systems of classification in any given moment, community, or group, but in every addition to ecclesiastical (canonical) expression and in the process of constitution of a dominant ecclesiastical cultural capital, which—as we will show in Chapter 8— may enter a period of crisis while continuing to be the point of reference for both the "orthodox" and the "heretical," with corresponding sociopolitical consequences in either case.

In conclusion, ever since the times of the classics of sociology, concern for the study of religion results from the fact that religion and religious forms are considered a basically social experience elaborated around what has been defined as a "religious order" and closely connected to material factors, interests, and structures. This religious order is connected—whether by organic solidarity, the Protestant ethic, or ideology as hegemony or as a passive consensus—to the basic processes of social reproduction. In our discussion, then, we have established that the main idea binding these four perspectives, which are not necessarily related, is a consideration of religion as a disciplinary order with its effects on the constitution of the workforce and its productive activities (the accumulation of capital) and on the negotiation of the basic values of the organized interaction of subjectivities, that is, on the constitution of political power and social domination.

Let us now see how an analysis of the origin, constitution, and operation of specific religious orders may contribute to an understanding of phenomena that are increasingly important in Latin America. From among these phenomena we have chosen three important topics with which to discuss the role of religion in the Continent: the Popular Church, in Chapter 6; the problem of tendencies within the Catholic Church (on the basis of a classificatory schema), in Chapter 7; and, finally, a proposed theoretical framework for understanding the connections among religion, Churches, and social structure, in Chapter 8.

## NOTES

1. For example, commentators have frequently insisted that in Latin America there is a close relationship between the fertility of women and attendance at religious services (as an indicator of religiosity). However, a study on Mexico

found otherwise: "It would be expected that greater attendance at religious services could be associated with a greater number of live births, given the position of the Church on the use of contraceptives and/or limitation of the family. However, according to the survey, this is not the case and, for the most part, among women who attend such services, the number of children they have had is independent of that fact" (CEED, 1970: 80). Aside from claims such as these, it is worth noting that religious questions are at the heart of the debate on family planning. In the case of Mexico, the connections between socioeconomic status, authoritarian personality, dogmatism, and religiosity have been studied even when the analytical categories used in the study are not solid and the empirical evidence obtained is insufficient to derive precise conclusions (Dillon Soares & Reyna, 1962).

2. See Chapters 6–8.

3. Although there are no systematic books or manuals of Latin American origin on the problem, there are numerous papers and articles and research projects that have been completed with varying success. See the excellent work of Luiz Alberto Gómez de Souza (1978: 15–29) for bibliography and references, although they do not pretend to be exhaustive. Luiz Alberto Gómez de Souza's study of Catholic students and politics in Brazil (1984) is one of the few exceptions. Likewise, Otto Maduro's analysis (1979) from a Marxist perspective remains among the few studies of sociology of religion as a discipline in Latin America.

4. The sociological tradition most consistent in the analysis of religious questions is in Germany where, not surprisingly, the strongest tradition in the sociology of knowledge is also to be found. The most relevant school is that gathered under the term *formal sociology*, in which may be placed Ernest Troeltsch, Georg Simmel, Werner Sombart, Ferdinand Tönnies, and, given certain criteria, Max Weber himself. The contribution of the French sociological school, with Marcel Mauss, P. Rivet, and Lucien Lévy-Bruhl, is also important. Some mention should also be made of the English functionalist school, including especially anthropologists of the stature of Alfred Reginald Radcliffe-Brown, Edvard Alexander Westermarck, and Bronislaw Malinowski; the American functionalist school, represented in some of the works of Talcott Parsons or Robert King Merton; and, more recently, the American phenomenological school, whose most distinguished representative is Peter Berger.

5. Let us recall here that, according to Durkheim (1915), the elements of morality are the spirit of discipline, adherence to social groups, and autonomy of will.

# 6

# The Popular Church and the Process of Conscientization: Reflections on Possibilities and Contradictions

The sociological analysis of religion, as we have already pointed out, must be founded on a certain "methodological atheism." For this reason, in spite of the many ideological and social implications of the polemics on theology and pastoral work within the Churches of Latin America, we intend to describe a significant part of those polemics on the basis of their belonging to a social discourse. We do not at any time intend to discuss the criteria of their validation or, still less, the validity of their origins, or their Biblical or theological sources.

In order to consider the question of the Popular Church, let us begin with a dichotomy that has a certain tradition in theological discussion: institution versus event. This discussion, which has had various terminological guises (institution vs. community, the ecclesiastical vs. the ecclesial, etc.), responds fundamentally to a profound ideological struggle within Christian communities. In the last analysis, these theological and pastoral polemics reflect an attempt at articulating both the cluster "faith–culture–society" and discussions that arise in the search for and determination of criteria concerning the theoretical orientation of Christian praxis, whether for the individual, the group, or the institution. The acknowledgment of this dichotomy as a theological datum has not been lost on theological reflection itself, as one Brazilian theologian asserts: "There is a true ideological watershed that is at the roots of the forms of historical mediation of the original Christian event when this event is crystallized in institutional form" (Dias, 1978: 3).

As a general rule, the sociological treatment of intra-Church ideological conflict is alien to theological reflection. From a sociological perspective, what is recognized behind a "conflict of theological interpretations"—apparently irreconcilable in this case—is not a mere question of superstructure, but a phenomenon that rests on the basic class conflict, in the central issue of any society in particular—in effect, in the horizons of class from which theological reflection is shaped. This is to say that this ideological conflict in some way expresses the different configurations of class conflict and the broader ethnic, gender, regional, or social conflicts of contemporary Latin American society. Hence we find there a "Theology of Praxis" or a "Theology of Liberation"[1] endeavoring to emphasize certain doctrinal aspects that not only constitute a doctrinal watershed, but seek to reorient and rechannel Christian praxis in general and the pastoral work of the Church in particular. Let us consider the principal features of this polemic in some detail.

## THE "POPULAR" IN THE THEOLOGY AND CHURCH OF LATIN AMERICA

Stated in theological terms, the fundamental tension within the Christian community is that which occurs between fidelity to the founding event of Christology (the Spirit) and fidelity to the historical praxis of the institutional Church—a praxis that, for some, has become ideologically conditioned by its insertion in society and is, as such, a mere civilizing crystallization that will always threaten fidelity to the original spirit of the Gospels. From this context there emerges a fundamental task of renovation: to condition the institution to the event, or, in other terms, make the institution ever more faithful to the spirit in the areas in which that spirit is currently expressed. At this point we have entered fully into the problem posed by the adjective *popular*.

In sociological terms, the theological dispute referred to above retains, as an elementary underpinning, the attempt by one sector of this Christian community to modify the conditions of the Church's institutional presence in opposition to the efforts of the other sector to maintain the civilizing terms of institutionalization. The counterargument wielded by each side is that in its own terms and no others is the "Christological event" expressed. While the former sector does not see the evangelization of human culture as possible in the Christological event given the institutional inertness and conservatism of the Churches and, above all, their ignorance or disregard of the popular sectors as intended recipients par excellence of the "message of salvation,"[2] the latter holds that the presence of faith in culture must basically occur in the same institutional terms as it has occurred for decades, and accuses the former of wanting to destroy the Church.

The basis of this discussion has gradually turned to the question of "the popular" and its theological implications. To avoid a hodgepodge of definitions and counterdefinitions as to what may be understood by "popular" in the context of the Theology of Liberation,[3] we will simply point out that incorporation of the popular into the thought of Liberation Theology represented a threefold theoretical endeavor. First, it was an attempt to construct an analytical perspective that did not compromise liberalism,[4] but at the same time did not incorporate the Marxist perspective in all its dimensions. Second, it was an attempt to locate the historical subject of the evangelizing praxis of the Churches (Scannone, 1975, 1976). Third, it represented an alternative in political organization. Without renouncing historically crystallized tradition (dogma), while at the same time endeavoring to retrieve the core of the "message of the Gospels" (the notion of the "people of God"), it was an attempt to regain possession of the construction of a Church that would distance itself from the institutional practices of the "official Church" without constituting itself as a parallel one. This desire to function within the institutional Church was not simply a principle or categorical imperative intended to prevent heresy and a subsequent schism. It was, by contrast, the product of political thought. As an alternative position still framed within the official ambit of the Church, it could in some way still use the apparatus of the institution. Outside the canons and formal institutions of the Church, the political effectiveness and the social significance of this theological orientation would simply become irrelevant. The complexity and importance of the subject evidently warrants a more precise study that would evaluate the ideological impact of this theological and pastoral project on the recent history of the Latin American Church and on the social movements connected with Church institutions. Here, however, we shall present a very preliminary evaluation of this threefold concern in Christian thinking on "Liberation."[5]

In Latin America, there developed a vigorous current of theological and philosophical thought that had and continues to have an undeniable social impact on Christians, especially on groups linked to the structures of involvement of the laity in the Catholic Church and on politically militant Christians working in marginal urban and rural areas. In the light of this trend, a need was recognized for adopting a social theory that would interpret the social framework within which the Gospel was to be preached—but a theory that would address the "oppressed" condition of the people to be evangelized. The fairly generalized adherence, above all toward the end of the sixties, of the "progressive" sectors of the Church to what could in the social sciences be called the "theory of dependence"[6] did not therefore come about by chance.

In addition to the above, given the political conditions of Latin America in the second half of the sixties, a radicalization of the youth in the Christian movements occurred in the first half of the seventies. Many of the politicized young adhered (all things considered) to a precise method of political struggle that they regarded to be virtually the only option possible as an instrument of social change in the Continent: the establishing of focal points of guerrilla activity.[7] At the same time, there occurred a reconsideration in ideological terms—perhaps restricted to the clergy and some middle-class members of the laity—of the conflict between the Church, religion, and Marxism, while, with different nuances in each country, there was an increased mingling of Christians and Marxists in social and political praxis. In this regard, the most consistent successes were due to the Christians for Socialism movement[8] in Chile and its impact on those who currently constitute the Party of the Christian Left, the Movement of Priests for Latin America founded in Colombia in 1971, and the Movement of Priests for the Third World founded in Argentina, which was clearly Peronist but had many members who adopted a method of analysis inspired by historical materialism.

## THE POPULAR CHURCH AND SOCIAL ANALYSIS

Two questions will be analyzed here. We will refer to the problem of theoretical categories and the theoretical framework for social analysis. One of the most interesting texts for the analysis of theological-Biblical categories in Church documents is by Gilberto Giménez (1975). Through semantic and semiotic techniques he studies the condemnation of the Christians for Socialism movement in Chile. He concludes by referring to the condemnatory document issued by the Chilean episcopacy in 1973, calling it a discourse or paradigm of binary oppositions, rigidly dichotomous, disymmetrical, and nonreversible in character (Giménez, 1975: 75). This paradigm of binary oppositions,[9] which in our opinion is not exclusive to the Chilean episcopal document but may be found in all Latin American theological thought, offers a wealth of material for discussing the categories incorporated with new dimensions by the Popular Church. Among the principal ones is the category of the poor, since around it will turn much of the theoretical elaboration of the Popular Church and Liberation Theology. Moreover, in it there also lie the possible connections of this new theology with critical models of social analysis.

As we have shown, a very close association developed between the theory of dependence and the sociopolitical outlook of certain sectors of the Church connected with the Popular Church (but not necessarily with movements such as Christians for Socialism). This is logical if one considers the theoretical disjunction prevalent in a way of thought such as the Christian—the disjunction between the supposed universality of the message of salvation and the historical subject to whom this message is directed, that is, the poor. The fact is that, when the main characteristic of the historical subject of evangelization in Latin America is sought, it is found to be the situation within the dominated sectors of society (that is, their being the object of social domination). At the same time, when the need to preserve the horizon of universal preaching of the Gospel is reaffirmed (to all people of the region, this is), many implications are generated in the theological discourse and the pastoral practice of the Catholic Church.

On the one hand, with the adoption of the dependence-liberation schema, it became possible to articulate a theological-social matrix recognizing contradictions that were related but analytically separable. From this perspective, two levels of contradictions emerge: first, that between empire and nation; and second, the social contradictions constituted by the confrontation between the people and the (monopolistic) bourgeoisie; and between the people and the (State) bureaucracy.[10] This kind of analysis made it possible to heighten social confrontation and thereby advance toward national liberation (considered the liberation of the people of God), while promoting an element of unity and organization with respect to precisely delimited segments of society that, in the end, would constitute the Chosen Ones. On the other hand, in many of the major formulations of this theology and social analysis, use of the schema of class struggle was explicitly renounced because it excluded universality. The thesis that the oppressed, by liberating themselves, also liberated their oppressor was therefore defended both implicitly and explicitly, and the categories *people*, *oppressed*, and *poor* were used to replace categories such as *working class*, *industrial proletariat*, or *subordinated social classes*.[11] The logical corollary was a high degree of ambiguity in the choice of alternative models of society. Capitalism was rejected as an unjust social system, but socialism was not fully accepted, for different reasons.[12] In the beginnings of the new theology, the strategic horizon of the social struggle was not very clear.

These political-theoretical determinations affected the social interpretation of reality. However, it is evident in this respect that, even when they relied on an analytical rationality distorted by voluntarism in some cases, anticapitalist Christians did not fall so easily into the process of social reification classically attributed to religious practices. This led many revolutionaries in the Continent to consider Christians as "strategic allies" in building socialism in Latin America. In a famous speech at Valparaíso, Chile, in 1972, Fidel Castro stated, "When all the similarities are sought, it will be seen how the strategic alliance between Marxist revolutionaries and Christian revolutionaries is really possible." (Castro, 1974).

The evolution of the ideological process among Christians and their analytical practices since the sixties[13] may be characterized as a transitional and ambiguous stage, especially at the level of the organic intellectuals of the Churches. At this stage of profound self-criticism, the mystifying element of religion has come under scrutiny, but the theoretical route from which to adopt a systematic or scientific theory of society has remained elusive. It is a state of rapprochement with psychology and sociology—especially among ministers (priests and pastors)—as social sciences essential to pastoral practice. However, notwithstanding these factors, in the opinion of many authors the Popular Church constituted a rapprochement between what we would call the "theory of revolution" and the praxis of the Christian faith (Girardi, 1977(a); various authors, 1976; Richard, 1978), with obvious consequences at different levels. The institutional Church, once the invaluable ally of economic power and the traditional groups of political power, began to be an institution that the dominant bloc and the armed forces in particular began to distrust. The Catholic Church, especially after the document on justice promulgated by the Latin American episcopacy in Medellín, Colombia, in 1968 (Segunda Conferencia, 1971), appeared as a threat to the status quo and established power.[14] All this had important consequences in the social praxis of the Churches, that is, in their pastoral options.

## THE POPULAR CHURCH AND INSTITUTIONAL PRAXIS

The social practices of the Churches, the pastorates—inserted here into the broadest possible context with a view to examining their repercussions—derive from theological interpretations that belong at the level of specialists and professionals of religion. There are different pastorates, corresponding to the different compromises of the institutions of the Church with society, which may be represented by typologies in the analysis of alternatives (Gera & Melgarejo, 1970; Büntig, 1968; Gómez de Souza, 1978). For the purposes of a sociological analysis, in order to show Popular Church's continuity with and difference from the traditional Church, the following may be distinguished: (1) the pastorate of Christianity, ritualistic and traditional, linked to the origins of Christianity in the Continent; (2) the progressive (or modernizing) pastorate, initiated with the developmentalist stage associated with the reforms after the Second Vatican Council, and (3) the popular (or liberating) pastorate, the expression of the pastoral tendencies originating with the Theology and Philosophy of Liberation.

The pastorate of Christianity is characterized by its origin in a world whose key value was tradition and whose symbol was the council of elders as the synthesis of knowledge and experience, a world with values socially recognized for the preeminence of the sacred as opposed to the secular. It is the result of an entirely rural society, without the great urban centers—and rural circumstances facilitated interpersonal relations. It derives, then, from a society in which primary personal relations predominated, with a high and direct social control. Finally, this pastorate gives expression to a society that is nonpluralist, let alone ecumenical. As a general rule, there was but one religious interpretation and this was Christianity according to the Roman Catholic version, and the civil authorities counted on the Church as an invaluable ally to maintain their mechanisms of social hegemony. As a pastorate—that is, as a religious practice in the strict sense—it combines characteristics that see Faith as a further element of the sociocultural heritage deriving from the Spanish conquest and colonization: these include a maximization of the value of the institution over that of the individual, clericalism, the priority of the pastorate for children (the pastorate of childhood and the catechism of initiation) over all other pastorates (such as those for adults, young people, or married couples), and a greater projection of the parish over organization at the level of the diocese.

The modernizing, or progressive, pastorate arose from a double phenomenon. On the one hand, it came from proposals of the Second Vatican Council, the principal landmark of religious renovation in the Catholic Church in the twentieth century, which generated all kinds of centrifugal and centripetal tendencies in the regional Churches (Marins, 1978). On the other hand, given the close dependence of ideological and political phenomena with respect to social projects, this kind of pastorate coincided in time with the thrust, formation, and growth of movements in developmentalist politics in Latin America, especially in the Southern Cone where it most vigorous political expression took shape under the Alliance for Progress. The characteristics of this pastorate are the following: it begins as a critique of the pastorate of Christianity, whence it not only endeavors to establish a new vision of the relation between the Church and the world, but is concerned above all with liturgical renovation, interconfessional dialogue, and the momentum of the ecumenical movement. In addition it promotes the design of a "pastorate of elites," with priority over a "pastorate of the masses"; the renovation of the catechism and religious pedagogy; the gradual incorporation of new techniques of audiovisual instruction; and, finally, a greater impetus to specialized pastorates, especially that for youth. In contrast with the pastorate for Christianity, the progressive pastorate has not been so closely linked to popular religious phenomena. It has been evaluated very critically in Church circles, especially since the gap between Church and society in Latin America does not seem to have been closing in spite of the efforts for pastoral renewal in this direction.

The dynamics of transformation experienced by the Catholic Church in the seventies showed the consolidation of a third tendency that we call "popular pastorate."[15] This tendency has been connected in particular to a theological approach that insists on pointing out the need to make the preaching of faith compatible with "liberating" social change and therefore provide concrete practices to the Christian groups who are radicalizing their sociopolitical options. In the light of this ideological perspective, pastoral work would be given a different task and orientation.

In order to define this task, it is appropriate to establish a contrast with the two pastorates already described. In some respects, the practice of the pastorate of Christianity may be associated with intra-institutional (Church) phenomena, without any intentional discrimination among social sectors with respect to its message. Its message apparently gives no priority to any group, although, in practice, it is directed to the power bloc—especially the most traditional holders of authority. The modernizing pastorate is connected and directed to the middle classes in particular. By contrast, the popular pastorate directed its message and turned especially to the marginal sectors living in the poverty-stricken slums, squatter and shantytowns, and forgotten cities of Latin America, and also adopted their political claims.[16] Thus the connection of the Church with the popular sectors seemed guaranteed. The "word of the Church," which had difficulty in reaching the workers inside the factories, maintained a much clearer presence among the social-political claims of the marginal communities of Latin America. The figure of the priest who lived in the poverty-stricken slums or shantytowns soon became a political symbol[17]—a religious, organizational, and political leader—so that the so-called prophetic dimension of the Christian tradition seemed to crystallize in a position that surpassed the customary theological attitude of denunciation in order to unite, and at times direct, the social-political praxis of the community (Concatti, 1975).

However, the path followed by the popular pastorate itself gives a new historical dimension to the overall process: the growing association in some countries between popular religious phenomena (particularly the popular pastorate) and the projects of populist regimes as movements that emerge in times of crisis in Latin America. The experience of Argentina is considerable in this respect. Take, for example, the following statement from the Movement of Priests for the Third World:

We affirm that the Peronist experience in Argentina and the longstanding fidelity of the masses to the Peronist movement are a key element to the incorporation of our people in that revolutionary process. We believe that recognition of this fact by all revolutionary forces will help to solidify the unity of all who fight for National Liberation. (Movimiento, 1970a)

The adherence of this sector of the Catholic Church to Peronism subsequently became even more apparent, as affirmed by Rolando Concatti, secretary-general of the Movement of Priests at the time, in a document titled "Our Option for Peronism" (Concatti, 1972). Significantly, the link between certain sectors of the popular pastorate and decidedly populist movements such as Peronism is not fortuitous, but the result of the elective affinity between the ideologies of both types of social movement. This point is fundamental. The characteristics of the ideology of the populist regimes are well known. It is an ideology of the State, legitimizing a State that presents itself as behaving above class contradictions and without representing any social class in particular. However, it is an ideology that derives its authority, as a basis for sustaining the social movement that inspires the popular sectors, from the notion of people as a fundamental analytical category. Generally it is associated with and promoted by a leader to whom is attributed a charismatic character. This charisma arouses the consensus of the masses around the person, words, and actions of the leader (for example, Perón, Goulard, and perhaps Cárdenas), who guides the movement from above, in spite of its internal contradictions. Political management is articulated through an ever increasing State bureaucracy, undoing the image of the classical liberal party in favor of the idea of a "national movement" with nationalistic characteristics and a general association with the "Western and Christian" tradition of thought. The correspondence of populist ideology with certain ideological propositions of the social doctrine of the Catholic Church is evident.

The social doctrine of the Catholic Church is directed to all the people of God and is not tied to one class in particular. Its entire social discourse is articulated around the notions of "common good" and "social harmony." The Church is always connected with the organization of people en masse, and its lay institutions operate on the basis of national "movements" (for example, Catholic Action in the fifties, University Christian Youth, etc.). It resorts to leaders who make charisma a matter of routine and assigns this function in institutional terms to priests and especially to bishops. There are a number of texts that are particularly illuminating on the ideological and programmatic correspondences between populist ideologies and sectors of the Church that administer a pastorate in the populist style[18]. However, until recently—in spite of these correspondences—the historical experience of the popular pastorate was not necessarily tied to the political horizon of the populist movements.

## THE POPULAR PASTORATE AND POPULAR EDUCATION

One aspect that has been closely connected with the origin of the Popular Church and the popular pastorate is the practice of popular education, although its projections undoubtedly exceed the theoretical and ideological limits represented by the Popular Church. One of the most articulated expressions of popular education is associated with the notions of "conscientization" and a "liberating education."[19]

Toward the mid-sixties and beginning of the seventies, popular education and its connections with the Church and the popular pastorate seemed little associated with populism. That is to say, it does not seem strictly possible to locate conscientization and a liberating education within the ideology and practice of Latin American populism, as some authors have nevertheless tried to do (Paiva, 1982). Other analyses have shown, rather, that the educational mode centered on popular education has become one of the most significant and independent sociopolitical phenomena of the past two decades in Latin America, clearly surpassing the frontiers of public education and constituting educational practices associated with projects of radical social change (Puiggrós, 1983, and 1984: 310–11; Gajardo, 1983; Brandão, 1980; Brown, 1978; Torres, 1990.)

Historically, popular education has been connected to the praxis of the Churches and other confessional groups by some of their greatest representatives (Freire, 1972). As educational methodologies, conscientization and the liberating education were devised, systematized and disseminated by educators of a clearly Christian origin. In its most general sense, the idea of conscientization was wielded as one of the very tactics of nonviolent struggle in the Continent by religious leaders of such stature as the distinguished Brazilian bishop Helder Camara (Camara, 1969; de Santa Ana et al., 1974). As methods for adult literacy and nonformal education, conscientization and the liberating education were used as mechanisms of social organization and agitation in marginalized social communities of the Third World and even in some advanced industrialized capitalist countries (Torres, 1982; 1990; Zachariah, 1985). Finally, as an "educational philosophy"—although it amply exceeded the objectives of a "new Christian education" in the confessional schools of the region—the liberating education had a very notable impact on Catholic education toward the end of the sixties, fully reflected in the section on education in the Medellín Final Document (Segunda Conferencia General, 1971). However, given the radical nature of many of its proposals, the liberating education was gradually abandoned as a model for Catholic education, having been accused—from a Thomist perspective, to be exact—for its lack of universality and its evident Marxist coloration (Cantero, 1975).

In brief, there was once a close connection between groups within the Churches and the proposal for conscientization and a liberating education. On the one hand, this was due to the progressive consolidation of a Popular Church toward the middle of the sixties that assumed as its mission the task of conscientizing and organizing the marginalized masses and the peasants of the region—a task at times developed outside socialist and communist parties and political movements in Latin America, and at times with strong bonds of association. This Popular Church developed as the informal, complex, and progressive coordinating of base Christian groups and diverse interrelated social sectors, but with a relatively definite class perspective. In general terms, the Popular Church holds a critical view of the capitalist mode of production and sees a strategic enemy in its repressive machines—especially the armed forces. It seems evident also that, by the mid-seventies, the progressive sectors of the Church were suffering clear failures and defeats, due in part to their political voluntarism, but above all—given the shortcomings of their interpretative theories[20]—to the visibility of their leaders and groups of members, who succumbed to the State's authoritarianism and terrorism unleashed as a reaction to these emerging elements of social "threat," especially in the Southern Cone. Many militant Christians, coming from experiences in the Popular Church, swelled the ranks of the principal guerrilla movements in certain countries and were decimated or had to go into exile, just as many others—without having been part of the guerrilla experience—were persecuted, jailed, kidnapped, or forced into exile because of their participation in the base communities and the political struggle of the time.

However, some indications suggest that this complex process led many elements of the Church to associate themselves with the Popular Church to prevent the latter from becoming an instrument of rapprochement between the Church as a social institution and the populist regimes or movements. Toward the mid-seventies there occurred a transitional situation, with a certain tactical imprecision in the policies developed by progressive Christian elements, as is evident in some analyses (Gómez de Souza, 1978). In some cases, as in Brazil, Church circles were among the few places of political-social reflection on civil society and undoubtedly produced a fundamental factor at an organizational level for the reconstitution of Brazilian democracy. In other cases, as in Chile, the Church publicly positioned itself as the enemy of the military regime, in spite of having supported its creation after the experience of government under Popular Unity and in spite of having systematically eliminated from its ranks priests of socialist or Marxist affiliation. The Chilean Church even exhibited a certain institutional capacity for political and legal maneuvering, and ended up coinciding on concrete political tasks with all the sectors in opposition to the State, as in the defense of human rights and political prisoners.

Without undertaking a more detailed analysis of national cases, our statements are necessarily general and hypothetical. A systematic history of the experience of the Church in Latin America will eventually contribute to dissipating some of the doubts and mysteries underlying the Popular Church. Nevertheless, at least two points are clear thus far. On the one hand, the constitution of the Theology of Liberation and its secular counterpart, the Philosophy of Liberation, has left an indelible mark on theology and—to judge from the internal debates of the Catholic Church—the subject is far from exhausted, but continues to be a source of polemics. On the other hand, it has also become necessary to pay great attention to the popular sectors of society in pastoral practices. As a result, through the very dynamics of the relationship with these sectors, their specific demands and their education—in effect, simply through the connection with their daily life—the experience of the Church and the popular pastorate became so radicalized that it was impossible for them to be used as instruments in projects of a populist character or to be manipulated by the new State authoritarianism of the seventies. With the emergence of the Popular Church, different alignments took shape within the Catholic Church, making the fabric of agreements and oppositions more complex, and demonstrating the need to identify better the internal tendencies of the Church, its different ideological orientations, and its political practices. Chapter 7 will be concerned with this task.

## NOTES

1. The content of a Theology of Liberation or of a Theology of Praxis has been systematically reviewed by many authors: see Gustavo Gutiérrez (1970a, 1970b), Oliveros Maqueo (1977), and Battista Mondin (1973). There are also numerous critiques: see, for example, E. J. Laje (1977a) and especially the document published by the Sacred Congregation for the Doctrine of the Faith, "Instruction on Certain Aspects of the Theology of Liberation" (1984).

2. An influential theologian of Liberation, Segundo Galilea, points this out clearly when he states, "The Church is killing the presence of God on the face of the poor" (Galilea, 1974: 29–45).

3. For a systematic treatment of the subject in theological terms, see Oliveros Maqueo (1977: 349–73). A statement by Enrique Dussel will serve to locate the focus of analysis of the Philosophy of Liberation at the beginning of the seventies:

The category *people*, which is not often considered as an interpretative scientific category, and still less a sociological one, is, I believe, a true category of interpretation . . . [T]he category *people* is much broader and includes the category *class*. . . . One must take the category *people* very seriously, not simply as the oppressed, nor as the totality of the system, for the essence of the people is the "eschatological externality" that causes it to see the system and to say "them" but does not feel identified with the system itself. (Dussel, 1974a)

4. Dussel remarks, "We say sincerely and simply that the face of the dominated, poverty-stricken Indian, of the oppressed mestizo, of the Latin American people, is the subject of Latin American philosophy" (Dussel, 1973: 114).

5. A very good summary of this theological current, written for the nonspecialist, has been given by J. C. Scannone (1973).

6. The category of dependence has been defined in the following terms: "Our development is conditioned by certain international relations definable as relations of dependence. This situation submits our development to certain specific rules that describe it as a dependent development. . . . Dependence is a situation in which the economy of a certain group of countries is conditioned by the development and expansion of another economy" (Dos Santos, 1976: 173, 180). For a presentation and methodological critique of the theory of dependence and "dependentism" in general, see Carlos Alberto Torres (1979b); for analysis of a concrete example of the connection between radicalized Christian groups and the theory of dependence, see Gustavo Ortiz (1977); for a broader view that presents the question theoretically, but from an epistemological focus different from that usually found in analyses of dependence, see Hugo Assmann (1973, esp. pp. 36–70).

7. In its time, the publication of the "Diary of a Guerrillero," by the Bolivian guerrillero Néstor Paz (1971) of the National Liberation Movement just before he was killed in Bolivia in 1968, was very celebrated and influential. The popularity of this document is a vivid testimony to the ideological atmosphere among certain radicalized Christian groups in which a strange amalgam of tendencies intertwined: ethical and mystical attitudes rooted in the most time-honored critical tradition of Christianity; a romantic eroticism, showing an early postconciliar reevaluation of the "secular" and the "carnal" not dissociated from the ethical procedures of traditional Catholicism; Marxist principles and positions, very rapidly learned, occasionally in a very bookish manner; and a nationalist stance adopted in pursuit of national liberation from foreign domination, imperialism, and dependence.

8. A movement arising in Chile and Peru that gained strength at the beginning of the seventies with the success of Popular Unity and that represented for some authors a new stage in the Marxist movement in Latin America. Undoubtedly, this theoretical reconsideration also suffered from swings in different directions that resulted from the internal disputes of the communist and socialist movements, with their national and international versions and the varying polemics that gave rise to what came to be called the "crisis of Marxism"; and on the side of Christianity, there was the systematic repression to which the Christian-Marxist attitudes gave rise in the Churches of the region. A regional critical history of these experiences remains to be written, but for

a documented analysis of the correspondences between Christian and Marxist perspectives, see the work of Porfirio Miranda (1978), Giulio Girardi (1977b), and the documents collected in the text compiled by Sacerdotes para America Latina (SAL) (n.d.).

9. Although the model (see Giménez, 1975) describes a number of binary oppositions, we will mention only the following by way of illustration: interior change—the transformation of structures; Christian charity—revolutionary charity; person—structures; sin—economic alienation (injustice).

10. On this line of reasoning, see Aldo Büntig (1973), Héctor Borrat and Aldo Büntig (1973), and Lucio Gera, Aldo Büntig, and Osvaldo Catena (1974).

11. Notwithstanding this fact, there are also attempts toward a materialist interpretation of Biblical tradition that have not been disseminated as widely as approaches based on dependence (see Fernando Belo, n.d.; Maurice Clévenot, 1980).

12. See E. J. Laje (1977b) for a critique of the socialist option for Christians based on the teachings of the Church.

13. It is essential to note the importance of the writings of the French Jesuit priest Pierre Teilhard de Chardin (1965; 1969) for this process, especially his preconciliar contributions to the theory of evolution, the origin of the human species, and the interpenetration of nature, humanity, and the divinity.

14. The much quoted "Rockefeller Report" to the U.S., prepared in 1969, warned of this by pointing out that the Churches warranted greater attention on the part of the United States because they were undergoing very pronounced internal changes whose direction could not be foreseen, though they showed all the signs of anticapitalist radicalization. The report even mentioned the military as an ally *ad unguem*, while the Church had ceased to be fully reliable.

15. Discussion of the meaning of the term *popular pastorate* is far from exhausted; and just as discussion of terms such as the *people* or *the popular* may involve serious epistemological and theoretical difficulties, we also find references to the popular pastorate in statements like the following that, in the end, are tautological:

The word popular is not intended to restrict pastoral action to the popular and humble segments of society, the peasants and the workers, for example. The word popular does not refer to individuals, nor to the sum of individuals as members of a sector of society, separating them from the totality People, which is the collective subject of history. The word popular designates pastoral action to the extent that it is directed to a totality we call people. (Altamira, 1975: 223)

16. There are many testimonies to pastoral work bearing this political stamp. See, for example, José M. Llorens (1972), Jether Pereira Ramalho (1977), and Diego Irarrázabal (1977).

17. It is relevant to recall well-known figures such as the Colombian priest Camilo Torres who died in a guerrilla shoot-out after putting his option for the poor into practice (see Torres, 1966), or the Argentinean priest Carlos

Mugica, leader of Peronist organizations in the slums, who was assassinated in May 1974 by the Triple A (Argentine Anticommunist Alliance) death squad organized by José López Rega, at the time minister of social welfare in the Peronist government (see Mugica, 1973, 1984).

18. See César A. Sánchez Aizcorbe (1973) for a highly documented study that endeavors to associate the social teaching of the Church and Peronist ideology as corresponding in their fundamental ideas, that is, in their notions of "social justice" and "organized community."

19. What we are calling the notion or process of "conscientization" may be associated with the method of adult literacy developed by Paulo Freire, which basically centers on "revealing the mechanisms of social domination" and making the oppressed conscious of the causes of oppression so as to develop a praxis of transformation of their social context (Torres, 1985: 73–96). In general terms, we shall understand here the process of conscientization as an educational and cultural process that is centered on the understanding and denunciation of the social mechanisms of domination and develops alternatives to dominant and hegemonic practices and ideologies; that is generated, practiced, or inserted in marginal urban communities and in rural areas in particular; that consists of educational processes developed through specific methodologies, such as participatory research or literacy centered on social problems, the results of which have many points of contact at a social level with the strategies of social transformation and political struggle pursued in the Continent toward the middle of the sixties and early in the seventies (Torres, 1990).

20. This limitation or theoretical weakness was repeatedly pointed out by various Christian groups associated with the rise and consolidation of the Popular Church. The clearest document in this regard, in which the need to adopt historical materialism as a methodology for social analysis is even suggested, is the Declaration of Christians for Socialism (Cristianos, 1972).

# 7

# Internal Tendencies of the Catholic Church: Typologies and Extrapolations

## THE CHURCH AS AN INSTITUTION OF RELIGIOUS MEDIATION

We have pointed out that one of the major problems confronted by a sociology of religion is that analysis of the religious phenomenon per se is not clearly distinguished from analysis of what properly belongs among studies of the institutions of religious mediation. Expressed in other terms, most analyses (including the classics like Marx, Durkheim, Weber and Gramsci) make no distinction between religion as such and the Churches. This is acknowledged by Aldo Solari and his collaborators when they state,

It should be pointed out that in analyses both by philosophers and "scientists" no distinction is ever made between religion and Church. When certain characteristics of Catholic values are asserted, it is taken for granted that the members of the Church partake of them and vice versa; the values observed in certain holders of them are considered those of the Church as such.

Problems that are taken to be obvious with respect to any social group, such as the possible conflicts between declared and real values, are rarely posed with respect to Catholicism. This fact is doubtless partly the product of a trend of thought that was more monolithic in the past than today, or in its having been perceived as being that way. (Solari, Franco & Jutkowitz, 1976: 277)

Moreover, a secondary but relevant problem occurs because it is not recognized that religion does not have the same meaning for all persons and all social systems; even when a definition of popular religious phenomena or of religion as such is attempted, it is overlooked that there exists something very complex and cannot be characterized as easily as the forms of religiosity.

This all implies that, when speaking of a particular religion and attempting to define its essential components, researchers often lose sight of the manner in which it is modernized, modified, or transformed with respect to the social structure. Perhaps this is why, in order to study the religious question in societies like those of Latin America, it is conventional to begin with the construction of typologies, preferably of the Churches, and the Catholic Church in particular, so that the entire range of the problem is reduced to the articulation of these typologies as elements of analysis and interpretation. The problem with this approach does not reside in its producing the typologies (from the classical ones based on "right, center, and left," to others that are more sophisticated), but in its omitting—and therefore taking for granted— the criteria used to elaborate them and their connection with broader theoretical-methodological frameworks.

In this chapter, we seek to review the question of the sociological typologies of the Churches, endeavoring to clarify from our theoretical perspective the internal tendencies current in the Catholic Church in Latin America. But to complete this analysis we must begin with a theoretical assumption, the importance of which we have not yet sufficiently argued. This is the assumption that the Church, understood at the level of its global organization, may be thought of as a "social system" with its own ends, the elements of which—according to the type of Church in question—maintain a relation of varying intensity among themselves, although each by itself gives rise to action and manifestations that refer to the overall Church (Mayntz, 1967: 64). Moreover, it is necessary to consider that religion organizes itself within a society as a pluri-functional or multiple system that intervenes in the configuration of society to the same extent that religion itself is being socially formed by the overall group of sociocultural institutions and manifestations. To use a phrase dear to functionalism, it could be said that the "social system of religion" may be thought of either in a broad or restricted sense.

In the latter sense, the religious confessions or denominations present in a society are "cultural modules"—within a broad social spectrum, although concentrated at the level of their specific normative frame of reference—promote the permanence of the mental and value structures, the ideologies, and the modes of conduct derived from a particular religious perspective. At the same time, in this system in a restricted sense, mechanisms of struggle or adaptation are maintained that mediate with the established "Church system," so that there are also mechanisms of socialization of axiologically oriented forms of conduct having a center of gravity that falls outside the Church system, as well as outside the family or the school as agents of socialization (Matthes, 1971, vol. 2: 22 and 102).

In the former, broad sense of term—considering the social formation as a whole—we find three different levels: (1) the concrete organization of worship by the institution (called "religious systems" in the functionalist view); (2) cultural modules that are religious and socially disseminated; and (3) different styles of religiosity. At the same time, the elements of social structure and the processes developed in it are submitted by the institution (the Church) to a certain ecclesial-symbolic re-reading in order to reconcile the three levels identified.

In brief, the assumption from which we start is threefold. First, the religious phenomenon has a complex and pluri-singular expression in society and is not therefore reducible, as already held by Durkheim and others. Second, the Church, constituted in terms of a formal organization, is part of the social system of religion and does not in any way exhaust all of its forms of expression—which is an invitation to distinguish between religion and Church as two different dimensions of the analysis. Third, considering the social system of religion in a broad sense (not in the strict sense as when one speaks of Church), there are several different levels in which the system expresses itself: in the Churches; in what we have called "cultural modules" that are religious in character and socially disseminated; and in the forms of religiosity that may vary from clearly individual practices to those that are the rule in sects or religions, or even have local, regional, or national characteristics.

Beginning with this assumption, we will understand that every typology of religious systems or Churches will have only a heuristic and operational value. To believe that such typologies contain all the elements of religion, religiosity, or a particular Church that may be verified in a given social formation is risky, since they may simply constitute a collection of value judgments, more or less interrelated coherently in classificatory terms, but without any value for the analysis and interpretation of concrete situations.

## TYPOLOGIES OF RELIGION AND CHURCHES

The first typology that seems consistent to us—even if it does not refer to the Latin American problem in particular, but to religion in general—is that proposed by Charles Y. Glock (1972, 1973; Glock & Stark, 1965). Having stated the difficulties in characterizing the religious phenomenon and in classifying people according to their religious orientation, Glock points out that his task is to trace a conceptual frame of reference for a systematic analysis of the different connections and religious activities. After analyzing some universal religions and showing the differences among them, he indicates the presence of certain more general dimensions within which the expression of religiosity is made possible. In this context, he distinguishes the dimension of the religious experience, the ritualistic dimension, the ideological dimensions, the intellectual dimension, and the dimension of the consequences of religious convictions.

The *dimension of the religious experience* is intended to show the fact that all known religions suppose, more or less explicitly, that the religious person has on some occasion directly acceded to the ultimate metaphysical reality or has experienced some deep feeling of a religious nature within his or her spirit. In this last instance, Glock mentions subjective religious experience, which has a certain value as a sign of individual religiosity and corresponds to some very specific manifestations of the religious phenomenon in the psychology of the individual and even in social reality, such as ecstasy, mysticism, or collective processes characterized as "miracles."

The *ritualistic dimension* includes the specific religious practices to which the members of a religion must adhere. They are forms of actions such as religious services of every kind, praying, participation in special sacramental rites, fasting, and so on.

The *ideological dimension* includes the demand that every religious person proclaim particular statements of faith, the content and scope of which vary not only with respect to different religions, but also within the same religion. However, each religion inevitably establishes a certain system of dogmas and then demands that its adherents profess them.

The *intellectual dimension* refers to the fact that all religions expect the religious person to know and be familiar with the fundamental dogmas of faith and the sacred writings. Glock points out that there is a close relation between this and the ideological dimension, since knowledge about a faith is a necessary prerequisite for accepting it. However, in his opinion, it is not necessary for the faith to emerge from knowledge about it, or for knowledge about religion to emerge directly from faith.

The *consequential dimension* is distinguished from the preceding four and given a special place in the author's classification. This category combines all the secular effects of religious faith: praxis, experience, and familiarity with different individuals. Glock indicates that in this dimension are included all the prescriptions of religion that determine what people must do and the attitudes they must accept as a consequence of their religion. Using the language of the Christian faith, he states that it is more a question of the relation of one individual to another than of the relations of the individual to God. Finally, he suggests that, in the absence of studies investigating religiosity, it is impossible to present satisfactorily the reciprocal relations among the five dimensions.

There are various levels of analysis from which to criticize this attempted typology. On the one hand, the unity of its five dimensions derives from the link between religion and the individual, which results in an intimist and subjective view of social facts. In this way, the importance of the connection that could be established between community religious practices of very specific social groups (popular religiosity among peasants, for example) is deflected from the typology and eventually blurred. On the other hand, the view of ideology as a systematization of ideas or knowledge (linked to the intellectual dimension)—while having the advantage of being understood directly from a commonsense point of view—nevertheless gives too much importance to the rationalization of knowledge and religious experiences (all of which is the subject of significant debate in contemporary sociology of religion). At the same time, it does not take into account the double dimension of the ideological identified in our Chapter 1, namely, "the ideological" as a dimension of analysis of every social fact and "ideologies" as forms of existence and practice of social struggle for control of social processes of production (de Ipola, 1982: 73). It is precisely in the area of "ideologies" that the "ideological" dimension of which Glock speaks acquires relevance within the context of social conflict in our societies. In this sense, the notion of social conflict and conflictive religious experiences in terms of a social structure are not at all reflected in the approach to the subject he proposes. Finally, except for the consequential dimension, his classification does not appear to include relations of articulation and hierarchization among the different dimensions—although, from all appearances, the consequential dimension has a residual character whereby everything that cannot be classified in the other four is to be placed in it, including the relations among the different dimensions. In this sense, the comprehensiveness of the typology lies not in the inclusiveness of its theoretically and empirically discernible dimensions, but in its usefulness for the analysis of concrete situations. Thus, Glock's proposal is formalist and, both in the language it uses and in its assumptions, begs the phenomenon it sets out to study and systematize.

Gregory Lensk's study (1961) suffers from similar problems. Intending to measure the religiosity of individuals, he also falls into the same vicious circle. In order to measure the degree of religiosity, Lensk creates four indicators: (1) participation in ritual; (2) doctrinal orthodoxy; (3) degree of devotion; and (4) degree of religious association. After analyzing certain empirical data, he shows that the relation among these indicators is very weak. In this study, as in the preceding one, religion is understood as an individual and psychological experience with a certain social impact. But neither the causes of its social persistence nor the causes of its reciprocal interpenetration with social processes and structures are analyzed. In choosing a methodology from which to approach the religious phenomenon, Lensk seeks to gain empirical evidence in order to use statistical analyses that are probabilistic in character. However, he begins, as a general rule, with the declarations of informants obtained from questionnaires; the verbalization of the replies are taken as indicators of real behavior, when, in fact, religious practices may differ considerably from the patterns of verbalized understanding of religious ideas and values. This is to say, not only is the problem one of using instruments that are not entirely adequate to measure the phenomenon (and perhaps the measurement of "levels of religiosity" may itself be questioned), but also there is an analytical formalism that prevents an adequate theoretical characterization of the phenomenon in question. In any case, at this juncture, we should quickly review some of the studies undertaken in Latin America.

The most complete analysis with which we are familiar is that by Iván Vallier (1967, 1971). In his studies, he elaborates a typology of religious elites and tries to confront it with the process of the development of Latin America.[1] On the one hand, Vallier considers the structural principle of Catholic activity according to whether it is hierarchical or cooperative. On the other, he takes into account the sphere from which the influence of the Church is drawn, whether external or internal. Combining these two dimensions, four possible cases are obtained that correspond to four types of religious elites.

The first type of religious elites are the "politicians," who combine a hierarchical principle of Catholic activity with external influence. The second type of religious activity are the "papists," who combine a hierarchical principle of Catholic activity with an internal sphere from which the influence of the Church is drawn. The third type of religious elites are the "pastors," who combine a cooperative principle of Catholic activity and an internal sphere from which the influence of the Church is drawn. Finally, the fourth type of religious elites are the "pluralists," who combine a cooperative principle of Catholic activity with external influence of the Church.

Vallier gives the name *politicians* to the traditional Catholic elites who have a highly hierarchical view of things and an external source of power, which is why they are oriented to the power structure of secular society, where they seek support, protection, and legitimization. The social group to which they relate is that of the upper classes. For this type, the laity has no importance unless it is constituted as a source of power. The politician-type Catholic does not favor change and prefers the preservation of traditional society. This type of religious elite is the one traditionally considered to be the most conservative sector in Church structure. By contrast, the other three elites mentioned by Vallier are more recent; and in this regard, he sees three stages of development in Latin America. In the first, the notion of social change must be legitimized by some kind of ideology; in the second, it is necessary to make that ideological compromise concrete through specific conduct, a mobilizing of the population, and so on; and in the third stage, economic and social modernization should be attempted and should be total. The change has to be accepted ideologically and practically by all important groups, and new levels of social integration should be created.[2]

The term *papists*, which has no pejorative connotations in Vallier, corresponds to a militant modern Catholicism that is oriented toward the "re-Christianization" of the world, that rejects traditional sources of political compromise, and that seeks to draw its religious influence from the religious community itself. The activity of the papist is centered on building a Church with an authority and the resources to gain influence and visibility in society: "Direct political compromises between the Church and the political parties are avoided and even prohibited. Thus the hierarchy of the clergy and the lay constitute a missionary elite interested in expanding the frontiers of 'Catholic-Christian' values" (Vallier, 1967: 167).

The *pastors* are composed of a small but growing group of elites who seek a formula to unite the priest, the people, and the sacraments in a spiritual body. Their ideological terms are "cooperation," "collectivity," and "communication"—all connected to the idea of producing a profound renovation in the life of the Latin American Church and influencing society through it.

Finally, the *Pluralists* have the principal objective of "developing policies and programs that allow the Church to contribute to the institutionalization of social justice on all fronts whenever possible" (Vallier, 1967: 168). They insist on the need to associate with any social group and other religious confessions that share the same ethical and social orientation.

Thus, the papists emphasize the nonparticipation of the Church in politics, thereby confirming their adherence to the social encyclicals of recent times, which point out that the "body of the laity" should be the bearer and agent of the new Christian values in society. Only a change of mentality would permit a change in structures, and the laity is not called upon to push for such a change. The pluralists place themselves within the process of social development; they contribute to social mobilization, are the vanguard of the Church on a social level, and propose a change in structures without overlooking a change in mentality. Finally, the pastors endeavor to concentrate their efforts in strengthening the spiritual life of the Church and contribute indirectly—although sizably, in Vallier's view—to the general process of social development in Latin America, to the extent that this pastoral tendency

combines the religious tradition of Latin America with the new forms of social integration [and] is particularly functional for the people and the groups who have in part become the urban masses. . . . If this pastoral tendency takes root in Latin America, the parochial church will gradually acquire many of the functions that the local churches have in the United States: a combination of roles and values that provide social identity, religious expression and cultural scrutiny. This kind of religious unity acquires special importance when societies have passed into the third phase: complete modernization. (Vallier, 1967: 178–79)

Although Vallier undertook research in Latin America for many years, his conclusions present problems that may be summarized as follows: they constitute part of an effort in empirical research that seeks to verify in the reality of Latin America many of the analytical assumptions and hypotheses derived from the social science of North America— hypotheses, that are, in the majority of cases, the product of North

American contexts. The transference of theories and hypotheses in sociology—especially for the purpose of verifying them—generates an optic that may cloud, if not distort, the phenomenon studied to such an extent that though data may be obtained pointing in a direction different from that of the researcher's theoretical-methodological assumption, he or she may end up sustaining it to the detriment of the empirical evidence.

The degree of emphasis Vallier gave to the connections among Catholicism, social control, and modernization led him to formulate value judgments that are often surprisingly abrupt, as when he refers to the future of the Brazilian Church (Vallier, 1971: 185–90). Although he anticipated the importance that the Church indeed came to have in the mobilization of civilian society against the military regime and defined—simplistically perhaps, but clearly—the struggle between "lefts" and "rights" as a confrontation of equivalent forces, he concluded his analysis by pointing out that "these newer and more flexible [political] compromises go back in part to the charismatic adventures of revolutionary Christians. This may be temporary. If this is the case, there are many definite possibilities of the Brazilian Church continuing along the paths of its development" (Vallier, 1971: 190). This amounts to saying that, once the internal dispute is resolved and a balance is achieved (perhaps with a safe domination of the centralist wing), once the mists that provoked the leftist disturbances have dissipated, the Brazilian Church will be in a condition to resume its contribution to social development.

Another typology, departing from types of religious beliefs and the relations of the faithful to them, is that proposed by Cándido Antonio Procopio Ferreira de Camargo (1971). He has constructed a typology of Catholicism based on a distinction between the "traditional" and the "internalized," which represent radically different functions with respect to both the form and content of their role in orienting the conduct of those involved, and their relations with society as a whole. The basic criterion of his typology is the "acquiring of consciousness."[3]

*Internalized Catholicism* is characterized above all by religious and social conduct that is consciously oriented by religious values, which leads Ferreira de Camargo to include all forms of "reactionary integralism" within this type. *Traditional Catholicism* is divided into the rural and the urban. He accepts the classic thesis of traditional Catholicism that the rural is a source of conservatism while the urban has purely ritual functions and lacks true influence—to the extent that it is not even capable of orienting and sustaining rural migrants, who must look to other sects for the axiological support lost when they were separated from the context and social order in which their faith and religious practice were formed. Within this category of traditional Catholicism three main tendencies are distinguished: (1) that which seeks, above all, a sense of spirituality in today's world; (2) that which primarily looks for social meaning in the modern world; and finally (3) a more pragmatic tendency that seeks a sense of adaptation to modern life.

Part of this typology, with modifications for the frame of reference of the Argentinean experience, may be found in some texts by Aldo Büntig (Büntig, 1968). A slightly different typology—but related to those of Ferreira de Camargo and of Büntig—is the work of Lucio Gera and Guillermo Rodríguez Melgarejo (1970), elaborated for pastoral rather than sociological purposes. The critique of these related typologies may be organized along two fundamental lines: (1) the lack of a political perspective on the religious problem and the Latin American Churches; and (2) the use of a simplistic and often incomplete approach to the constitution, development, and crises of alternative pastorates and the internal tendencies of the Church. By contrast, the work of Pablo Richard (1978) is a fundamental advance toward a political analysis of the Catholic Church in Latin America, reflecting many of the later contributions made within the framework of the Christian left.

## ELEMENTS FOR A CRITICAL TYPOLOGY OF THE CHURCH

Based on the following point of view, Richard attempts to construct an alternative model for the elaboration of a typology of the internal tendencies of the Church:

We can certainly elaborate a theoretical instrument of analysis that will allow us to order, systematize and thereby understand the diversity of social and political roles of the Latin American Church at the present time. This instrument, necessarily provisional and hypothetical, would have to be verified by historical reality. The provisional and hypothetical classification that we shall establish is based on two relationships: "Church–State" and "Church–Social Classes." (Richard, 1978: 19)

He distinguishes four types or forms of Church practice: (1) the conservative; (2) the social-Christian; (3) the socially compromised; and (4) the politically compromised. Let us review the characteristics of each of them.

*Conservative Church practice* combines the following characteristics:

1. It is a formal, sacramentalist, ritualistic Church, centered on family or individual moral problems.
2. It rejects the "modernization" of the Second Vatican Council.
3. It is bound to the old conservative oligarchy.
4. It fulfills the classic role of the Church as the ideological apparatus of the State, granting an unconditional legitimacy to authoritarian regimes and military dictatorships.

Richard identifies two forms of this practice: (1) that which is conservative by its adherence to traditions; and (1) that which is conservative, but with an explicitly pro-militaristic and integralist stance.

The *social-Christian Church practice* has the following characteristics:

1. It is bound to the more progressive sectors of the *criollo* bourgeoisie and the middle classes.
2. It is open to social problems and a defender of the social doctrine of the Church.
3. Ideologically, it is close to a reforming liberalism that considers socialism and communism as a moral enemy.
4. It grants a conditional legitimacy to authoritarian regimes and military dictatorships.
5. Politically, it is very close to the Christian democracies.

This practice is expressed in three forms: (1) that on the right, which is similar to conservative practice, but more critical; (2) that in the center, where the Church ceases to fulfill the role of the ideological apparatus of the State and takes on the position of mediator with respect to it, fulfilling the political role of tribune of the people without depriving State action of its legitimacy, but struggling for the recognition of mutual legitimacies (State–Church); and (3) that of the left, which drops the role of tribune and may assume that of legal opponent of the regime.

The *socially compromised Church practice* includes the following characteristics:

1. It grants no legitimacy to authoritarian States or military dictatorships.
2. It is an anticapitalist practice.
3. It fights for clearly antibourgeois and anticapitalist politics, but does not support a route toward socialism.
4. It defines itself as a "popular" and "evangelical" Church.

5. Its fundamental social option is for the popular classes.

6. Politically, it fluctuates, at times subordinating itself to social-Christian practice, at times assuming more politically comprised positions, depending on the degree of State repression.

Finally, the characteristics of the *politically compromised Church practice* are the following:

1. Christians who support it not only consider that the dominant system and capitalism are not legitimate, but explicitly argue in favor of an option for socialism.

2. They maintain that they should become part of popular organizations in indifferent terms—that is, as a Church, they should not assume a specific political role.

3. This practice rejects all pretension to political power.

4. It becomes a source of constant denunciation and a "force for undoing the legitimacy of the capitalist system."

This typology is based on a more suggestive theoretical framework than the previous ones, giving priority to more theoretical and political criteria in order to understand the connections among the State, the social classes, and the Church. It seems a very worthwhile typology when used to analyze one particular facet of the problem, namely the question of Church praxis and its political impact on social formations. But we must also stress once more the need to make all possible criteria explicit in order to establish a typology. Although Richard's types seem correct, he nevertheless incurs the error of not considering the political practice of the traditional right, which, from every point of view, is a "politically compromised Church practice." In this sense, the very notions of politics and compromise may come to be questioned in his theoretical scheme.

## CRITERIA FOR A COMPREHENSIVE TYPOLOGY OF THE CATHOLIC CHURCH IN LATIN AMERICA

Thus far, we have stated first, that the Church is a hierarchy of power; second, that it reflects a social stratification and receives the impact of class struggle on social formation, to such a degree that we might say that the struggle is "interiorized" in the institution of the Church along with other relevant social conflicts with which it is articulated; and third, that it develops and actualizes a system of social functions on the basis of specific normative principles, at the same time forming part of a system of religious action in society that is neither circumscribed nor exhausted by the Churches, even if they are one of its most relevant manifestations.

On the basis of these assumptions, is it possible to construct a typology that will orient concrete inquiry into the Churches and religion in Latin America and will, at the same time, give an account of the multiplicity of factors that this inquiry implies? It is still difficult to respond to this question. However, we believe that there are four distinct criteria from which four systems of typologies may be elaborated that would therefore refer to four different centers of analysis.

- First, we propose to consider a technical-theological criterion that will account for the religious institution's theoretical position with respect to social (education, labor, social life, political life, etc.) and ethical-moral attitudes, particularly at the level of human sexuality and its impact on phenomena that for now we may call sociodemographic (for example, the relations between religion and fertility, birth control, abortion, euthanasia, etc.). In short, the entire theological discussion of dogma and morality enters here.

- Second, we propose an internal Church praxis that would include the application of canons and norms for rites and liturgy, the limitation and understanding of the role of the hierarchy and religious elites as well as of the faithful and the ministers, deliberations on the missionary aspects of the Churches, criteria even for determining strategies for recruiting faithful and ministers, criteria even for determining the strategy for investment of Church funds, and all the internal administrative questions concerning the functioning of the Churches as formal secondary institutions or complex organizations.

- Third, we propose consideration of a strictly ideological and political criterion. Under this heading we would find the entire problem of social class within the Church: the recruitment of faithful based on the preconceived choice of a particular class; social areas of apostolic activity (rural sectors, the workers, marginal and nonmarginal city dwellers, the middle classes or segments of the oligarchy, and/or the financial, commercial, or industrial bourgeoisie); the relations between religious praxis and socially dominant and subordinate classes (where we find the problem of the social function of religion with respect to the power bloc and the basic problem of the practice of the Churches and the construction of a class hegemony); and the problem of religion and social response, the questions of the Popular Church, religion, and revolution, or religion and counterculture. Here we will also find the problem of the connection between Church and State, including the different positions with respect to formal political-administrative relations (concordats, pacts, etc.). Then there are the problems related to the levels of the religious phenomenon and social consciousness—among which questions such as religion and social fetishism, religious legitimation of the State and the mode of production, and, in effect, the ideological-religious bases of social domination stand out in particular. The question of the sociopolitical vision of Christians and Christian hierarchies,[4] and the role of the Church in political life, play an important part under this criterion. The work by Richard is an evident contribution here.

- Fourth, we shall find something that we may call the criterion for analysis of the "insertion of the Church," that is, the phenomena that result from the implementation of Church practice in social formations. Although this entails a level of generalization that is perhaps much broader than the other three criteria, it will allow us to explain, for example, the political-cultural role of the national, regional, and even parochial Churches, certain vicissitudes particular to the Church of the region, and some specific social practices (work with marginalized ethnic, racial, or linguistic minorities, for example)—in fact, all those elements that permit an analysis of the connection of Church practice with immediate or national community, and some of the empirical evidence of its action, as a complex organization within the institutions of civil society as a whole.

As is clearly evident, these four criteria or focuses of analysis are very considerably more than a taxonomy of different environments of Church action, or levels of study of the Churches as social institutions. It is also evident that they do not address homogeneous aspects. While the first and the third refer to more ideological or theoretical processes, the second and the fourth refer to processes of the internal or external praxis of the Churches.

## IDEOLOGICAL TENDENCIES OF THE CATHOLIC CHURCH IN LATIN AMERICA

In order to obtain a somewhat more complex and perhaps more operative typology, we have combined—as indicated in Figure 7.1—the more ideological or, if one prefers, the more "normative" criteria. The defect of every typology is its schematic character, but the advantage that the one presented in Figure 7.1 may have is that, in spite of having been elaborated from data about the Catholic Church, it may allow for consideration of the Protestant Churches and may be helpful in undertaking a comparative analysis of Church ideologies in Latin America.

Within the ideological-political criterion we have distinguished three currents: (1) the "traditionalists," which is synonymous with the term *politically conservative*; (2) the "*aperturistas*," which refers to a broader and more ambiguous position in political-ideological terms; and (3) the "radicals," which refers to a militant position in political and ideological terms regardless of nomenclature or ideological direction.

**Figure 7.1**
**Proposed Typology of Internal Tendencies of the Latin American Church**

| | | Traditionalists | Aperturists | Radicals |
|---|---|---|---|---|
| | | | **Political-Ideological Criterion** | |
| **Technical-Theological Criterion** | Conservative | Neo-Christianity | Social-Christianity<br><br>Christian Democracy Development | Traditional Catholic Right |
| | Renovationist | Charismatic Spiritualism | Populism | Socialism |

Within the technical-theological criterion, we have distinguished the "conservatives" from the "renovationists," between whom the line of demarcation is established by the fact that the former give most of their efforts to preventing all significant change in dogma, canons, and Church praxis, while the latter systematically promote them. The combination of these two criteria provides configuration shown in Figure 7.1.

We may call the first category or type *neo-Christianity*, corresponding to a position and a Church praxis that has traditional characteristics in political-ideological terms. It presupposes that culture is imbued with faith, it rejects all kinds of evangelization in favor of catechism, and it sees the world on the basis of a static and ingenuous view, while also understanding the opposition between science and faith to be unreconcilable. Its clearest historical manifestation in Latin America is "Colonial Christianity." Although deeply rooted in the popular sectors, its weight in terms of Church practice is becoming more limited, and in its "purest" forms it is tending to disappear from the Church superstructure.

By contrast, the *traditional Catholic right* repeats most of the values espoused by neo-Christianity and coincides to great extent with the same world view, but radicalizes its option, bringing it into the realm of the "social" without ever losing sight of a Manichaean view of social reality— insisting on the action of the devil in the world—and, finally, maintaining a corporativist position with medieval overtones. Its political horizon is clearly nationalistic. The traditional right endorses a corporative capitalist stance and the need for a rigid and strict social stratification. Social mobility is a risk in itself that may contribute to the destruction of values, norms, and traditional structures. Nevertheless, the world (the secular) is not antagonistic, but must be systematically infused with a Christian presence so that a conservative Christian political order may occur. The olitical expression of this tendency is not far from fascism.

*Social-Christianity*, an aperturista view, recognizes that capitalism certainly produces some evils, and it suggests correcting them; but in the long run, it tends to legitimize capitalism. It is anticommunist, in common with neo-Christianity and the traditional Catholic right. The most tangible evidence of its practice are the Christian-Democratic parties on the Continent. Politically they are centrists and reformists—very close to the views of the political third party (*tercerismo*), but with differences about what the role of the Church should be in the process of economic development and social change in Latin America. Their class position is very close to that of the nationalistic bourgeoisie that endeavors (not without some friction, on occasion) to renegotiate the condition of economic dependence with the imperialist powers, seeking to capture greater room for its own involvement in internal markets. Its political horizon is that of a democracy under the tutelage of the military sectors. Ideologically, it thrives on the tradition of spiritual humanism since Erasmus of Rotterdam, including Giovanni Battista Vico, extending as far as Jacques Maritain, and occasionally including Giovanni Gentile. Its position is antisocialist, to the extent that socialism implies a modification of private ownership amounting to creation of a "mortgaged society," and it finds the materialist or atheistic positions of many militant socialists particularly irritating.

*Charismatic spiritualism* is one of the most recent novelties of the Christian world. The charismatic movements maintain the need for a militant spirituality and conversion of consciousness, and, above all, the need to project the Church through exterior signs and become part of the experiences of secular life—views that are especially reinforced in gatherings of the initiated in which "the breath of the spirit is allowed to work." Nevertheless, it is an essentially traditional political stance: politics is the work of politicians and citizens should not concern themselves with it, but only with their personal affairs. Religion is a point of inflection in human affairs where the secular and the sacred combine.[5]

Next, we find *populism*, which has important antecedents in Latin America. It corresponds to the social pact whereby a nationalistic bourgeoisie is supported by working-class sectors in order to assert the hegemony of the internal market over the indigenous production of goods and services, seeking to displace monopolistic international capital from its entrenched positions. The fundamental ideological category is the term *the people*, and the analytical framework may be characterized as the "theory of dependence" and, to a lesser degree, a non-Marxist theory of imperialism. Populism's intention is the modification of the capitalist system, while seeking an alternative route to "collectivized socialism." In this regard, it is very similar to the political third party.

Finally, there is the *socialist* perspective, which uses historical materialism as an instrument of analysis and has the "poor and oppressed" as the basic sectors toward which its pastoral practice is oriented. Generally, the socialists in the Churches are radicalized in their political positions and systematically confront the State apparatus. Their long-term objective is to construct a new historical bloc with a worker–peasant hegemony. The militants of this tendency actively participate in political parties and popular movements of the Continent.[6]

Table 7.1 includes these six types or categories and compares them according to sociologically significant parameters. Obviously, this proposal for a typology requires broad discussion and, above all, concrete research in order to show its possible heuristic value.

## NOTES

1. For a relatively extensive bibliography on the sociology of religion in Latin America until the beginning of the seventies (although regrettably with serious omissions), see Gerhard Drekonja (1971).

2. An interesting critique of the theoretical positions of Vallier and other authors of the same current of thought may be found in the excellent text of Luiz Alberto Gómez de Souza (1978). See also Jaime Rodríguez (1978).

3. A very broad and systematic critique of Ferreira de Camargo may be found in Gómez de Souza (1978), which we have used to structure many of our comments. The contributions of Gómez de Souza to the critical sociology of religion in Latin America—with his abundant theoretical documentation and, above all, his extensive experience in Brazil, Chile, and Mexico—are without doubt among the most stimulating, systematic, and complete that may be consulted. He reviews and critiques the work of Thomas Bruneau (1974), Emmanuel de Kadt (1970), and Thomas Sanders (1966), among others, and calls attention to Luigi Einaudi, Richard Lawrence Maullin, Alfred Stephan, and Michael Howard Fleet for their work on the study commissioned by the Rand Corporation that has the suggestive title *Latin American Institutional Development: The Changing Catholic Church* (1969).

4. In Chapter 8, we propose some hypotheses for an analysis of social stratification and the class origin of priests and ministers that undoubtedly throws some light on the question of how the sociopolitical vision of the hierarchies is constituted. Like many of the hypotheses presented in this book, greater

**Table 7.1**
**Ideological Tendencies in the Latin American Church**

| | Proposed Types or Categories | | | | | |
|---|---|---|---|---|---|---|
| COMPARATIVE PARAMETERS | NEO-CHRISTIANITY | CHARISMATIC SPIRITUALISM | SOCIAL CHRISTIANITY | POPULISM | TRADITIONAL RIGHT | SOCIALISM |
| POLITICAL-SOCIAL IDEOLOGY | Christian Occidentalism (based on Thomist philosophy); universalism | Liberalism of its own making | Christian liberal democracy; third party | Reconciliation of class (Bonapartism); third party | Militant conservatism in the style of Maurras and Action Française | Socialism |
| INSTRUMENT OF SOCIAL ANALYSIS | Traditional humanism; culturalist analysis | Unconcerned with the social; lacks a framework of analysis | Structural functionalist analysis | Syncretism; anti-imperialist; revolutionary nationalism | Oligarchical nationalism; theory of elites | Historical materialism |
| LINK WITH SOCIAL CLASSES | Supported by traditional agrarian bourgeoisie | Middle-class and popular sector phenomenon; used by capitalism | Urban and rural middle classes; "national" bourgeoisie | The people, working and marginal sector; popular classes | Traditional oligarchy; upper classes | Working-class marginal sectors; peasants |
| RELATIONS WITH THE STATE | Harmonious and legitimizing (especially if the State professes Catholicism) | Legitimizing | Critically legitimizing (producing friction) | In the long run legitimizes capitalism (non-antagonistic disagreement) | Legitimizing but critical of liberal models | Nonlegitimizing (antagonistic disagreement) |
| CONCEPT OF CHURCH'S "MISSION" IN LATIN AMERICA | Individualist and triumphalist: salvation of the soul | Inculcate the Christian "Spirit" in social structures; change of consciousness | Christian presence in politics; reform of structures and change of consciousness | Linkage of the Church to popular sectors | The Church as a support of the power bloc | The Church as critic of the System: the voice of voiceless; CONSCIENTIZING |

empirical research is necessary in order to verify their versatility, explicative value, and analytical usefulness.

5. The political importance of these charismatic Christian tendencies is sporadically highlighted by the press in Latin America. One of the most recent and tragic episodes that have taken place when this kind of orientation is linked to the State may be found in the experience of Guatemala under the dictatorship of General Efraín Ríos Montt from 1981 to 1983.

6. During the eighties, many militants representing anticapitalist or socialist positions in the Catholic Church, and in the Philosophy and Theology of Liberation have embraced political positions closer to Social Democratic agendas rather than socialist, Communist, or anarcho-syndicalist ones. This new political emphasis is related to the ever growing criticisms of Marxism as a theoretical framework, and the development of post-structuralist and post-modernist theoretical approaches (Giroux & McLaren 1989; Laclau 1985; Sherover-Marcuse, 1986). Criticism of Marxism as a theoretical approach is also linked to the growing dissatisfaction with "real socialism" as expressed in the former Soviet Union. The Communist system was eventually dismissed in the context of popular dissatisfaction and activism, but also due to the complete economic and technological bankruptcy of the system. The progressive sectors of the Catholic Church are not immune to these historical changes, and many political implications will follow.

# 8

# Hypothesis for a Theoretical Framework for Religion and Churches in Latin America

=========

The religious experience of Latin Americans has by and large been analyzed as associated with and inscribed within the ideological-cultural processes of the social structure. This is to say, from a certain point of view, that religion and the Churches have been studied as part of the ideological-juridical spheres of capitalist societies. All things considered, this seems inadequate today for a critical sociology of religion and the Churches, especially since such an analytical approach favors the study of religious forms from the perspective of their correspondence with the processes of cultural, political, and ideological reproduction of the capitalist mode of production. The noncorrespondences and contradictions that emerge among religious forms and Church practices with respect to the more general question of the reproduction of the social relations of production and the generation of alternative expectations and social practices are omitted and, to a certain extent, ignored.

The legitimizing effects of religion with respect to the social structure have been studied in some detail where they exist, but the contradictory effects of a denial of legitimacy by those religious forms in light of a change in perceptions and appeal, and consequently in social practices also (and thus a change in the religious forms themselves), are almost always ignored. In general, religion has been studied from critical perspectives as a significant part of the "will for political domination" associated with established political power. However, there are now criteria, expectations, and concrete processes in various Latin American countries that invite us to consider religion as a significant part of the "will for transformation" associated with a new political power or with the generation of a new historical bloc. That is to say, it is proper to consider and study religious and Church processes from critical perspectives as part of the new areas of struggle, or arenas of social conflict, so that, by understanding them, it may be possible to broaden the historical and social coordinates that promote changes leading to a fundamental democratization of the social and political structures of the region.

In the following discussion, we will outline some reflections that are presented as hypotheses concerning religious forms in Latin America. Although they are necessarily provisional, they are intended to draw attention to the importance of elaborating a systematic theoretical framework on religion and the Churches in Latin America that will direct and guide empirical research, on the one hand, and, on the other, will contribute significantly to an understanding of the social and political struggle involved in creating new forms of religion that are popular and democratic in origin and meaning.

## RELIGIOUS FORMS AND SOCIETY

Throughout this book, we have pointed out that religion and religious forms are basically a social experience, the individual elements of which are adaptations of a "social consciousness" predetermined by established social patterns and norms. At the same time, however, this experience depends on the basic process of socialization of the individual, and cultural tradition of society, and its attendant political circumstances. In other words, it is still valid to state that religious experience depends on the empirical-cultural process by which people appropriate their material existence, produce their own way of life, and rationalize their empirical experience. Religious experience is expressed and often achieves its specific validity as a very personal experience. But even intimist experiences are connected in their greater dimensions to the complexity of social life, and one of the fundamental purposes of a critical sociology of religion is to discover how these meaningful connections occur.

In this way, among the forms of social consciousness, the social structure includes religious consciousness, which is in turn organically inserted into the process of social struggle. To the extent that they constitute one of the basic elements in the construction or support of social hegemony, religious forms will also be organically inserted, with a specific role, in the process of social domination. Insofar as, according to Marx and Engels, "the dominant ideas of an age are the ideas of the dominant classes," religion will reflect important themes of the dominant ideologies. In this regard, the old Althusserian hypothesis that ideologies address and constitute individuals may now warrant, insofar as religious forms are concerned, a more detailed elaboration.[1]

However, the effect that takes place on religious consciousness as a result of its reflecting the dominant ideology as its own is not mechanical. Within the corpus of every religious doctrine, the device by which the religion may constitute itself as part of the apparatus of the State has many determinants. This is to say that the process of reflecting the dominant ideology, and its effect, are not mechanical because every ideological appeal is re-elaborated within the religious or ecclesiastical corpus via double conditioning. On the one hand, certain conditionings derive from the objective developments of the social structure (i.e., every religious ideology is historical and is continuously actualized); on the other hand, conditionings arise from the internal dynamics of the Churches as institutions that organize worship and legitimize dogma and sacred rites. To this extent, every religion may tend to distance itself from the overall ideological material that constitutes the atmosphere of social hegemony, in the same way that—resorting to an analogy from statistics—the observed frequency of a phenomenon may be different from its expected frequency on a normal curve.

As institutions that participate in building social hegemony and are the support of the entire apparatus of domination of the political society over the civil, the Churches possess a relative autonomy without ceasing to be institutions of civil society. In a few cases, far from expressing any national consensus on the system of State domination, they are in fact able to express rebellion and even channel social dissatisfaction against the State—a characteristic that is very likely to occur whenever there is a crisis in hegemony, as Pablo Richard has pointed out very clearly:

The Church has its own identity and a relative autonomy within historical processes. Social and political conflicts are certainly reproduced within a specific dynamic and with particular characteristics. The analysis of the Church must therefore dialectically combine these two fundamental methodological principles: first, the fundamental determination of the economic, political and social in church phenomena; second, the relative autonomy and identity proper to the Church. (Richard, 1978: 14–15)

This goes much further than the observation made by Karl Marx that misery in religion is, on the one hand, the expression of real misery and, on the other, a protest against it. A certain type of religion may be not just a sufficient element but even an indispensable one at the outset and consolidation of a revolutionary process in social formations profoundly bound to religious traditions. In this context, Anatoly Lunacharski's prescription concerning the need to revolutionize social relations and to revolutionize religion is more clearly understood (Lunacharski, 1976). Unfortunately, in the analyses like that of Richard, although the question of relative autonomy (which is where the possibility of connecting religion to the social struggle really lies) is clearly presented, it is subordinated to structural factors in every circumstance—whereas in practice the relation is much more complex, having multiple subordinations that result from historical circumstances of social formation and the very practice of religion within it. The subordination of the transformation of religious consciousness to the transformation of structural conditions necessarily amounts to reductionism and a historical fatalism that no history of social revolutions justifies.

The above, however, does not prevent us from pointing out that religion is determined by the social structure in which it expresses itself. Nevertheless, this determination is not necessarily unilateral and does not provoke unavoidable historical conditionings. Thus, every religion has a class profile but, at the same time, has a particular impact on class structures. This may be seen in the differences in recruitment between lay members and ministers and pastors in the different Christian Churches and sects. These differences are also reproduced within a particular Church, even when, in general terms, the Churches are eminently multiclassed and therefore define themselves as pluralist.

Within themselves, the Churches live and reproduce the basic class, gender and race conflict and the ideological conflict of society as a whole, even when—it must again be pointed out in order to avoid the reductionist thesis that the Church as an institution is only a reflection of the social process—there exists a relative autonomy in the social, political, and ideological processes of the Church as a social structure. In other words, it is appropriate to speak of a certain Church logic that is difficult to understand under the decodifying optic of the rest of the ideological processes of a capitalist society. In this way, the Churches have a social stratification similar to that of society, to the extent that they encompass all classes and social class groups—from which it may be derived that the practice of one class may prevail over that of the others and express itself with greater force in Church praxis. Considering the class of origin both of their ministers and bishops and of the lay directors of their classic organizations (e.g., Catholic Action, Catholic Student Youth, Catholic University Youth), it would seem that the petite-bourgeoisie is the dominant social sector in the Churches of Latin America, with immediate consequences at the doctrinal and pastoral level, as well as in the ideological perspective of the Churches, and even in the language of their documents.

Luiz Alberto Gómez de Souza (1975) offers a very stimulating analysis of the criteria of reproduction of the hierarchical cadres of the Catholic Church in Latin America, drawing attention to the class makeup of the clergy. On the one hand, the existence of a very significant proportion of secular priests from the traditional agrarian bourgeoisie or the industrial and financial bourgeoisie together does not seem evident. On the other hand, a significant number of clergy from the industrial working class is not observable either. In some regions, like Peru, Ecuador, Bolivia, Mexico, and Central America, there is a significant incorporation of members of the peasant and even indigenous sectors in the clergy. However, it would not seem hazardous to hypothesize that the greater part of recruits into the Church come from the petite-bourgeoisie, the children of small business families, liberal professionals, white-collar workers, State bureaucrats, and small farmers—in fact, the children of the emerging classes under competitive capitalism. This leads Gómez de Souza to suggest a certain elective affinity among the Churches in rectifying the ranks of social agents to the benefit of one particular pastoral praxis and the petite-bourgeoisie. Of course the attribution of class does not inevitably determine the class horizon or consciousness of class from which each priest or bishop presents his religious practice, but it does seem plausible to suppose that a certain political culture and a particular cultural capital will have important consequences in his choice of political and social options (Gómez de Souza, 1975: 77). It would seem even more likely, however, that this attribution of class—the reflection of which in terms of social consciousness is all the more significant—would give a special stamp to the policies of the Church concerning the political alliances to be established.

As mechanisms that select and expel their members according to a great variety of formal rules and informal principles, the Churches are social institutions. As institutions, they are also structures that constitute the matrix for the organization of other institutions (Poulantzas, 1976: 140, n. 22). By operating, to a greater or lesser degree, as ideological apparatuses, the Churches tend to establish themselves as mediating structures. That is, they may articulate basic systems of hegemony that—if we suppose that there is a low level of autonomy among the Church systems—become important sources of support for obtaining and producing a basic consensus among social agents. This consensus would not necessarily express itself as decided support for the regime currently in power, but would in any case be a consensus that gives global acceptance to the dominant mode of production and the capitalist form of State. If, however, there existed conditions for the relatively high autonomy of Church institutions, their power to convene a definite consensus would diminish notably. There might even arise phenomena that would propose the formation of a new historical bloc and the development of processes and actions that could be characterized as anti-hegemonic. The development of the Theology of Liberation and its movement toward the poor as the historical subjects of conversion, or the development within the Church and community structure of what has come to be termed the Popular Church, could be read in these terms.

At the level of the Churches in Latin America, in the past two decades there has appeared a new and unusually vigorous phenomenon: the discussion of Church praxis is acquiring an increasingly greater importance over the dogmatic-doctrinal discussion of theology. This has occurred because theology is pursued no longer in a specifically theological place such as the theological faculties or appropriately ecclesiastical institutions, but in the communities and in the poor quarters and marginal areas of the cities. Juan Luis Segundo has pointed out that "pastoral conditioning submitted liberation theology to a double haste or urgency: the first theology of liberation was *a kind of urgent theology formed with a certain pastoral haste*" (Segundo, 1975: 94; original emphasis).

Expressed in other terms, the basic preoccupation of the new currents in the Catholic Church in Latin America is the search for a pastorate that will resonate with the social structure and respond to its demands to a greater extent. No longer placing so much emphasis on providing greater "theological rationalization" to its central groups represents a Copernican shift in the experience of the neo-Christian Church. Around the dogmas of faith, the Church always sought to consolidate the advances obtained by conversion in Latin America, an area with about 300 million Catholics—approximately 42 percent of all Catholics in the world. Hence, the basic practice it promoted was the catechism of initiation as a device for maintaining the cycle of traditional faith at both the family and social levels. Today, the concern for conversion responds to the opposite phenomenon. The ground that was thought conquered and consolidated no longer seems to be so, and the turbulent social and political modification of Latin America does not really contribute to "expanding the faith," at least from the traditionalist perspective. Existing pressures on this internal tendency of the Catholic Church are also associated with a greater ecclesiastical self-criticism that derives from liberal, social-Christian, and developmentalist sectors and has led to a progressive retreat, at least in official documents, from the former triumphalism of the Church.

However, without contradicting the above, we must point out that this self-criticism is also associated with greater expression of class and other social conflicts as an ideological conflict within the body of the Church. Theological disputes no longer present themselves at a technical level within a single paradigm, but between paradigms of contradictory origins and different social bases; and this confrontation arises from discussion on and from Church praxis, rather than from theory and abstraction. Elaboration of theory (regardless of the level in ecclesiastical terms) follows the concrete praxis of sectors of the Church, always sustains it, sometimes justifies it (independently of the political horizon from which it is elaborated), and in some cases endeavors to indicate courses of action open to base communities.

## CHURCHES, CRISIS, AND HEGEMONY

As institutions that create and support hegemony, the Churches, like the political parties, represent organic intellectuals of the social classes. The historical experience of Latin America would state that, at the level of the hierarchies, they are generally organic intellectuals of the bourgeoisie. By contrast, in terms of some lay and clerical structures and at the level of the ecclesial base communities, many of them seem inclined toward becoming organic intellectuals of the subordinated sectors of society, or at least a source of reflection and criticism undertaken by civil society on political society and, in a few cases (as in Nicaragua), part of the reconstruction of a new State in a society in transition.

These circumstances are at the root of the crisis through which the Churches of Latin America have been passing since at least the early seventies. While one of its elements is positioned as representative of the dominant social groups, formulating an ideological discourse in terms of values directed toward civil society and appealing to those who are part of its consensus through a praxis that is intended to provoke and call upon the whole of society, another element is attempting to forge a new historical bloc in collaboration with extra-ecclesiastical social and political forces. This sector rejects the official ideological discourse of the hierarchies and undermines their project for hegemony at the level of the Church as an institution, through the development of an ideological counterdiscourse. All this would seem to suggest the construction of a counterhegemony and an ecclesiastical praxis that essentially hinges on the marginalized and peasant sectors of society and on the Catholic student sectors. There is, of course, a large sector, a "silent majority" that keeps swinging toward either pole, giving the issues at hand an historical process.

In order to measure the scale of the "ecclesiastical crisis" in Latin America, it is necessary to reflect on its character and specificity. First of all, it is necessary to take into account that a historical bloc is constituted around the system of hegemony of the prevailing class—which excludes the fundamental interests of the subordinated classes. Thus, the problem in creating a new historical bloc is that of creating a new system of hegemony based on a new prevailing social class (or a new set of alliances oriented to forming that class or part of it as a prevailing class). The eruption of an organic crisis in a historical bloc generally leads to modifications in the connections and alliances among classes and sections of classes. Hence, the formation of a new historical bloc is not a mechanical phenomenon but a real undertaking requiring the positive resolution of at least two major conditions:

1. The eruption of an organic crisis in the historical bloc, that is, the breaking of the organic link between structure and superstructure, so that intellectuals no longer represent the social classes. This crisis may be provoked by the subordinate classes (whether or not they are organized) or may be a consequence of the political failure of the governing class.

2. The creation of a system of hegemony that combines the subordinate classes. If the crisis is spontaneous and the subordinate classes are not organized, the dominant class will regain control of the situation and the old society will be maintained, at least provisionally. Then again, in the absence of any organization, the organic crisis will not occur in the first place. There is, however, one proviso. According to Gramsci (1975–77), not every crisis within the historical bloc is necessarily an organic crisis, since, for this to occur, the break must encompass the prevailing classes.

All these concepts can be related to the Church without resulting in an exaggerated "tour de force." We may begin with the assumption that the

Catholic Church in Latin America, as a regionally and temporally limited structure, can be understood as a particular historical bloc, different, for example, from the Churches of Western Europe, or the Catholic Church in the United States or Canada. The second element in our observations would be that, as already stated, the Church contributes to the elaboration and consolidation of social hegemony—which warrants a third element: according to neo-Christianity, the flexing of the system of hegemony should amount to support for the basic dominant class, and should accompany the creation of the power blocs, marching to exactly the same beat. However, with the modification of the system of hegemony— the changeover of classes in the bloc in power—a relocation in the position of the Church has also occurred that was first expressed on a large scale by the subordinated social classes. Fundamentally, this was the result of combining the working class and the popular sectors in general with the industrial bourgeoisie within the "populist pact"—which also facilitated linking the Church to the "popular" element of the alliance, insofar as ritualistic and magical practices were concerned.

A fourth element to be considered, as already stated, is that the Church reproduces not only the multiclass character of society, but also its class conflict. Thus, to create a new historical bloc it is necessary to create a new system of hegemony. This is the importance of the so-called Popular Churches, which contain within them—in a practical state—the seed of a new system of hegemony that is to be implemented in the historical bloc. At the same time, the importance of popular Catholicism in Latin America becomes very clear, although the phenomenon of the Popular Churches seems a relatively heteronomous one with respect to the dynamics of civil society overall.

For the possible construction of this new historical bloc, what has happened in recent decades should be reviewed in the light of two theoretical conditions previously proposed:

1. On the one hand, it is evident that the basic intellectuals of the Church no longer represent the dominant classes in an articulate and effective form— particularly the bourgeoisie of the bloc in power. This organic crisis is the product of a double phenomenon: the activation of the subordinate classes and the growth of the Popular Church not as a parallel Church, but as a new challenging reality within the institution (with variations, according to countries); and the political failure of the ecclesiastical governing class, since its attempts to adjust the Church to the evolution of society have also failed.

2. On the other hand, the creation of a new system of hegemony that is still closely bound to an intense ideological struggle is prefigured by the rise and development of Liberation Theology and its concern for the poor. This leads to a new situation where the emerging system of hegemony (now at an ideological and cultural level) seeks to combine the subordinated classes designated by the term *poor* in a counterhegemonic ideology.

In a strict sense, it is not an organic crisis that is occurring in the Church, but a crisis of hegemony that, as we have maintained in this book, is very closely bound to the economic and political phenomena of the Continent and, especially in the Southern Cone, to the development of new models of the authoritarian State. Some national Churches—ones that were once a function of the capitalist mode of production in its premonopolistic or competitive stage, and never did express themselves clearly as the organic intellectuals of the bourgeoisie in a liberal democratic regime—have begun to challenge the "regimes of national security." The Chilean Church is a case in point. Basically, the economic model supported by the military dictatorship had characteristics that made it exclusive in social and political terms and features that tend toward the concentration and centralization of capital in economic terms. It has cast aside the expectations of classes and sectors of classes ideologically represented in part by the Catholic Church, among which should be included segments of the middle class, part of the working class, peasants, marginalized urban dwellers, and important elements of the national entrepreneurial class. In much this same way, throughout the region, the functional character of the Church in premonopolistic capitalism has collided head-on with a model of oligopolistic accumulation, and challenged the totalitarian character of the regimes of national security, even when they call themselves Christian.

The fundamental motive for this challenge in Chile and elsewhere is an awareness in the different ecclesiastical tendencies of the Church—even among the liberal and social-Christian pastoral tendencies—that these regimes do not leave a wide margin for the traditional social action of the Churches. In some cases, it is even believed that they represent an ideological alternative to the Churches given that to a certain extent they create their own ideological apparatuses and discard, in terms of the social consensus, the function borne by the Churches as mediators. By the same token, as the authoritarian features of the model of domination are accentuated, these States are required to resort to various corporative mechanisms of coercion, rejecting the ideological mechanisms of the consensus—for, in contrast with the fascist regimes of Europe, authoritarian regimes based on the doctrine of national security lack a broad mass support.

The prevalence of this crisis of hegemony in the Churches of the region would explain the constant references to "unity" made in the speeches of Pope John Paul II during his travels in Latin America. The crisis of hegemony within the Church is not in any way remote from the hegemonic crisis that constitutes one of the keys for understanding the political and social struggles of the seventies and eighties in Latin America. By coming to understand that hegemony has a class character and is essentially ethical-political, the social sciences have given new currency to the study of religion—particularly the phenomena of popular religiosity. Phenomena that were underestimated for their reifying, fetishistic, and alienating character—and were, in fact, taken to be of little importance— are now beginning to be studied as part of that national-popular component of every historical bloc of which Antonio Gramsci (1980) spoke and which is a substantial component in the construction of a new historical bloc in Latin America. The implications of this conclusion will become apparent through the discussion presented in our next and final chapter on the role of the Catholic Church in Argentina.

## NOTE

1. Referring to ideologies in general, Emilio de Ipola (1982: 11) makes a similar comment; and beginning with a thematic and theoretical continuity of the same nature as Althusser's hypotheses on ideology, Göran Therborn (1980) develops a comparable argument.

# 9

# The Catholic Church in Argentina

The purpose of this chapter is to analyze the Catholic Church in Argentina as an institution of religious mediation intersected by a number of ideological tendencies that correspond to concrete historical crystallizations or projects for Church action promoted by lay Christian groups, members of religious orders, priests, and bishops.

Any analysis of the Catholic Church in Argentina, even as an institution with specific rules and regulations, implies an analysis of the connections between Church and State. By the same token, any analysis here of the ideological and pastoral tendencies of the Church—given that we have previously omitted a detailed discussion of the patterns of theological interpretation related to pastoral action—implies an historical-structural analysis. Hence, the discussion that follows, to the extent that it studies the experience of a national Church during the past two centuries and is restricted by the space available to us, can only refer to some of the most notable aspects of the Church–State relationship and Church ideologies, and does not in any way pretend to be a complete historical interpretation.

In this chapter, we will show that the Argentine Church, as a Church of Christendom[1] and a traditional intellectual force, has subtly influenced the constitution of common sense of both the popular and hegemonic classes. However, since independence in 1816, and especially during liberal governments from 1853 to the beginning of the 1930s, it was hemmed in by an oligarchical state dominated by the agrarian historical bloc. In that context, although the Church was able to exert a certain cultural influence, this was not sufficient to constitute political hegemony, with the result that it played merely a symbolic and marginal institutional role, constantly subject to the vicissitudes of the legal status of patronage.

With the upsurge of integral Catholicism in the thirties—particularly its association with Argentine nationalism and alliance with the military—some sectors of the Church thought they could see militant Catholicism as a new way of tying their cultural influence to a stable hegemonic political model. The Peronist experience modified this process significantly. During the years 1945–55, the Church in Argentina went from a period of connection with the political power—a connection tinged with difficulties but mutually beneficial to the Church and the political regime—to a time of crisis and wholesale confrontation, especially during the last year of government under Peronism. With the fall of Perón, the opposition between Peronism and anti-Peronism lay dormant within the Church and was revived with the rise of Tercermundismo (Third Worldism) only after the changes that occurred toward the mid-sixties following the Second Vatican Council.

The authoritarian pact between the Church and the military corporation that came to power in 1966 did not prevent polarization within ecclesiastical circles, as the result of the formation of a Popular Church that would be linked to Peronism and would promote national socialism. Following the experience of the third Peronist government (removed by a military coup in 1976), a new version of the authoritarian pact—in which the traditional Catholic right sought to reconcile cultural and political hegemony once and for all—again fragmented and divided the Church in Argentina, this time over the question of human rights.

The most recent period of democracy does not seem to have brought any radical change to the pattern of concert and conflict between Church and State, although the official Church must confront the situation—unprecedented at least since 1955—of democratic constitutional change orchestrated by legitimate political parties in a pluralistic, nonmilitarized environment. In this context, it seems that the Church's capacity to appeal to society has diminished. The institutionalization of democracy doubtless gives rise to important challenges for the Church in Christendom that repeatedly seeks to influence both cultural values and the political regime of the day, although, on the other hand, its actions may also affect the stability of democracy itself.

## CHRISTENDOM

The "discovery," conquest, and colonization of Latin America entailed the active participation of the Christian Church as a disciplinary order. Since we pointed out the predominant characteristics of the pastoral of Christianity in Chapter 6, we shall emphasize only three of its aspects here: (1) the relations between natural order and Christianity as a Church; (2) the fundamental anthropological dualism of this notion of natural order; and (3) the practical implications of this dualism with respect to the cultural specificity of Christianity.

The notion of Christendom is based on the existence of a natural order, as defended by one of the best known Catholic antimodernists in Argentina, Carlos A. Sacheri, for whom natural order does not result from blind chance but has a hierarchy—"a harmony manifested in all beings and in all phenomena" (Sacheri, 1975: 22). This natural order makes it possible to establish a natural law "made up of all those principles that men know spontaneously and with certainty by applying their natural reason to the knowledge of their own being and to property that is natural and necessary to them" (Sacheri, 1975: 25). It is essential and different from the nonessential order formed through the positive law created by a competent authority. In such a view of Christianity, natural law (and natural law alone)—characterized by immutability, knowability, and universality—must be the foundation of positive law, and humanity inclines toward natural law as a result of three particular characteristics: first, a tendency to preserve life; second, a tendency to propagate it; and third, a tendency toward human, intellectual, moral, social, and religious perfection (Sacheri, 1975: 28). Finally, one of the fundamental principles of natural order and therefore of Christianity is the distinction between a temporal order, whose administration falls to the legitimate authorities, and a supernatural or sacred order, which, in the last analysis, is ineffable and whose preservation is the basic mission of the Church, aided by the grace of God (Sacheri, 1975: 187). This distinction is at the root of the dualist anthropology of Christianity.

The foundations of Christendom—especially the Church that arose in the Counter-Reformational wake of the Council of Trent—acquired institutional effect in Argentina from the time of the conquest and colonization, and survived the turbulent conflicts between liberals and Catholics in the second half of the nineteenth century until approximately the first three decades of the twentieth. However, their ideological traces have endured longer through the pens of Catholic nationalist journalists such as Bruno Jordan Genta and Carlos Sacheri and especially through the corporatist ideologies of groups connected with the armed forces. The founding premise of Christendom that derived from the Council of Trent and became deeply rooted in America was *extra ecclesia nulla salus* (there is no salvation outside the Church). Thus, the sword and the aspergillum were intimately related to the conquest, colonization, and constitution of social order in the New World. Moreover, the Church that accompanied the conquistador was not only antireformist, but also centrist, based on the premise of one Church, one religion, one king, one bureaucracy, and one army.

There is an important tradition of analysis of Latin American culture that I shall term the "patrimonialist approach," whose main concern is centered on the process of political legitimation and the distribution of power and authority in society, and in particular on the question of culture itself: ideology, the social history of ideas, values, and their effects on the configuration of political power and its administrative expression as government. This approach focuses on the philosophical foundations of norms and institutions from the colonial period to independence in Latin America and the persistence of the same traits in the present. Similarly, it compares the historical antecedents of the Iberian and the Anglo-Saxon political-ideological ethos. This tradition contrasts the Hobbesian-Lockean liberal traditions of North America and some European experiences (based on contract theory and government by consent of the governed, checks and balances, inalienable rights, equality), with the Spanish-Iberian tradition whose dominant influences have been Thomism (natural law, Catholicism, scholasticism, the hierarchy of laws and states) and Machiavellianism (personalism, princeship, centralized state-building and royal authority). This patrimonialist and culturalist approach (e.g., Wiarda, 1973, 1974; Veliz, 1980; Morse, 1981, 1982; Uricoechea, 1980; Paz, 1961; Pike & Stritch, 1974; Meyer, 1977; Schmitter, 1975) concludes that, since Latin America stems from an Iberian cultural stock—from the same branch of history and culture, the same religion and language—this, in addition to the persistence of Thomism and Machiavellianism in political thought, should to a great extent explain the so-called authoritarian traditions rooted in a Thomist-Machiavellian outlook. This authoritarian tradition will be expressed in the persistence of a state bureaucracy in corporatist States[2] having a preindustrial origin and temper.[3]

In a well-documented study, Enrique Dussel argues that the metaphysical, ontological, and logical dualism of Christianity underlies the notion of natural order and its practical results during the process of colonization in Latin America.

The necessary co-existence of Christianism with the Roman culture of the Mediterranean led it to take a fundamental step: it evolved from Christianism to Christendom even before Constantine gave superiority to the Christians. This transformation means the following: Christianism governed the formation of a new culture (Christendom) which is no less than an entire complex of mediations (language, instruments of logic, economic, political, pedagogical and erotic systems, etc.) in relation to a fundamental existential project. One of the equivocal moments of the culture we have called Christendom is its anthropological dualism. (Dussel, 1974b: 160)

[The anthropological dualism of Christendom] distorts political relations because it locates fellow humans within the rationalized totality of the *system*. The Other comes to be interpreted from this as a being placed at my disposition by virtue of the right I have to dominate him in order to communicate civilization, being and reality to him. In this way, the man [formed by] Latin, Hispanic Christianity arrived in America in the fifteenth century and alienated the Indian through a principle that Sarmiento would formulate ontologically in the mid-nineteenth century as "Civilization or barbarism." The politics of domination became a pedagogy of alienation. (Dussel, 1974b: 287)

As Antonio Donini points out, "The relations between Church and State in Argentina were born with the mark of the ideal of Christianity of the Hispanic conquest and colonization" (1985: 53). Shortly thereafter, quoting Dussel, he emphasizes,

The intentional world structure of the Hispanic was that of European medieval man, plus certain elements from the Arab world. One of these was a tendency to unite the objectives of the State and the Church indissolubly. It should be noted that the Islamic doctrine of the Caliphate required this unity, this religious-political monism, but the same monism was also proposed by several other schools of regalism. . . . There existed in Spain, then, something like a "temporal Messianism," according to which the destiny of the Nation and the Church were united, the Hispanic Nation being the instrument chosen by God to save the world. This awareness of being the chosen people—the permanent temptation of Israel—was the basis of the religious policy of Isabel, Charles and Philip. (cited by Donini, 1985: 53)

As so correctly pointed out by Dussel, this anthropological dualism resulted in the spiritual (religious) and political monism that has not only marked the links between Church and State in Argentina, but left a deep imprint on Latin American culture as a whole: the imprint of authoritarianism. For Donini, the ultimate expression of this monism is to be found in the fact that "these relations are defined in the Constitution of 1853, in spite of its clear liberal inspiration. Article 2 affirms, 'The Federal Government supports the Roman Catholic, Apostolic Church' and the same article requires that, 'in order to be elected President or Vice-President of the Nation, it is necessary to belong to the Catholic Church' " (Donini, 1985: 117). The relations between political and spiritual power in the ideology of the Church of the Christian society are clear. As Alejandro Mayol and his colleagues point out, "Temporal, political and economic power made use of spiritual power for its own ends. The latter provided it with two valuable elements: a theology of order and the authority and a mystic content in the struggle against its foes" (Mayol, Habegger, & Armada, 1970: 10).

Alongside this fact, in the context of the transcendence that could be acquired through grace in a uniformly Catholic world "where every pattern of social life pressured the individual to fit into an official religion and morality" (Mayol, Habegger, & Armada, 1970: 20), the concept of the temporality of human affairs was no longer necessary. Thus, among the principal characteristics of the theology and pastoral organization of Christianity were self-defense against heresy, distrust of the sensuality of the temporal, and suspicion of any initiative that might undermine its institutional status, such as Masonry, atheism, pansexualism, modernism, or socialism (Mayol, Habegger, & Armada, 1970). In practice, this self-defense is founded on two basic notions: the exaltation of authority within the institutional Church (especially with the development of the Jesuit order and strict obedience to the papacy); and the links between the Church and the world, whereby "the backing of the political, economic and military powers" would be sought (Mayol, Habegger, & Armada, 1970: 23).

The civilization promoted by Christendom in the River Plate provinces suffered a rude blow with independence, given that the vast majority of priests were foreigners, tied to Spain, and therefore owing their loyalty to the Spanish crown and/or the Vatican. After the independence movements, of the 15,000 priests and religious on which the Vice-regency of Upper Peru—Peru, Bolivia, Argentina—could previously count, less than 500 remained in the region to continue their pastoral work. The reduction in religious personnel severely limited the preaching and practice of Christianity, in addition to the fact that the Church then had to negotiate with a new temporal power and was still seen as an ally of the old metropolitan order associated with the kings of Spain.[4] To this should be added the challenge that positive science presented to faith. With the combined impact of the French and industrial revolutions, Christian ideology was challenged by the vigorous presence of European liberalism in the formation of the new nations. In Argentina, the decline of postindependence Christianity did not immediately imply the separation of Church and State, nor the loss of influence on the formation of Argentine culture by Catholic intellectuals, as we shall see. The Catholic Church, its intellectuals, and its clergy placed themselves in the center of the great debates of the nineteenth century that have deeply marked the political history of Argentina: Federalists versus Unitarians and Catholics versus Liberals.[5]

## THE CATHOLIC CHURCH AND THE GENERATION OF 1880: CHRISTENDOM BESIEGED

The birth of the Argentine State came about with independence from Spain on May 25, 1810, and was consolidated by the Declaration of Independence in Tucumán in 1816. As Christian historians point out,

Happily, there was a constant unanimity among the Congressmen at Tucumán that the form of the State of the River Plate Provinces should be Christian. All of them, without exception, some more strongly than others, made firm, clear and sincere declarations on the necessity of uniting Christian principles with political principles in our country. Our political law would therefore be a Christian political law. And this healthy resolution became particularly evident in the interest that the Congress of Tucumán showed in attaching the Argentine State to the Catholic Church. (Romero Carranza, Rodríguez Varela, & Ventura Flores Pirán, 1975: 433)

However, this unanimity was not won without cost. The Argentine Congress demanded that a number of Spanish bishops—Monsignor Rodrigo de Orellana in Córdoba, for example—be restored to their appointments by civil and ecclesiastical authorities, thereby continuing the royalist tradition of patronage,[6] "provided they recognize the authority of Congress and swear to the Independence of the country" (Romero Carranza, Rodríguez Varela, & Ventura Flores Pirán, 1975: 435). Orellano replied, however, that he could recognize neither. He removed himself to Rio de Janeiro and from there to Spain, where he was named bishop of Avila by the king.

The congressmen of Tucumán had attempted to link themselves with the Vatican and have it reconstitute the ecclesiastical hierarchy of the new country directly. However, not wishing to break its alliance with Spain's

King Ferdinand VII, the Vatican declined to dissociate from the concept of royal patronage, with the result that the negotiations of the Argentine Congress were fruitless.[7]

In this atmosphere, the Minister Bernardino Rivadavia proposed an ecclesiastical reform for the province of Buenos Aires, which, in practice, mandated that religious houses could not have less than 16 or more than 30 members and that those not complying with these numbers were to be closed, their properties and rents to go to the government of Buenos Aires. The principle of the intervention of civil power into ecclesiastical affairs was thereby established, following the lead of that governing patronage, a principle of organization that functioned in practice for 146 years. It was not modified legally until an agreement developed by Chancellor Miguel Angel Zabala Ortiz during the 1963–66 constitutional presidency of Arturo Humberto Illia—although, since Illia's administration was deposed by a military coup in June 1966, the final decree between the Vatican and the government of Argentina was signed by General Juan Carlos Onganía later that year (Mignone, 1988: 57). As one historian of Catholicism in Argentina remarks, the situation after independence was very confusing:

The situation remained clouded for many years, but the full force of regalism came to flourish in the period of Argentine history that was dominated by Bernardino Rivadavia after 1820. By the end of 1822 Rivadavia had established state control over the Church in almost all of its personnel and property aspects. Churches and Church property came under the jurisdiction of the government, and not only the diocesan clergy but also the religious orders were subjected to the most detailed regulation by public authority. At the time the cost of maintaining Churches and their clergy was assumed by the government. Some students see in the Rivadavia moves the logical extension of the *patronato* into the creation of a national church with its clergy firmly tied to the national authority rather than to Rome. (Kennedy, 1958: 19)

The classic antinomy of liberals and conservatives was reflected in Argentine political history as an antinomy of liberals and Catholics. In his study of Catholic thought in Argentina—written from an anti-Rosas stance—comparing Catholic thought with nationalist thought in opposition to liberalism, John J. Kennedy states,

Catholic thought tends to concentrate in the two great formative periods of the nation's history, from 1810 to roughly 1830, and from 1853 to 1890. During the [Juan Manuel de] Rosas tyranny between these two periods there is some significant Catholic writing, but like most worthwhile Argentine endeavors of that time, it was the work of exiles. And after 1900 Argentine Catholic writing takes a different turn. It becomes more formally philosophic, and with a few exceptions abandons the national orientation which had characterized the earlier periods. (Kennedy, 1958: ix)

A number of Catholic figures sought to accommodate Christianity to the new social and political conditions, although not always in ways that were in accord with the new principles of national organization or prerevolutionary Church practices and customs. Gregorio Funes (who lived from 1749 to 1829), dean of the Cathedral of Córdoba, was a political figure who ultimately collaborated with Rivadavia's reform.[8] He held the position of president of the Constituent Assembly of 1819 and is accredited with having been the first defender of universal suffrage in Argentina. Father Juan Ignacio Gorriti was fundamental to the movement for independence, having been the chaplain of General Manuel Belgrano's army and a decided representative of the federalist position. Another notable Catholic was Facundo Zubiría (who lived from 1796 to 1861), a well-known dissident and unitarian from the province of Salta, who was therefore opposed to provincial autonomy within confederation and to the Constituent Assembly of 1853, given its provisions on relations between Church and State. Felix Frías and Fray Mamerto Esquiú should also be mentioned. The former, a noteworthy intellectual who lived from 1816 to 1881 and became one of the most influential journalists of the time, reconciled his Catholic convictions with a liberal and rationalist stance and eventually became a national senator. Fray Mamerto Esquiú, a distinguished orator and bishop of Córdoba who died in 1883, gave religious approval to the Catholic nationalism that appeared during the government of Nicolás Avellaneda from 1874 to 1880, and argued that Catholics should support the new Argentine State. Toward the end of his life, Esquiú sought to emphasize recognition of divine intervention in the human history of Argentina as a way of countering the increasing laicism that would reach its maximum expression with the Generation of 1880 and the governments of Julio Argentino Roca (from 1880 to 1886) and Juárez Celman (from 1886 to 1892) in particular. Finally, a word should be said about the most important Catholic intellectual of the second half of the nineteenth century: José Manuel Estrada, who lived from 1842 to 1894, endeavored to link Christianity and liberalism. He was director of the Department of Education for the Government of Buenos Aires and later head of the Catholic Association of Buenos Aires (1884), which was dedicated to organizing Catholic opinion against the laicized positions of the administration of Julio Argentino Roca.

As already indicated, the liberal Constitution of 1853 established the principles of national organization and the separation of Church and State, but also made Argentina a Catholic nation and imposed the Catholic religion as a requirement for election as president of the republic. After 1853, the relations between the Argentine State and the Catholic Church, which had been dominated by the civil power through the exercise of patronage since the government of Bernardino Rivadavia, became stormy.[9] As proposals for massive immigration began to be considered, Juan Bautista Alberdi and other statesmen argued that it was necessary to guarantee freedom of worship in order to attract non-Catholics. They felt that the country needed to take drastic measures to increase its population; the country's productive area had expanded considerably after the first campaign in the desert against the Pampa, Tehuelche, and Mapuche Indians conducted by then Minister for War and the Navy, General Julio A. Roca (under the government of Avellaneda), who attacked the native peoples in April 1879 and successfully pushed the agricultural frontier as far as Patagonia.[10]

As a function of freedom of worship, the Congreso Nacional Pedagógico (National Congress of Pedagogy) of 1882 resolved to remove religious instruction from the schools. This action was also in accord with the increasing predominance of positivist thought[11] clearly expressed through the creation of the Normal School in Paraná on June 13, 1879, during the presidency of Domingo Faustino Sarmiento, and subsequently through the Law of Common Education of 1884, or Law 1420, which was intended to organize primary schools under the rubric of popular education (Lafforgue, 1980: 91–106). Sarmiento declared, "We must educate the sovereign. Popular primary education is what civilizes and develops the level of peoples. All peoples have always had doctors and learned men, but have not been civilized because of it. The schools are the bases of civilization."[12] This notion of educating the sovereign was founded on a pedagogical positivism that, at the time, confronted the beliefs of the Catholic faith with experimental science.

It vindicated the value of the natural sciences from which it derived: the use of the experimental and inductive method; the unity of the sciences; the possibility of promulgating universal laws; the concept of "evolution" as a real and physical principle that governs the entire development of the cosmos. It raised the cult of science and the negation of the metaphysical as the condition necessary to affirm the possibility of indefinite progress. It caused material and economic interests to prevail over moral and spiritual ones. In pedagogy, it was concerned with the accumulation of means to make Pedagogy an instrumental discipline. It saw the teacher as one who applied didactic principles and the pupil as a being who could be interpreted according to psychological and physiological laws. (Perazzo, Kuc & de Jové, 1984: 96)

Along with the separation of Church and State and the principle of freedom of worship (endorsed by the removal of religious instruction from the schools), another serious source of confrontation between Church and State was the Civil Marriage Law, introduced during the administration of Juárez Celman and promulgated on November 2, 1888. This law affected one of the prerogatives of the Catholic Church, and even contained "a clause that was yet more harmful to Catholicism: that which established the penalty of imprisonment for a priest who married without heeding the act of civil matrimony by the contracting parties" (Romero Carranza, Rodríguez Varela & Ventura Flores Pirán, 1975: 350).

One decisive moment in the confrontation between the Catholic Church and the State—which provoked a break with the Vatican—occurred in 1884 when the Argentine government expelled the papal nuncio. To this should be added the conflict experienced by some segments of the Catholic population when the government developed a policy of inviting Protestant teachers from the United States to run the normal schools for young women—not to mention the irritation felt by the hierarchy of the Church as a result of attacks in the newspapers, especially in the Córdoba daily *El Interior*, that were considered irreverent (Auza, 1975: 296–98).[13] In addition to the expulsion of the apostolic delegate, Roca's government provoked countless conflicts with Catholics through its visibly anticlerical legislative actions, which were founded in part on the Masonic tradition of many of its prominent members. Among these abrasive actions should be included the dismissal of the respected liberal and most distinguished Catholic of the time, José Manuel Estrada, from his position as professor of constitutional law at the University of Buenos Aires, as well as the removal of Rafael García as professor of civil law from the University of Córdoba and the expulsion of Emilio Lamarca from his chair of political economy at the University of Buenos Aires. All were persistent critics of government policy in the Catholic newspaper *La Unión*.

The liberal project of the Generation of 1880 placed the Church on the defensive, limited its prerogatives, modified the legal statutes concerning the relation between Church and State, and used patronage as a means of control. The period of confrontation between Catholics and liberals anticipated both the texture and dynamics of the most conflictive subjects in the relation between Church and State during the twentieth century: ethical-social control in matters concerning the family, and the question of Catholic education. It should also be noted that these conflicts were equally and intimately linked to the introduction of capitalism in a social formation controlled by the agrarian historical bloc, "which occurred without removing the foundations on which the ascendancy of the traditional agrarian classes rested" (Boron, 1990: 39).

In the context of an incipient capitalism that smacked of latifundismo, and faced with the predominance of liberalism and the attacks on the Church, some laypersons—especially Pedro Goyena and José Manuel Estrada—attempted to organize the Catholic project around a political party. However, these initiatives were systematically discouraged by the Church hierarchy, which, rather than provoking a political confrontation, sought to win cultural influence over the governing elite through Catholic secondary schools presided over by European religious orders (Forni, 1987a: 215).

## FROM POLITICAL INTERREGNUM TO CATHOLIC INTEGRALISM

The beginning of the twentieth century in Argentina is marked by the presence of an oligarchical pact in an agricultural exporting country with an incipient industry that had won a privileged place in the world system under British hegemony. According to Atilio Boron,

As a result, Argentine capitalism developed under the attentive eye of a latifundist oligarchy that changed into an agrarian bourgeoisie but retained, like the Prussian Junkers, an undisguised adherence to many of the features constituting the old order of things, among which the latifundio stands out. This hegemonic element of the oligarchical "pact of domination" was also made up by the marginal landowners from the interior who could not find a niche in the international market to guarantee them profitable sales, by the "compradora" bourgeoisie based in Buenos Aires, who exercised a crucial intermediary role in Argentina's expanding international commerce, and, finally, by imperialist capital, principally British, that provided the immense financial resources necessary to exploit the national wealth and controlled a good part of the fixed investment in the country. (Boron, 1990: 40)

The country that the liberal Generation of 1880—with "liberal orthodoxy and oligarchical domination" (Oszlak, 1982: 215)—had imagined as a prosperous, fortunate, and attractive land for masses of immigrants and capital seemed a reality at the beginning of the century.

Indeed, during the second half of the last century and the first quarter of this one, Argentina was an attractive land for immigrants and foreign capital. Between 1857 and 1914, it gained 3,300,000 immigrants, predominantly from Europe. The total foreign capital in the country at that time reached almost $10 million (1960 = 100), representing 8.5% of the total amount of foreign investment in the world, 33% of the total amount of foreign investment in Latin America and 42% of the total investment of the United Kingdom in the region. (Torres, 1991a: 869)

Considering this historical context, it is not surprising that, a century later, a publication by Christians involved in base communities in Argentina should try to characterize the period of the history of the Argentine Church between 1900 and 1945 by describing it as "the Church of the Oligarchy" (Memoria y Esperanza, 1980: 19). However, it is precisely during this period that the hegemony of the landowning class—and its political apparatus, the conservative party—began to be challenged on several fronts. Different anti-oligarchical tendencies began to combine around an emerging radical party representative of elements of the middle class, the children of immigrants, and the popular classes (Jauretche, 1973, 1981; Peña, 1971; Puiggrós, 1965, 1971a, 1971b). The political struggle of the radical party bore fruit with the establishment of universal, secret, and compulsory suffrage, which culminated in the election of Hipólito Yrigoyen to the presidency in 1916.

Culture was a second very important area of struggle that, with the advent of university reforms in 1918, had national and international repercussions.

The University Reform of 1918 greatly influenced the university atmosphere throughout Latin America. Starting in Córdoba City on March 13, 1918, as a violent strike of university students, the reform had a number of specific goals: the substitution of traditional professors by implementation of a new system of teacher appointments and their terms on the job; the modernization of teaching methods; the participation of students and alumni in the university government; the creation of endowed chairs for invited professors; the exemption of students from the obligation to attend theoretical classes; and the opening up of examination dates. The reform quickly spread beyond the university environment. Starting as a way of democratizing the university, it soon became a contribution to the political and socio-economic democratization of societies still dominated by conservative, pro-oligarchical parties. The reform was an expression of the newborn middle class of Argentinean society, represented politically by radicalism. Its new program tied to modernize the university, a fief of oligarchical and conservative forces. (Torres, 1991a: 873)

Labor and the working class—especially elements that were socialist or anarcho-syndicalist in origin—began, with the backing of nuclei of European workers, to confront the State and were brutally put down in Buenos Aires during what has become known as *la Semana Trágica* (the Week of Tragedy) in 1919. Later, in 1921 in Patagonia, the army put down a revolt of agricultural workers in a particularly brutal fashion, with the summary execution of leaders and activists.[14]

The radicalism that represented the urban middle class of the coast, certain middle-class landowners and farmers of the interior, and the marginal elements of the upper class in the interior developed contra-dictory policies with respect to the working class and the Socialist Party founded in Argentina in 1896. As Tulio Halperin Donghi observes,

At the same time as it encouraged moderate tendencies for renovation (from whose progress a drop in the impact of conservative elements on the life of the country was expected) radicalism fought, often with brutal energy, against those who directly or indirectly seemed to pose a revolutionary threat to social order. In 1919, intervention by the army culminated in the Semana Trágica, at the beginning of which some union leaders and, above all, many of their adversaries had thought the installation of Soviet power in Buenos Aires a possibility. The outcome was an act of repression that caused hundreds of victims among workers and included the voluntary collaboration of conservative minded organizations. The suppression of the strike of rural workers in Patagonia in 1921 was even more unnecessarily savage. (Halperin Donghi, 1975: 330)

The social convulsions of the beginning of the century—which some analysts attribute in great part to the "alluvial" effects of immigration, with its economic and demographic impact becoming a politically destabilizing factor (Oszlak, 1982; Romero, 1975)—should not cause us to overlook that these struggles occurred in an Argentina that during the first three decades reached its highest levels on the economic and social indicators, all of which came tumbling down with the crisis of 1929 and the loss of hegemony by Britain in the world system. Argentina's privileged position has been documented by Carlos F. Díaz Alejandro:

In 1928–29, Argentina was eleventh among the major trading nations. Exports per capita were $90 annually in terms of the American dollar of 1928–29, in comparison with $105 for Australia and $125 for Canada. With 26 inhabitants per motor vehicle, it exceeded the United Kingdom in the number of vehicles per capita, in spite of the relative lack of roads in the country. The illiteracy rate, calculated as a percentage of the population of 14 years of age or more, which had dropped from 77% in the census of 1869 to 36% in that of 1914, was around 25% around 1929 (and reached 14% in the census of 1947). By 1929, Buenos Aires had become one of the great cultural centers of the Spanish speaking world; its newspapers and publishing houses were often the first to publish the works of the most outstanding cultural figures. For example, several important essays by Miguel de Unamuno first appeared in *La Nación*. In the same year, the mortality rate in Argentina, 13.1 for every thousand inhabitants, was not far from that of Canada (11.4 per 1,000). (Díaz Alejandro, 1970: 66)

The year 1930 and the nationalist military coup headed by Lieutenant General José Félix Uriburu[15] marks a double break in the political experience of the country: the end of a pattern of accumulation of capital and economic growth based on a policy of agricultural exports as a function of a farming oligarchy in alliance with others to create a pact of oligarchical domination; and the end of a period of political stability inaugurated in 1862 under constitutional rules. It also marks the beginning of what one astute commentator defined as the dissolution of the liberal culture (Boron, 1990: 45).

Thus far, we have argued that the Church's project of Christendom was beleaguered by the lay, positivist, and Masonic project of 1880. Toward the beginning of the twentieth century, with the oligarchical State in full splendor, the Catholic Church in Argentina—reduced to playing an essentially ceremonial role—had lost political weight and found itself not only harassed, but, quite simply, penned in.[16]

The ideology of the Church in Christendom is constituted by two basic principles: the close combination of Church and State, and the identification between faith and culture (i.e., the Catholic faith and European Christian culture) (Scannone, 1975).[17] In this context, confronted with the turbulent changes at the end of the nineteenth century, the Roman Church launched a campaign: the re-Christianization of the world, which implied a militant evangelizing attitude, and the effective presence of Catholics in a modern world that was hostile and threatening to them, and increasingly secular. Thus there emerged the integralist, antimodernist, and ultramontane position that created integral Catholicism in Argentina between 1930 and 1946. Two institutions played a relevant role: Acción Católica Argentina (Catholic Action of Argentina) and the periodical *Criterio*.

In 1928, in his role as the new papal nuncio and representative of the policies of Pope Pius XI (who in 1923 had promoted the creation of a lay structure capable of supporting the complex evangelizing tasks of a highly bureaucratized Church still imbued with a medieval mentality), Monsignor Cortesi suggested the appropriateness of founding Acción Católica to the bishops. A collective pastoral letter of the Argentine episcopacy ratified the decision on December 1, 1928. Acción Católica Argentina, organized in the style of its Italian counterpart, was officially introduced at the parish level in April 1931, with participants divided according to age and sex (i.e., men and women, boys and girls).[18]

At virtually the same time, there was an attempt made to come up with the means of spreading in society at large the Catholic thought that had matured in countless social encyclicals—especially Pope Leo XIII's *Rerum Novarum*, which offered the Catholic response to the problems of the age by appealing to the social teaching of the Church and was categorically opposed to liberalism and socialism (Chiesa, Soneira, Sosa, et al., 1982). This means turned out to be the Catholic periodical *Criterio*, founded in March 1928, which was initially edited by laypersons (Atilio Dell Oro Maini and Enrique Peres Osés) and later, from 1932 until his death in 1957, by the priest Gustavo Franceschi, one of the most influential intellectuals in the development of integralist thought in Argentina. Fortunato Mallimaci regards *Criterio* as part of an "intransigent and integral Catholic movement" (Mallimaci, 1988: 14). In its first issue, the editors asserted,

*Criterio* responds to a movement, affirms and defends a doctrine, has its own method. *Criterio* is born of a movement of ideas. . . . [I]t expresses the decided will of a numerous group of Catholic citizens, who are encouraged by the highest authorities and aspire to satisfy adequately the urgent needs of an organization.
. . . It is a new, doctrinaire and popular organ for the diffusion of a healthy doctrine, for the exaltation of the essential principles of our civilization, for the restoration of Christian discipline in individual and collective life. *Criterio* propagates Catholic doctrine in all its integrity and in the purity of its true sources. This is not to say that *Criterio* is a purely religious newspaper: it would not suffice the objectives proposed to have everything well defined in that respect and leave everything else to chance. The Catholic definition of religious matters outlines the fundamental directions to be taken when facing problems of another order, presented by immediate, temporal reality, but does not provide concrete and definite solutions. . . . *Criterio* is not a journal for

dilettantism or divagation; it is not a showcase for contradictory opinions: it is a clear and frank newspaper, an organ for definition, the instrument of a discipline. The method selected has two characteristics: to look for the thread of ideas in every problem, institution or event, to confront them with the doctrine adopted, and to give to the reading of its pages a clear educational and integral meaning. (cited by Mallimaci, 1988: 14–15)

All the important elements of ultramontane Christian integralism are present in this editorial: (1) the idea of a movement (with alliances, strategies, tactics, method, etc.); (2) the idea of doctrine to guide (the social doctrine of the Church marked by its antiliberalism, antisocialism, anticommunism, anti-Masonism, antimodernism,[19] etc.); (3) the collaboration of the laity and priests in this attempt to affirm, reestablish, and restore Catholic culture in modernist temporal structures; (4) a militant, challenging, polemical force based on the "true" and "essential" principles of Western Christian civilization and profoundly intent on restoration; (5) antiecumenism (Catholicism as truth and as preaching the only truth); and (6) use of information media to educate with respect to an integral philosophical and theological position.

The periodical *Criterio* showed that Catholics were confronting enemies on two fronts: liberalism, which had already had its moment of glory and was in open retreat (Mallimaci, 1988: 20); and socialism and communism, which—given the disturbing events of the Mexican and Russian revolutions and the growing social struggle in Argentina headed by anarcho-syndicalist workers—appeared to be a formidable opponent that was not just secularist, but materialistic and atheistic.

Mallimaci distinguishes between two tendencies in Argentinean integralism. One of them is concerned with social questions and is represented in the person of the editor of *Criterio*, Father Franceschi, who in the long run was tolerant of the positions held by Jacques Maritain[20] that gave rise to the foundation of the Christian-Democratic Party in Argentina in open opposition to the integralist tradition. The other tendency—of corporatist or even fascist origin—was that which ended by adopting a rabidly nationalist stance in the person of Father Julio Meinvielle, an acerbic polemicist and contributor to *Criterio*, who also marked the political life of Argentina.[21] Mallimaci's assessment is that "the attempt by intransigent Catholic intellectuals to introduce themselves into the nationalist cultural movement and give it their own interpretation from within, until they made it practically the dominant one of the whole movement, is perhaps one of their most important achievements" (Mallimaci, 1988:

21). Perhaps one of the contributions of European nationalism to the emerging Catholic nationalism of Argentina was anti-Semitism, which must be added to the collection of philosophies to be brandished by the integralist creed.

Argentine nationalism—especially the version learned from Europe and from the French poet and theorist Charles Maurras—endorses the importance of the Church as a bastion of the conservative restoration, but its advocates are not necessarily integralist Catholics. As Mallimaci correctly points out (1988: 25), there is a very strong nationalist vein in the Círculos de Cultura Católica (Circles of Catholic Church), frequented by members of the patrician class and the old Argentinean oligarchy, and in Acción Católica, comprised mostly by the middle classes. From the perspective of integralist thought, Acción Católica can be seen as an expression of Christian philosophy based on the theocentrism opposed to the anthropocentrism prevalent in secular circles (Casiello, 1948: 319). It was not by chance that integralism played a relevant role in the military government of Uriburu, which broke the tradition of constitutional governments.

As we mentioned, the military government paved the way for the fraudulent stability of the political regime and the oligarchical state. After rigged elections, General Agustín P. Justo assumed the presidency on February 20, 1932, inaugurating a fateful period in Argentine political life described by the journalist and historian José Luis Torres as the "infamous decade." In the meantime, integral Catholicism was organizing itself under the motto "Long Live Christ the King"; and ultimately, as Mallimaci observes, "for several years during its history, the Catholic movement has developed on the basis of a model that rejects the liberalism–socialism, capitalism–communism alternatives and has assiduously sought a third way, a third formula that is not even a middle ground, but something different" (Mallimaci, 1988: 41). The central question, however, was the extent to which the Church—which before the crisis of liberal Argentina had been a powerful institution of cultural hegemony, forming the common sense of the middle classes and certain popular sectors[22]— would have any capacity for convening and organizing the masses. The International Eucharistic Congress held in the city of Buenos Aires— with the Cardinal Eugenio Paccelli, the future Pope Pius XII, present as the personal representative of the pope—would give a positive reply to this question. Reports on the Congress, held October 10–14, 1934, show the participation of thousands of people; newspapers speak of more than a million and a half taking part in the religious ceremonies. The event culminated with the consecration of Argentina to "Christ the King" by the president General Justo.

This mobilization of the masses—especially the middle classes and popular urban sectors—marks a turning point in the history of the Argentine Church and reflects the strength shown by the renewed Catholic integralist institutions. (Monsignor Franceschi, editor of *Criterio*, was one of the official speakers at the Congress.) In addition to the comfortable relationship established with the regime of General Justo, it made the Church a new and formidable ally of the political power, capable of formulating the principles of a new political order. The holding of the International Eucharistic Congress of 1934, which reflected the end of laicism in Argentina for Catholic integralists, shows not only the effects of the apostolic renaissance and the increasing connection between Church and State, but also, more importantly, the growing association of two institutions intimately linked to political domination in the country: the Church and the armed forces.[23]

With the emergent of a militant Catholicism came the multiplication of dioceses and the foundation of parishes as the means of providing the necessary infrastructure for the task of re-Christianizing the country, which was also linked to its Argentineanization now that the massive arrival of foreign immigrants had diminished. When thanking Cardinal Santiago Copello for his work as head of the Archdiocese of Buenos Aires, the president of the College of Parish Priests of the city stated, "When you were named Vicar General of this Archdiocese in 1928, our capital had 39 parishes. Today, in 1939, there are 105. We can rightly say, Your Excellency, that the city of Buenos Aires owes most of its parishes to you" (Mallimaci, 1988: 10).

It is remarkable how much, toward the end of the thirties, Catholic integralism was concerned with the form that a Catholic social order could adopt without being either fascist or communist, but Christian. The Spanish Civil War and the triumph of General Francisco Franco with his corporatist model offered (along with Antonio de Oliveira Salazar in Portugal) experiences that Catholic nationalists kept their eye on as the possible third position that they so much desired. An important member of the hierarchy, Monsignor Miguel De Andrea (who lived from 1877 to 1958)—considered the "social bishop" in Argentina, to whose initiative were owed such institutions as the Women's Technical Institute and the Young Athenaeum, in addition to his having headed the Círculos Católicos de Oberos (Catholic Workers Circles)—began to argue for a democratic corporativism[24] in his writings *El catolicismo social y su aplicación*

*(Social Catholicism and Its Application), Las causas que favorecen la difusión del comunismo (Causes That Favor the Spread of Communism),* and *La Justicia Social (Social Justice),* and in his lectures and sermons (Kennedy, 1958: 143). De Andrea as well as anticommunist campaigns of Monsignor Franceschi[25] in the pages of *Criterio* (supporting Franco against the Popular Front), together with the growing popularity of Father Meinvielle and the nationalist-fascist professor Bruno Jordan Genta (who would be named rector of the Universidad del Litoral after the coup of 1943), show the markedly right-wing orientation of social Catholicism and integralist thought.

By the same token, the cultural and political presence of integralism and the traditional Catholic right were a fact in the political and cultural life of Argentina. With respect to the cultural environment, Floreal Forni (1987a: 217) correctly remarks on the new presence of Catholic intellectuals toward the beginning of the forties, with popular novelists such as Gustavo Martínez Zuviría, who wrote under the pseudonym Hugo Wast, and Manuel Gálvez, who sought to describe the popular nationalism of the governments of Juan Manuel de Rosas and Hipólito Yrigoyen. Among those who contributed to the presence of integral Catholicism are Julio Meinvielle, whom we have already mentioned, and the Jesuit priest Leonardo Castellani, who fluctuated ethically and politically between two different positions. On the one hand, in some of his writings he celebrated fascism as a philosophy ultimately compatible with the traditionalist Catholic ideology he lauded. On the other, he praised the emerging ideology of Christian-Democracy inspired by the poet Léon Bloy and his protegée Jacques Maritain, the lately converted (to Catholicism) French philosopher and creator of neo-Thomism, who by the close of World War II was to be the French ambassador to the Vatican.[26]

Christian-Democratic initiatives during the first decades of this century were the activities of a handful of Catholic intellectuals and professionals from the middle class who could not succeed in gaining acceptance by the middle class as a whole. The Catholic social presence in the working class, until the beginning of Peronism, was limited to a small group of urban workers concentrated in Buenos Aires in particular; and in symbolic-religious matters, the most important element of worker culture was ceremonial ritual, which coincided with the anthropological identity of Christianity and coexisted openly alongside laicism and anticlericalism. "The working class district at the beginning of the century is a place in which the rudest and most aggressive anticlericalism coexists with the celebration of the feast days of patron saints" (Forni, 1987a: 225).

Néstor T. Auza shows, with regret, that the different experiences initiated at the beginning of the twentieth century to create a Catholic political presence in Argentina—although not totally fruitless—did not succeed in amounting to a popular, massive political movement. One of the first initiatives had been the short-lived Unión Patriótica (Patriotic Union) from 1907 to 1908, which emerged as a result of the Second Catholic Congress of 1907[27] with the purpose of promoting universal suffrage. The Unión Patriótica ultimately presented candidates for the elections of March 8, 1908, but was defeated, although Auza attributes the defeat to electoral fraud (1984: 46).

A second attempt was made by the Unión Católica Electoral (Catholic Electoral Union), which presented its own candidates for an election of deputies in 1913, but won few votes. Nevertheless, given the introduction of the Sáenz Peña Law (which instituted universal, secret, and compulsory suffrage), this episode indicated a realignment of political parties and gave birth to the Partido Constitucional (Constitutional Party), which was formed between 1913 and 1918. This party united Catholic intellectuals, could count on the unofficial support of Monsignor De Andrea and the members of the Unión Democrática Cristiana (Christian Democratic Union),[28] and also tried to obtain the support of the Círculos Católicos de Obreros (Catholic Workers Circles), but it was finally unable to evolve as a party of the masses and disappeared in 1918.

The next attempt to form a Catholic political party—again reflecting the influence of the Catholic political struggle in Europe (in this case, in Italy and France)—was the creation of the Partido Popular (Popular Party) in 1927, which was the first effective forerunner of a Christian-Democratic party in Argentina although it was restricted virtually to the electoral struggle in the federal capital. Partido Popular ceased activities definitively in 1945 after having presented itself for municipal elections in Buenos Aires in 1928, 1930, 1931, 1932, and 1934, obtaining the meager quantity of 2,819, 2,263, 3,509, 2,263, and 9,086 votes in those years and electing only one councillor: José Pagés in 1932 (Pagés, 1956: 27–30). In 1934, after a change in the election law, it received far below the minimum number of 30,000 votes needed to elect a councillor.

Another attempt to influence social and political matters was the organizing of the Círculos de Obreros, founded by the German Redemptorist priest Federico Grote (see Sánchez Gamarra, 1949), which were intended to give birth to a Catholic social movement. In a product of German Catholicism of the end of the nineteenth century, Grote's specific intentions were to avoid the spread of socialism in working-class culture and stimulate a philosophy based on mutualism and cooperativism that would combat the Masonic sects, anarchico-syndicalism, and socialism—philosophies that, in Grote's opinion, sought to alienate the worker from God. As organizer and spiritual advisor, Father Federico Grote was at the head of the Círculos de Obreros until 1912 and tried to prevent the addition of the adjective *Catholic* to their title. After Grote was removed by order of the metropolitan curia, De Andrea remained at their head until 1919, after which they were directed by Monsignor Santiago Ussher (Auza, 1984: 80). The activities of the Círculos de Obreros—especially their public lectures—were very intense: for 1917 they recorded 256 meetings attended by more than 250,000 persons (Auza, 1984: 90–91). In addition to reporting these meetings, Auza also reviews the list of initiatives for social legislation (beginning with a petition to Congress for a law supporting rest from labor on Sunday) undertaken by social Catholicism in Argentina. Many of them, along with the demands for labor legislation promoted by socialists through the voice of the deputy Alfredo Palacios, were to be adopted and made law under Peronism. Other institutions, such as Vanguardias Obreras Católicas (Vanguard of Catholic Workers) and the Liga Social Cristiana (Christian Social League), also reflected the same social interests and concerns.

In taking stock of the past hundred years of political and social action by Catholics in Argentina, Auza must regretfully admit that a series of errors were committed—including, among others, the imposition on the few organizations that existed "the realization of objectives for which they had not been created," "the excessive zeal or the blindness of many leaders and of some members of the clergy with leadership roles that prevented or made the creation of new tasks difficult," and, finally, the presence of too many personal attacks and coteries with narrow outlooks, all of which led to "the closing of institutions and division among Catholics, which produced a resentment that required several years to heal" (Auza, 1984: 65–166).

The events of World War II with the increasing possibility that the Axis would be defeated, placed nationalist forces in Argentina in a compromised situation. The change in British hegemony (which had played a role in the economic growth of the country and its link to the World System) and the subsequent pressure exerted by the United States on Argentina to join the war, overshadowed national polemics, translating them into European problems. Beyond this, it is important to note that the comparative advantages of being a country that sold meat and grain in the middle of a war in which the opposing armies needed to secure their provisions at all cost,[29] and the fact that the shortage of imported manufactured goods as a result of the war itself had revived industrialization as a substitute for imports, allowed Argentina to overcome the crisis of 1929 and emerge as a strong country with respect to gold reserves at the end of the war (Díaz Alejandro, 1970; Murmis & Portantiero, 1971).

Forni argues that, with the country's combination of decidedly neutral army officers concerned with promoting an industrial project (Potash, 1971) and trying to maintain the sale of beef and grain to all participants in the conflict, the conditions were created for a new military coup inspired by Catholic nationalism: "Argentina threw itself into a national, popular project, contrary to the hegemony of the United States that was to be imposed on the entire western and dependent world. . . . The two year period of 1943–44 was the Golden Age of militant Catholicism" (Forni, 1987a: 219).

As a result of the new coup commanded by the Catholic General Edelmiro J. Farrel, who was supported (or at least joyfully received) by the ecclesiastical hierarchy, the writer Gustavo Martínez Zuviría entered the Ministry of Education in 1943; and Martínez Zuviría reestablished religious instruction in the schools, drastically reversing the liberal program of 1880–84. It was in this government that Juan Domingo Perón began to stand out—a young colonel in the army who would later be three times constitutional president of Argentina.[30]

The complex relation between the military and the hierarchy of the Church turned into crisis with the increasing political activism of the subaltern sectors of society, as symbolized in the first Peronist demonstration of October 17, 1945, which forced the government to free the charismatic Colonel Perón from military prison and set in motion dynamics that would lead an alliance of the Labor Party with a faction of the Radical Party and an Independent Party, under the Perón–Quijano candidacy, to the presidency in 1946, inaugurating the cycle of Peronism in power.[31]

In addition to priests who disseminated pro-Peronist opinions and were essentially populist,[32] Peronism included among its intellectuals the first priest constitutionally elected in the country as a federal deputy, Father Virgilio Filippo, a well-known anticommunist activist and parish priest in Belgrano, who took to Peronism as the best antidote for stopping the march of socialism in Argentina[33] (Beltrán, 1987; Filippo, 1948). The noted Catholic historian Ernesto Palacio was also among the Peronist deputies, and other well-known Catholics joined the movement. One of them was the jurist Arturo Sampay, who was to be the principal writer of the Peronista-inspired Constitution approved in 1949, a document Sampay defended with consummate legal arguments, combining Maritain's neo-Thomism with the principles of democratic liberalism. Another supporter of emerging Peronism was the Catholic novelist Leopoldo Marechal, who later used his novel *Adán Buenosayres* to dwell on the national and popular elements attributed to the Peronist experience and to link Peronism with Christianity in a systematic way, portraying it as a natural result of the makeup of the popular classes and the impact of the Church and the faith (rather than the hierarchy) on culture.[34] Finally, Floreal Forni refers to other important Catholic intellectuals who joined Peronism:

Among the youngest were Cafiero, Castiñeira de Dios, Fermín Chávez, a generation marked by nationalist and social concerns, formed in the school of militancy headed by the new movement. On its fringes, ever ready to return, this group of cadres formed in the golden years of Catholic militancy reappeared at moments when Peronism was an option for power. (Forni, 1987a: 221)

Thus began the stormy years of the first and second Perón administrations, in which the pastoral figure of the Church appeared fundamental to the electoral triumph of 1945[35] and Perón's profession of Catholic faith showed—according to Father Filippo (1948), one of the most ardent defenders of the congruity between Peronism and Christianity— the progressive assimilation of the social teaching of the Church in the doctrine of Peronism. Father Filippo has described how and why he backed Perón initially. Invited to a dinner at the Ambassadeurs Hotel, where a group of entrepreneurs were honoring then Colonel Perón, Filippo was invited to speak.

The moment was compelling and a serious responsibility. An atmosphere of malevolent ill-will had been created around General Perón which made him seem like a leper to everyone. . . . If I spoke, those who would say that I compromised the priestly body of which I am part by my very presence at the function would not be wanting. . . . While I awaited my turn to speak, I concentrated my thoughts, asking for inspiration from on High, and God enlightened me. For three months I had been preaching every Sunday to the men of my parish in Belgrano, enlarging on the encyclical of Pope Pius XII on Christian Democracy. There was nothing more natural than that, before a man who gradually and with a tenacity worthy of admiration, had been turning the proposals of the Pontiff into reality, I should present a synthesis of the aspirations of the Pope with respect to the redemption and social elevation of the lower classes. In brief, I traced the theoretical objectives pointed out by Pius XII, which, when put into practice, would permit the people of the spirit to enjoy a real democracy, not just the purely literary and propagandistic one of an artificial fascination that they had had until now. At the end of my speech, Perón stood up and said, "My work will be accomplished taking the Encyclicals of Leo XIII, Pius XI and Pius XII as its basis." From that moment, I gave myself entirely to collaboration with his cause. (Filippo, 1948: 8–9)

Filippo's profession of anticommunist, anti-Masonic, and antiliberal faith leaves no room for doubt: confronted with the choice of, on the one hand, supporting the idea of a Christian-Democratic party that was growing strongly in Europe and could count on the support of the Vatican magisterium, or, on the other hand, trying to understand and participate in an autochthonous social process in which, to his way of thinking, the social doctrine of the Church was being taken up and applied,[36] he opted for the latter. His decision reflects not only a personal choice, but also the waxing and waning of Christendom in Argentina—and the dearth of political and social projects that were genuinely Catholic in origin, character, and presence and could effectively capture a mass following and the political imagination of the popular classes.

With the historical possibilities of the Church of the traditional right and integralism exhausted—and the chances of establishing an ultramontane neo-Christendom, a working-class social Catholicism, or a Christian-Democrat alternative based on a popular party in the European style with massive electoral support, all overtaken by social and political events— the rise of Peronism was to create a new twist in the ideological lines of the Argentinean Church. With it came new possibilities: a social-Christian ideological perspective that would have a certain influence in the exercise of power, as well as for an ideological tendency in the Church that could be characterized as populist.

## THE CHURCH AND PERONISM (1946–1955)

The international context of the postwar era as relevant to Argentina was that of attempts to rebuild Europe under the Marshall Plan, an emphasis on new forms of democratic organization among nations, and disputes between the United States and the Soviet Union during the Cold War. It was also a period of intense struggle for national liberation, especially in Africa and Asia, with the emergence of independent nations in the Third World and the formation of alliances (following the Bandung Conference of 1955) that sought—ingenuously perhaps, given the precariousness of the economic and political circumstances of the latecomers to the World System—to maintain a geopolitical nonalignment with respect to the confrontation between the great powers.[37] Within this political context there occurred, especially in Latin America, a complex process of renewed intervention on the part of the United States, whereby nonaligned Third World positions (i.e., neither liberal democratic capitalism, nor socialist or communist) were considered to be not only suspect, but an obstacle to the reaccommodation of North American hegemony in the World System and especially the economic link of the United States to Latin America within the framework of a policy of import substitution.[38]

In general terms, the so-called populist regimes of Latin America (Ianni, 1975) that emerged in association with the model of import substitution were not supported by U.S. policies of the time. They seemed too close to the mass appeal of European fascism, with its antidemocratic flavor and desire for geopolitical expansion. They had a redistributionist political economy that could alter the models of increased reproduction of capital and the accumulation of capital itself within their countries (Canitrot, 1975). The power that the worker aristocracies acquired at certain phases of development in these populist movements seemed difficult to offset, from the perspective of Capital; the utopia of an anti-imperialist Latin American unity whose spheres of hegemony would be arranged in regional blocs, as Peronism proclaimed, could have economic and political repercussions in the entire area that were not welcomed by the U.S. Department of State; and finally, given their ability to mobilize the masses and given the charismatic pragmatism of leaders such as Perón who were inclined to improvise, these movements were politically unpredictable and difficult to manage from private boardrooms or through bilateral agreements between countries.

It is within this international context and given the fabric of Argentina's cultural and political past that the links between the Church and Peronism are to be understood, then. So far we have argued that relations during Perón's first government from 1946 to 1952 were at times cordial and at times conflictive. One of the sources of conflict during his first term was the role played by Evita (Perón's second wife) in the Peronist movement.[39] With her charitable works, her tireless travel among the people, and repudiation (as an instinctive reaction rather than as a result of a calculating or cold-blooded attitude) of the upper classes and the oligarchy (Luna, 1980: 251–56)—and above all through the social action pursued by the Evita Foundation, in practice had displaced many of the unsophisticated and not very extensive social works of the Church, and had alienated organizations such as those that collaborated in the Sociedad de Beneficiencia (Charities Society) in the capital—Evita was attracting people to her who were linked to the farming oligarchy and some who were closely linked to the Church (Navarro, 1981).

Juan José Sebreli (1990) argues that the campaign against the Church began surreptitiously with Evita, who had perceived the hostility of the Church and the army toward her activities, and began to confront it. Sebreli's argument is that both the Church and the armed forces were bent on attacking Evita, in part because she represented a feminist model for Argentina that could not be accepted by corporations functioning on the basis of a camaraderie among men, and in part because they were suspicious of her connections with the working class and fearful of the possible radicalization of Peronism.[40] This conclusion seems to have been endorsed by Perón himself, who argued that the persecution and calumny against Evita was fostered by recalcitrant elements of the Church (Perón, 1958: 68). Nevertheless, relations with the Church at the beginning of Perón's government were ostensibly cordial. Although there is no precise information and the subject is open to speculation, it is reasonable to assume that a politician as pragmatic as Perón would not fail to have noticed that the contents of the collective pastoral letter written on November 15, 1945, contributed to the electoral triumph of Peronism and the Perón–Quijano ticket forging a kind of tacit alliance between the movement and the official Church (Donini, 1985, 55).

The sociologist Floreal Forni, who was both a Catholic and a militant Peronist,[41] argues that most analyses of the origin of Peronism give insufficient credit to the contribution of political cadres and intellectuals from Acción Católica and other organizations, and do not even show the noticeable convergence of Perón's intentions with the social teaching of the Church. His central argument is that, in spite of conflictive relations, a review of the history of Argentine would show, on the one hand, that the Church (represented by certain intellectuals, some members of the clergy, its social teaching, and popular Catholicism)[42] was important to the consolidation of Peronism and, on the other, that the Peronist government was one of the most audacious projects to be explicitly founded on the social teaching of the Church.[43] Forni criticizes José Luis Romero for comparing Peronism with fascism (Romero, 1975) and places him among the "ideological extremists of illuminism," and he considers the analyses undertaken in the vein of sociological scientificism of a functionalist bent, as epitomized by Gino Germani (1962), to be mistaken. He is also opposed to analyses that make the historical origins of Peronism out to be clearly Forjista,[44] attributing it, therefore, to the nationalist, radical, and anti-imperialist movement that initially supported the radicalism represented by the political figures Arturo Jauretche (see Neyra et al., 1965) and Raúl Scalabrini Ortíz (see Galasso, 1970, 1985). This would amount to a Peronism (with Forjista and syndicalist roots), produced by the influential analysis of the prolific historian Rodolfo Puiggrós (1965, 1971a, 1971b) and the analyses of Abelardo Ramos (1959, 1961, 1981) and J. J. Hernández Arregui (1957)—especially the latter—with the result that Peronism is reduced to "one of the tendencies of revisionism while being adopted in the same terms by one of the tendencies proposed by a popular pastorate within the official Church" (Forni, 1987a: 213).[45]

In spite of Perón's conflicts with liberal elements in the Church (centered around the figure of Monsignor De Andrea) and with the ultranationalists of integralist origin (centered around Julio Meinvielle), Forni argues that, in his speeches, Perón was the first to offer the explicit adherence of an Argentine ruler to the social teaching of the Church, a posture that culminated both in the corporatist social Constitution of 1949 and in the concept of the Comunidad Organizada (Organized Community) presented in the address delivered by Perón during the World Philosophy Congress held in Mendoza in 1950 (Perón, 1974). Forni concludes that in these documents and speeches

there is embodied a concept that, with some exaggeration of its features, could be called "social corporatism," a social-Christian version of the welfare state that, although "conservative" or "traditionalist" in many of its forms, was in practice much more advanced than the neo-liberal position of the Christian democracies that were emerging in Europe. In fact, this position, highly compatible with post-crisis Keynesianism, has its only suitable precedent in Roosevelt's New Deal. (Forni, 1987a: 221)

Concurring in part with the analysis of Gerardo Farrell (1976)[46] that Peronism appeared in Argentina as authentic national social-Christianism, Forni argues that this was doubly meritorious: not only because it was the first expression in the form of a State of the social teaching of the Church, but because it was headed by a group of syndicalist leaders with a strong anticlerical tradition who were, to a large degree, alien to Catholic culture (Forni, 1987a: 221; Auza, 1984). However, in Forni's opinion, it was precisely Perón's concept of syndicalism (of a strong united union, with obligatory membership, but nonconfessional, structurally designed on the basis of the fascist syndicalist experience) that would appear as an alternative to the mutualist version—based on the notion of charity, unsympathetic to the creation of workers' unions—prevalent in the ideas of Pope Pius X. For Forni, the Peronist version of syndicalism was "the clearest center of potential conflict with the Church" (Forni, 1987a: 222), notwithstanding the fact that Hernán Benítez reported from his trip to Rome in 1947 that Pius XII unreservedly praised Perón's undertaking (Benítez, 1953: 376).

In summary, the greatest sources of conflict with the Church hierarchy during Perón's first government were not only the appropriation of the theses of the social teaching of the Church (warned against by Franceschi in *Criterio* and claimed for itself by the new Christian-Democracy, see Parera, 1967), but also the Peronist version of unified syndicalism based on a third alternative to democratic liberal capitalism and socialism.[47] On the other hand, the antiliberal aspect of Peronist doctrine was expressed in the vindictive criticism of the oligarchy fostered by some segments of Peronism (especially Evita), thereby anticipating the antisystemic peculiarity of a popular national mass movement that John William Cooke (1970a, 1970b, 1972) would capture in his famous definition of Peronism: the accursed fact of a bourgeois country.[48] The popular antiliberalism and anticlericalism of Peronism were to alienate the Catholic middle class in particular.

Shortly after the intensification of the confrontation between the Church and Peronism, Father Hernán Benítez, Evita's confessor, lamented that many Catholics were shortsighted:

We have not been attentive in paying [Perón] the credit he is due. A worker's world has been served to us on a platter. . . . Today's Catholics do not see ourselves having to fight, as we did until a decade ago, against the liberalism and irreligiousness of the ruling classes, against a sectarian press and radio, against the dark forces of masonry, against state regalism, against laicism in the state school curriculum, against satirical anti-religious campaigns, against a loose tongued socialism and communism, nor even against economic stringency, since the national and provincial governments favor the construction of seminaries and churches with an open hand. . . . Is Catholicism more favored in any other country in the world? (Benítez, 1953: 369)

Forni also argues that the epicenter of the potential conflict between the Church and Peronism was the thesis of "two Christianities"—one for the people, the other official—fed by the parable of the pharisee and the publican and the parable of the good Samaritan. This thesis, by distinguishing between the letter and the spirit of Christianity, between primitive Christianity and the institutionalization of Constantinian Catholicism, would have great critical force and a much greater impact on the mood of anticlericalism (which Forni believed he detected in the world of the Argentine urban worker) than the agnostic critique of religion attributable to Marxism and Marx's vision of religion as the opium of the people. On the other hand, this Peronist version of popular Catholicism—much closer to the anarchist and socialist critique of the institutional Church—celebrated the simple, telluric, country Christian values of the people while stigmatizing liberal and European rationalizations of the middle classes and the pro-oligarchical positions of the official Church. This would be highly offensive to the Argentine Church and give rise to misunderstandings on both sides (Forni 1987a: 224, and 1987b: 197).

The chronicle of conflict between Peronism and the Church, especially during the second government from 1952 to 1955, is well known and there are several alternative explanations why Perón became openly antagonistic to the Catholic Church in spite of being a Catholic himself and having maintained relatively cordial relations with the hierarchy, even to the extent of promoting the teaching of religion in the schools in 1947 at the beginning of his mandate.[49] The explanations for the conflict and for the anticlerical campaign of 1954 run from electoral reasons (to put an end to the internal disputes of factions who were after the presidential succession) to totalitarianism (as the necessary conclusion of a political philosophy that could not accept the presence of a cultural and normative apparatus as powerful as the Catholic Church). Responsibility is also attributed to Perón's entourage, where the atheists in his government—such as Méndez San Martín as minister of education; Angel Borlenghi, head of the High Council of the Peronist Party; and the Vice-president Alberto Teisaire (a Mason, according to some)—could have influenced him. Another type of explanation—psychosocial in nature—suggests emotional or egotistical reasons to the effect that the sixty-year-old Perón was still mourning the death of his wife, who died in July 1952. Finally, some weight is also given to the theory that Perón's prestige was at issue, according to which, given his constant brushes with some Catholics and clergymen,[50] he saw himself called upon to exercise an exemplary punishment against the institutional Church or risk a loss of popular prestige (Beltrán, 1987: 126–27).

In reality, Perón never explained the conflict, although the historian Tulio Halperin Donghi maintains that the heart of the problem was

Perón's anticipation of a probable massive intervention by the Church in the working world in an attempt to compete with the Peronist unions (see Beltrán, 1987: 128). A careful reading of Perón's speech of November 10, 1954, to the assembly of provincial and territorial governors and representatives of Argentine labor organizations would support Tulio Halperin Donghi's hypothesis.

The conflict between Perón and the Catholic Church—described by Hernández Arregui as the greatest political error of the Catholic Church in Latin America (Hernández Arregui, 1957: 219)—placed countless lay and religious organizations who supported the growing anti-Peronist front in an uncomfortable but temporarily acceptable marriage with traditional liberals and socialists, who had always been fought by the Catholic Church. One source of conflict was the founding of the Christian-Democratic Party in July 1954.

Forni considers the dispute between Christian-Democracy (i.e., the Church) and the Peronist movement to be the spark that set off the conflict. He does elaborate the point, however, saying that Perón was legitimately concerned with the international repercussions of this politicization of Catholic forces and indignant at what he might have considered (as reflected in the passage from Hernán Benítez cited above) ingratitude on the part of the Church (Forni 1987b: 206–7).

The creation of Christian-Democracy during a meeting on July 9, 10, and 11 in 1954 seems a step backward in comparison with the Constitutional Convention of Peronism in 1949 (Parera, 1967: 73),[51] although the Christian-Democratic position was based on the neo-Thomist thought of Maritain (who was very much in vogue in the world at the time and visited Argentina for the second time in 1947) and, for some militants, was also inspired by the philosophy of Catholic personalism represented by Emmanuel Mounier.[52] Perón, visibly upset in his famous speech of November 10, 1954, accused Christian-Democracy of being a coalition of conservatives, liberals, nationalists, communists, and clergy eager to defeat Peronism at the polls (Kennedy, 1958: 209; Beltrán, 1987; Chiesa & Sosa, 1983).

Perhaps, as Forni argues (1987b: 206), the parallel attempt to create a moderate nationalist association—the Unión Federal Demócrata Cristiana (Christian Democratic Federal Union)—should have been cause for greater concern to Peronism than the Christian-Democratic Party, since the UFDC constituted an initiative intended to raise the social-Christian banners waved by the Justicialista movement and could have been a neo-Peronist alternative. But it failed. One of the causes of its failure was the scant support of the hierarchy, especially of the two cardinals (the Argentine primates)[53] who preferred to continue with the Argentine Church's secular policy of trying to influence politics and the State through control of cultural hegemony, instead of seeking security through the creation of a Catholic political party, which would not necessarily have been under the guaranteed control of the hierarchy, but would, of course, have created difficulties in the relation between Church and State. In spite of this, to the extent that Christian-Democrats sought to develop an anti-Peronist opposition, they were subject to persecution (Forni, 1987b; Parera, 1967: 78).

The relations between Church and State in Peronist Argentina from 1946 until 1954 followed a path based on a reasonable understanding of questions concerning family legislation and education. The matter of religious education—the crux of the understanding between Perón and the Church (Kennedy, 1958)—was resolved first through Martínez Zubiría, an organic intellectual of the Church, with the introduction of religious instruction in the State schools (Forni, 1987b), and then through the presence of Oscar Ivanisevich, a man very close to the Church, in the Ministry of Education. The understanding on this matter is reflected in the passionate defense by Father Filippo of the position of religious instruction in the government's second Five-Year Plan (Filippo, 1948), where it is asserted that religious and moral instruction in public schools "will be realized organically through courses proper to the different levels of education and the formation of specialized teachers" (Perón, Mende, Teisaire et al., 1954: 490). By the same token, the Peronist Constitution of 1949—of which the Catholic jurist Arturo Sampay was the architect— takes a position on the family, divorce, the Church, and education that is not only acceptable to the Church, but pays tribute to it. As Forni points out,

Sampay's presentations to the [Constitutional] Convention—from the critique of Alberdi's negative liberalism to the proposal that culminated in Chapter IV on the social function of property, capital and economic activity—struck the highest note in the contribution of Catholic social thought to Peronist ideology and its system of legitimation. (Forni, 1987b: 211)

It was in the second half of Perón's second presidency[54]—with the promulgation of the divorce law in 1954, the legalization of prostitution, and the suspension of religious instruction on April 14, 1955 (promoted by the minister of education, Armando Méndez San Martin)—that the more deeply contrasting shades in the relation between Church and State were accentuated. At that time, the Confederación General del Trabajo (General Confederation of Labor) adopted anticlerical positions and denounced the Church for having infiltrated anti-Peronist forces. It is quite possible (given his increased animosity toward the hierarchy) that Perón may have thought he could take cultural hegemony out of the hands of the institutional Church, using his popularity among the working classes, the support on which he could count among some of the nonhierarchical elements of the Church, and the links between popular Catholicism and the social-Christian values advocated by Peronism, which were clearly detected by some populist priests.[55]

In any case, toward the middle of 1955 these traces of religious conflict—which we might characterize as an increasing number of skirmishes—had become a war, declared between Church and State on the occasion of the Corpus Christi demonstration.[56] On June 11, 1955—in spite of the government's attempts to prohibit them—150,000 people, with the participation of political and militant activists of an enormous variety of political parties and currents of opinion, marched in the traditional Corpus Christi procession in what amounted to a political demonstration with religious overtones. The demonstration was suppressed by the police; and by the end of the day, groups of trade unionists and people from the popular classes were setting fire to churches in Buenos Aires (Beltrán, 1987: 126–27).

After the burning of the churches, the *New York Times* on June 17, 1955, reported a formal decree of excommunication against Perón. In fact, the decree of Pope Pius XII did not specifically excommunicate Perón, but all government authorities who had "trampled on the rights of the Church" (cited by Mecham, 1966: 250). Apparently Perón sought without success to have the decree lifted. In spite of this, John J. Kennedy maintains, in a book written a few years after the Revolución Libertadora of September 1955, that the Church did not contribute decisively to the downfall of Peronism (Kennedy, 1958: viii). A very different story is told by J. Lloyd Mecham, who remarks, "Undoubtedly Perón's attack on the Church must be regarded as a contributing cause of his downfall" (Mecham, 1966: 250).[57]

In any event, it is public knowledge that many Catholics supported and jubilantly welcomed the coup led by the Catholic General Eduardo Lonardi that inaugurated the Revolución Libertadora of September 11, 1955.[58] Thus, one of the most contradictory episodes in the relations between the Church and the State in Argentina came to an end, but without eliminating the possibilities for a populist Church.

## FROM THE REVOLUCIÓN LIBERTADORA TO THE REVOLUCIÓN ARGENTINA: THE CHURCH AMID THE COUPS (1955–1966)

With Perón in exile, the Peronist movement in disarray but not wiped off the face of Argentina, and the Revolución Libertadora led by the Catholic nationalist General Lonardi, a new marriage between Church and State would seem to have been in the wings. However, this relationship was short-lived, since a change of leadership brought General Eugenio Aramburu and Admiral Isaac Rojas to the head of the executive authority on November 13, 1955. With this change of government, traditional liberal elements regained control of policy, in what one left-wing Catholic commentator has called the "liberal restoration" (Mayol, Habegger, & Armada, 1970: 109).

However, there is one other factor that cannot be overlooked: the alliance between the military corporation and the Church as a corporatist power bloc that had been inaugurated with the integralist experience of the thirties. Once the Peronist interregnum was over, this alliance was to intensify again, evolving into what Boron has called the "authoritarian alliance," which, in his view, entailed a decline in public life and the beginning of a prolonged period of political instability and illegality that would last until the eighties (Boron, 1990: 97).[59]

While the Church sought to reaccommodate itself within the national context to the changes brought about by the Revolución Libertadora, the new government, once it had dealt with the remaining public traces of Peronism, prepared to call elections and reconstitute a democratic government, initiating a period of democracy based on prohibition of the majority parties—a situation that virtually guaranteed institutional instability.[60]

Arturo Frondizi won the elections of February 23, 1958, and collected the Peronist vote[61] through a developmentalist project for government based on the expansion of certain industries (especially petrochemicals, steel, and the motor industry) with wide support from foreign capital and the involvement of Argentine petroleum and coal producers. His first conflicts with the Church came with the attempt to repeal Article 28 of Decree Law 403 of December 1955 according to which the private universities—most of them Catholic—were permitted to grant professional degrees. There were disturbances in the streets, and the validity of the article was finally confirmed in October 1958. After November 11 Frondizi governed virtually under a state of siege. The Peronist unions openly withdrew their support for the fragile government in January 1959, and Frondizi's administration had to confront one general strike after another.[62] To distract attention from internal conflicts, the government showed great diplomatic activity, as the Continent was shaken by the reverberations of the Cuban Revolution and the conflict between Cuba and the United States. After the conference in Punta del Este where the Alliance for Progress was launched in August 1961, Frondizi on August 17 received the head of the Cuban delegation, the Argentine-born revolutionary Ernesto "Che" Guevara—which provoked all kinds of criticism, including the resignation of the chancellor and considerable resentment among the armed forces, who were suspicious of the left-wing affiliations of the president and many of his advisors and members of cabinet.

On March 18, 1962, elections were held for governors, legislators, and municipal authorities; and in the province of Buenos Aires, they were won by Andrés Framini (1982), a workers' leader representing the outlawed Peronist Party. The armed forces demanded federal intervention on the part of the president in five provinces where the electoral results had favored Peronism. The president agreed, but ten days later the armed forces also demanded his resignation. When he refused to resign, Frondizi was arrested on March 29, 1962, and held in military prison on the island of Martín García. On the afternoon of that same day—by virtue of the law governing the absence of a head of state, and as a result of one of the most paradoxical legal maneuvers in contemporary Argentine history—the presidency was assumed by Dr. José M. Guido, the first vice-president of the Senate. Thus began a period marked by a series of crises, culminating in the confrontation between the blue (nationalist) and red (liberal) factions on September 20–23, 1962.[63] As it happened, the primary mandate of Dr. Guido's interim government was to call elections; but until the assumption of power by Dr. Arturo Humberto Illia as constitutional president on July 7, 1963 (after elections from which the Peronists abstained) there were countless palace conflicts and attempted military uprisings that were put down by then commander in chief of the army, General Juan Carlos Onganía.

Dr. Illia's Unión Cívica Radical del Pueblo came to power with only 2,394,196 votes, which represented a mere 26 percent of the electorate, showing the loss of legitimacy of the political system.[64] In October 1963 the president annulled all contracts signed by Frondizi's administration with the petroleum companies. In May and June of 1964—a few months after the radical government took power—the Peronist unions unleashed a plan of attack that paralyzed 11,000 industrial plants.[65] Harassed by the unions and pressured by the armed forces, the government seemed ineffective. The spiral of wages and prices was impossible to contain and it was precisely the issue of an undisciplined workforce, combined with the prevalent opinion that there was a "power vacuum" to be filled, that led elements of the armed forces to overthrow the constitutional president.[66]

On June 28, 1966, a junta of commandants of the armed forces overthrew President Illia in a palace coup in which not a single shot was fired. On June 29 at 11 A.M. General Onganía was sworn in as head of the executive power and read the Statute of the Revolución Argentina, declaring that an era had come to an end. It should also be noted, however, that Cardinal Antonio Caggiano, primate of the Argentine Church and military vicar, had been playing an important role as mediator between the government and the armed forces (Dussel, 1979b).

The first six months of Onganía's government, under the administration of Felipe Tami, undoubtedly amounted to a social-Christian government of the right; it was based on militant cadres, many of them linked to the armed forces and nationalist in character, but also connected to the Cursillos de Cristiandad and Opus Dei. The journalist García Lupo even spoke of the Cursillos de Cristiandad[67] as a secret party that was represented through the periodical Cité Catholique and based on the preaching of a Catholic integralist, Jean Ouiset (García Lupo, 1971a: 12). Four of the ministers appointed in 1966 under Onganía's dictatorship were clearly organic intellectuals of the Catholic Church, including the influential finance minister Jorge Salimei and the minister of the interior E. Martínez Paz. On December 30, 1966, however, Guillermo Borda became minister of the interior and on the following day Adalbert Krieger Vasena was appointed finance minister. Thus, the liberal elements in the government began to displace the Catholic nationalists. Adalbert Krieger Vasena went on to implement one of the most ambitious models of hegemonic consolidation of monopolistic capital that had ever been seen in Argentina, even attempting a transfer of income from the agrarian bloc to the industrial bloc, which fomented serious conflicts among important power groups in the country (Torres, 1978).

Monsignor Gerónimo Podestá, bishop of Avellaneda—a progressive who was to be removed from his position a few years later in the midst of scandal, given his position on celibacy and his apparent relationship with his secretary[68]—declared at the outset of Onganía's government that "Catholics who participate in the revolutionary government do so as citizens of Argentina, with a healthy patriotic purpose, but not as representatives of the hierarchy" (Selser, 1972: 88; Mayol, Habegger, & Armada, 1970). Among the first measures of Onganía's government, in an action backed by the Catholic philosophy prevailing in his cabinet, was its intervention of July 29, 1966, into the national universities that were considered bastions of liberalism and socialism. In practice, this marked the beginning of the dismantling of professorships and first-class research teams, whose members began to migrate abroad. At the same time, it unleashed countless conflicts in all the country's universities, including the Catholic University of Argentina (Selser, 1972: 227–44).

Some analysts argue that Onganía's government represented an attempt to reestablish Christendom, linking it to a center-right democracy (Dri, 1987). Others see it as advancing a new ideological model of domination that was emerging on the Continent at the time. This model would use the ideology and doctrine of national security to establish military governments that, following the precedent of General Castelo Blanco in Brazil, would be not ephemeral or transitional governments but, on the contrary, regimes based on an absolute nationalism, keeping a close rein on the relationship of the State, power, and security and attempting to transform the political economy of the countries of the Southern Cone once and for all (Richard, 1987: 97; Comblin, n.d.: 5, 34, and 44). Some Christians saw links between these governments and the proposals of the Trilateral Commission formed by the United States, Western Europe, and Japan (Dussel, 1979b: 17). As Enrique Dussel asserts, "The purpose of the 'Revolution of 1966' is to unite the army and the Church" (Dussel, 1983a: 245; Richard, 1987: 104). Moreover, as we have already mentioned, on October 10, 1966, patronage (and Church dependence on the State) was brought to an end with the signing of a concordat between Rome and Argentina.

By contrast, in a caustic assessment of the Onganía government, the journalist Gregorio Selser claims that he "inaugurated an atrabiliously confessional and paternalistic regime that represented itself as order and efficiency, but spread disorder and incompetence" (Selser, 1972: 7).

## THE CHURCH AND TERCERMUNDISMO (1966–1976)

After four years of deliberations that had begun in 1962, the Second Vatican Council of Bishops ended in Rome. With it, the winds of change in the Catholic Church blew with unheard-of vigor and the project of Christendom was made to confront one of its deepest crises. It was in the context of modernization, on August 15, 1967—reflecting intense struggles among diverse ideological, theological, and pastoral factions—that the bishops of the Third World (eighteen of them in total, including Dom Helder Cámara, the bishop of Recife, Brazil) released their own pastoral letter as a group. This document unleashed extraordinarily dynamic processes in Latin America, including Argentina, where it became the catalyst for all the forces of change that were fermenting and gave rise to the Movimiento de Sacerdotes para el Tercer Mundo (Movement of Priests for the Third World)[69] and a new accommodation between elements of the Church and Peronism.[70]

The letter released by the bishops of the Third World was undoubtedly one of the most important documents produced by a group of Church hierarchies in the postconciliar period. It set the tone for what would eventually be the Medellín Document, a product of the Meeting of Latin American Bishops in Medellín, Colombia, on August 26, 1968.[71] The social context of that meeting could not have been more explosive. The Cuban Revolution offered a successful guerrilla route for the transformation of social order, and this had a profound impact on an influential handful of Catholic Latin Americans. The leading and most highly symbolic figure in this generational process was the Colombian priest Camilo Torres, who proclaimed, "Every sincere revolutionary must acknowledge the armed struggle as the only route that remains" (Torres, 1966: 375).

The Chinese Cultural Revolution of the sixties showed that revolutions could go through successive stages of transformation, in a continuing struggle against the sclerosis of the revolutionary order. But the 1968–69 uprising in Czechoslovakia was crushed by Soviet tanks, and the optimism generated by "socialism with a human face" disappeared. Student protest was intense; there were student movements in almost seventy countries, the movements in May 1968 in France and in October 1968 in Mexico having a profound impact in Latin America. The deaths of John F. Kennedy in 1963, and of Robert Kennedy and Dr. Martin Luther King, Jr., in 1968, cast a shadow on the possible outcome of civil strife within the Western democracies and turned the Protestant pastor King into a martyr of the social struggle. A coup led by General Juan Velasco Alvarado inaugurated the Peruvian Revolution on October 3, 1968, while the echoes of the movement for freedom of speech born at Berkeley—one of the elite universities of the U.S. education system—still resounded. Ernesto "Che"

Guevara had been killed in Bolivia in 1967 and had become a mythic figure of the revolution in Latin America. These events and the renewal that was occurring at an accelerated rate within the Church as a result of Vatican II and Medellín could not fail to have an impact on Christians throughout the Continent.

The appearance of the Sacerdotes para el Tercer Mundo in Argentina was motivated not only by the letter of the bishops of the Third World and the processes of Church renewal, but—more concretely—as a response to Onganía's government under the neoliberal economic administration of Krieger Vasena.[72] As part of a plan of industrial conversion and reduction of the public sector, the government closed the sugar mills in Tucumán, leaving 20,000 workers unemployed and profoundly affecting the regional economy.

Successive meetings of the Movimiento de Sacerdotes para el Tercer Mundo allowed it to consolidate a focus of criticism within the Church structure, and a Popular Church began to develop founded not only on practical policies, but also on doctrine. The first meeting of the movement was held in Córdoba, Argentina, on May 1–2, 1968. Here it was decided to send a letter to the Catholic bishops through the Episcopal Council of Latin America, a letter in which the prevailing social, political, and economic system in the majority of countries was held responsible for the poverty of the faithful. The second national meeting was held on May 1–3, 1969, in Colonia Caroya, Córdoba, at which eighty priests from twenty-seven dioceses were registered. The third meeting occurred in Santa Fé on May 1–2, 1970, with one hundred seventeen participants (Dussel, 1979b: 111). In little less than three years, the movement had attached itself to the Theology of Liberation and assumed a preference for socialism and a clear anticapitalist and anti-imperialist position, and many of its members declared their support for Peronism in a statement that was also signed by Father Rolando Concatti, who held the position of secretary-general at the time (Movimiento, 1970c, 1972 & 1973).

The episcopal hierarchy could not allow all this and the turbulent changes within the Argentine Church to go by unacknowledged. On August 12, 1970, it gave its first pronouncement on the Movimiento de Sacerdotes para el Tercer Mundo through a declaration of the Executive Commission of the Argentine Episcopate on "the difficult internal situation which our country is going through" (Documentos del Episcopado Argentino, 1982: 120–27). Among other things addressed by this declaration, it calls upon the Sacerdotes para el Tercer Mundo to cease offering a woeful spectacle to "our faithful and our fellow citizens" (Documentos del Episcopado Argentino, 1982: 122) and to seek actions in common. The movement was censured explicitly for having declared its intention

to adhere to a revolutionary process . . . adopting an option for a Latin American socialism that necessarily implies the socialization of the means of production of economic and political power and culture. [This] does not correspond to and is not legitimate for any group of priests, on account of their priestly character, the social teaching of the Church, to which it is opposed, or the nature of a social revolution that implies acceptance of violence as a means to achieve the liberation of the oppressed as quickly as possible. (Documentos del Episcopado Argentino, 1982: 124)

The movement replied in a meticulously phrased letter to the bishops signed by then Secretary-general Miguel Ramondetti, which, after regretting incorrect interpretations by the Permanent Commission of the Episcopacy and accepting the call to reflection, invited them to engage in a pastoral and theological dialogue. Beginning with an explication of the principles that gave rise to the Movimiento de Sacerdotes para el Tercer Mundo, the letter then offered the movement's view of the mission of the Church, religious truth, the Christian sense of liberation, and the mission of the priests, suggesting a theological and Biblical reinterpretation of social revolution, with some emphasis in the discussion on adherence to socialism and the question of violence (Movimiento, 1970b).

While the debate intensified inside the Church, social tensions reached uncontrollable levels and the student struggle for autonomy continued. On May 29, 1969, striking workers from the industrial plants in Córdoba marched to the center of the city, where they were met by university and secondary students, numerous men and women from religious orders, as well as by people of various social levels, in protest against state authoritarianism and the economic model introduced by Krieger Vasena. This mobilization of people—which became known as the Cordobazo— marked the beginning of a series of street uprisings, or *puebladas*, that challenged the military government's attempt to discipline civil society for force.[73] Repercussions among the unions were not long in coming. The Confederación General del Trabajo (General Confederation of Labor) was split in two, giving rise to Confederación General de Trabajadores (General Central Confederation of Workers), known as CGT de los Argentinos, spiritedly led by a young graphics worker and militant Christian named Raymundo Ongaro.[74]

Conflicts within the Argentine Church were intensified by incidents such as the confrontation between Bishop Guillermo Bolatti of Rosario and thirty-three priests that culminated in an unprecedented showdown in Cañada Gómez, Santa Fé, on June 17, 1969. Bolatti had sent a new priest to a parish where the parishioners supported the incumbent and refused to hand the position over. The police intervened, five persons suffered gunshot wounds, and twenty were arrested. Never in the history of the Argentine Church had police intervention been required to resolve a conflict (Dussel, 1979b: 108).

The episcopacy struggled to regain the initiative and issued a new theological perspective in the San Miguel Document of April 26, 1969, whereby the bishops sought to apply the documents of Medellín and the Second Vatican Council and the encyclicals *Gaudium et Spe* and *Populorum Progressio*. The text is symptomatic of the kind of concerns that were affecting the traditionalist, conservative Church as it felt pressured to respond to the winds of renewal and the distressed conditions of the country: "Following the example and the mandate of Christ, the Church should be especially close to the poor, the oppressed and the needy, by living their poverty and renouncing all that may seem to be a desire for domination" (Documentos del Episcopado Argentino, 1982: 85).

This document, exhibiting such a compassionate tone, and founded on the notion of liberation, was without a doubt the most advanced social statement ever produced by the hierarchy of the Argentinean Church. However, while the institutional Church endorsed a critical reading of the political and social situation in Argentina (revealing the emergence of the Theology of Liberation not at the level of erudite theologians or in the specialized environment of diocesan seminaries, but in pastoral discussion), the political situation of the country under military dictatorship continued to deteriorate. On March 29, 1970, on the first anniversary of the Cordobazo, the former president Lieutenant General Eugenio Aramburu was kidnapped and later assassinated by a group known as the Montoneros,[75] some of whose members—it would later be discovered when two of its principal founders, Carlos Ramus and Fernando Abal Medina, were killed in combat—were former members of Acción Católica, as also was their leader Mario Firmenich. This discovery evidently provoked both stupor and surprise in military and religious circles, given that the "subversion" had hitherto been considered Marxist in character.

A member of the Movimiento de Sacerdotes para el Tercer Mundo, Father Alberto Carbone, was arrested and implicated in the disappearance of General Aramburu and was later sentenced to two years' imprisonment. Two other priests, Carlos Mugica and Hernán Benítez, both of whom preached at the funerals of dead *guerrilleros*, were also detained temporarily. At the same time, while urban guerrilla conflict made its appearance on the political scene, the disputes between factions of the Peronist unions reached new heights when important union leaders were murdered, including José Alonso and Augusto Timoteo Vandor, head of the important metallurgical workers union. The death of such influential leaders also removed those who could negotiate with the military government and made the dynamics of politics that much more complex—all of which had immediate repercussions for relations between the Church and State. What gave the times their particular character, however, was the emerging tendency of the Church to criticize the military dictatorship and the capitalist system. Thus began the Popular Church in Argentina.

The philosophy of Carlos Mugica,[76] who was a *villero* priest,[77] an important political and religious leader of the time, and a member of the Sacerdotes para el Tercer Mundo, illustrates the kind of new program that was emerging within the Church and shows its increasing association with popular and populist tendencies. Mugica argues that the problems of Argentina can only find a solution within a true revolution of mentalities and structures, and such a revolution must recognize the Christian values of Peronism (Mugica, 1973: 22). In the course of his analysis, Mugica cites all the sources that inspired him, including the Bible, the Colombian priest Camilo Torres, Che Guevara, and Jesuit priest and physical anthropologist Pierre Teilhard de Chardin, and the Brazilian bishop Helder Cámara, alongside Marx and Freud, "that is to say, all those men who have been concerned for Man and the human adventure" (Mugica, 1973: 29). However, this list of thinkers and "prophets," in which the names of Helder Cámara, Martin Luther King, and Camilo Torres are repeated many times, only makes sense if the Gospels are read in the context of Argentina, where Peronism—insofar as it manifests as the political option of the poor—is the crystallization of all Christian values.

What judge will allow me to tell if Peronism is today the historic moment through which Christ calls to me, through which I am to show my love for my people and my brothers? This judge is the people, the common people, the oppressed. The category people almost coincides with the category poor, although it does not cover it entirely. I know, from the Gospels and from the attitude of Christ, that I must look at human history from the perspective of the poor. And in Argentina, the majority of the poor are Peronists. (Mugica, 1973: 35–36)

Mugica, who came from a comfortable family, points out that the process of drawing near to Peronism coincided with his turn to Christianity (Mugica, 1973: 34); and when talking to his students, he used to say—paraphrasing Saint Thomas Aquinas—that political action is the noblest of all activities (Mugica, 1973: 35). He saw the Cultural Revolution in China as an evangelical revolution, and he suggested that the charismatic role of the Christian is to be "the voice of those who have no voice"—aware of the risks, but also knowing that "for the Christian, death does not exist." A man of strong personality, Mugica appealed to his listeners in his Sunday sermons, drawing parallels between the Bible and socialism. One of his many celebrated phrases was that Lenin was to Marx what Saint Paul was to Jesus. Unafraid of using any theoretical argument to facilitate his reasoning concerning the struggle for justice, when confronted with Lenin's objection to religion (in *Socialism and Religion*) Mugica concluded that the objection was important, but not applicable to primitive Christians or to base communities (Mugica, 1973: 71).

In the explosive context of Argentina in the seventies—when an entire generation of young people had grown up under the shadow of the Catholic Church and at the same time under successive military takeovers that prohibited freedom of speech, reading, and discussion of the different political philosophies—the opinions and preaching of a young, talented, and charismatic priest who was publicly taking positions on the greatest social problems of the day (e.g., the situation of the shantytowns in Buenos Aires) had enormous power in strengthening convictions and stimulating social mobilization. Above all, his position on violence—a central issue that afflicted the consciences of many Christians—was very influential. Mugica argued in 1970 that "the conclusion cannot be drawn from the Gospels today that the Christian should use force against the established disorder. But neither can we conclude that it should not be used" (cited by Dussel, 1979b: 354). This exegesis, by assuming that every Christian has a need to look for a personal reply to the question of violence, broke the hegemony of a doctrine imposed by the priests and the bishops and celebrated free will and the freedom of conscience.

In fact, however, Mugica belonged to the most orthodox element of the Sacerdotes para el Tercer Mundo, associated with the popular pastorate and opposed to a more political element that proclaimed the need for direct political action. The return of Peronism in 1973

entailed a crisis for the Movimiento de Sacerdotes para el Tercer Mundo. Its periodical *Enlace* ceased to appear. Indeed, from August 1973, the movement had two principal factions: one, associated with the "popular pastorate," from the coastal region, that rejected married priests, had a vertical structure, was more in the line of "orthodox" Peronism, and condemned all violence in a communication of April 29, 1974, when it expressed the opinion that "under a legal government, violence is absurd if the government is popular," although, on October 7, it rejected violence when it comes from the government itself. The other group, from the interior—Córdoba, Mendoza (Rolando Concatti's *Nuestra opción por el peronismo*, Mendoza, 1972), and Santa Fé principally—is more critical and is more inclined to socialism. This tactical division is indicative of a strategic split. (Dussel, 1979b: 353)

Pablo Richard argues that the movement was seeking an ecclesiastical identity and had no desire to constitute itself as a political party. In 1972 it could count on 800 members and 200 sympathizers, approximately 20 percent of all priests working in Argentina (1987: 102).

With all the intense ideological and political struggle occurring in Argentina at the end of the sixties, one specific area that became important in the Church was the youth pastorate. At first, this endeavor was approached as a typical expression of a spiritual Church; but in spite of having mobilized a great number of young people (especially in Buenos Aires), this pastorate was soon overtaken by the social contradictions of the time.

The pastoral renewal inspired by the Medellín Document delivered the coup de grace to the youth wing of Acción Católica and there appeared "all kinds of youth groups and associations, without much structure, but considerable vitality" (Memoria y Esperanza, 1980: 57). Youth camps, youth clubs, popular schools, and youth movements multiplied, trying to adapt for young people the methodology of the adult courses of instruction on Christianity such as *Palestra* (Arena) or *Encuentros de Vida* (Challenges in Life) (Memoria y Esperanza, 1980: 57). Many of these movements were promoted by different religious orders, giving rise to the danger of elitism and of competition among the orders to monopolize and control them as a way of resolving the "vocations crisis" endemic to the Argentine Church.[78] To remedy this situation, the organizing of *Semanas de la Juventud* (Youth Weeks) was proposed, where the youth could meet to discuss various questions and end with a party or a meal of fellowship. However,

the result of most of these experiences was that, given the impossibility of providing any profound response to the expectations of the young, the movements were weakened as enthusiasm diminished. They changed to offer spiritual alternatives or became radical through the inclusion of groups that inclined to a more concrete social or political practice. (Memoria y Esperanza, 1980: 58)

As a way of confronting the problem, the Argentine Episcopacy resorted to initiating the Colombian experience with Central Católica de Juventudes (Central Catholic Youth Organization), founded by the Colombian priest Father Fernández ("Pafel"), which included the active participation of full-time lay workers as "Missionaries to Youth." This organization was based on the notion of youth as a social body—a new estate, therefore—from whose constructive rather than destructive rebellion could be created a new mentality (Central de Juventudes, 1970). Quite simply, the idea was to use the youth pastorate to build a new Christian civilization. An elite group of young people from the principal movements already recognized within the pastorate as a whole was sought out as the foundation of this new organization. And at the same time as the work with young people proceeded, special courses for men and women in religious orders were held in 1970 in Tucumán and Buenos Aires so that they would be qualified to devote themselves to pastoral work among the young. This effort experienced the same misfortune as previous ones, however: the vicissitudes of Argentinean political life, as well as the complicated ideological and political struggle in the universities, initiated a period of hyperpoliticization of Catholic youth that constrained the development of this kind of youth pastorate in the seventies. As a result, all such efforts languished, until disappearing entirely toward the middle of the decade.

In the meantime, the debate within the Church—especially the positions advanced by the Sacerdotes para el Tercer Mundo—had repercussions among the ideologies of Christendom. The Catholic right furiously denounced the "Clandestine Church," represented by the Sacerdotes para el Tercer Mundo, as a modernist project (heresy, in other words) that proposed a Marxist-Castroite and Maoist formula for Argentina (Sacheri, 1970a: 113).[79]

Political conditions in Argentina had deteriorated badly by the early seventies. The executive power changed hands twice under the military government. After the Cordobazo, Onganía's model of integralist, nationalist Catholicism—in spite of the liberal orientation provided by the appointment of Adalbert Krieger Vasena—had been discredited, and he was removed from office by the chiefs of the armed forces on June 8,

1970. On June 13, 1970, General Roberto Marcelo Levingston, who had been military attaché at the Argentine Embassy in Washington, was invited to head the Revolución Argentina; and—in marked contrast to the policies of Krieger Vasena—Aldo Ferrer, a progressive economist who advocated a nationalist model combined with economic Keynesianism, was named minister of finance.[80] This project was also worn out by 1971, when renewed signs of social discontent (including a second Cordobazo in 1971) put pressure on a government that had done little but heighten the chronic crisis in the Argentine State, by making it both a crisis of representation with respect to the ruling class and a crisis of the legitimacy of the State with respect to the governed.

The relations then prevailing in Argentine politics had generated a hegemonic stalemate—a fragmentation within the dominant bloc—which was the product of secondary contradictions and in critical moments took the form of a hegemonic vacuum (in terms of leadership), although in the long run the political-economic process ended up benefiting the dominant faction within the bloc: monopolistic capital (Portantiero, 1973: 83). This fragmentation of the dominant bloc is radically expressed in what Guillermo O'Donnell characterized as the colonization of the State by civil society (O'Donnell, 1982), whereby the changing political-economic coalitions in civil society affected the political economy of the Argentine State, turning it, as a pact of domination, into an arena for conflict and, as a self-regulating administrative system, into an ineffective apparatus with too many dimensions to it (Torres, 1978). The arrival in 1971 of General Alejandro Lanusse (who represented the liberal faction of the armed forces) as head of the executive power and virtual leader of the Revolución Argentina produced an attempt to find a political way out of the crisis, while still attempting yet again, to limit and control the participation of Peronism.

On the political scene, the spontaneous mobilization of the masses predominated over the organizations established to channel their demands, and the struggle in the streets increased (Balve, 1971). From the point of view of Lanusse, the situation was moving beyond the control of the armed forces—which suggested an urgent political solution through the transference of power to civilians (Lanusse, 1977).

In the end, the attempt to marginalize Peronism during the ensuing elections failed; and on March 11, 1973, the candidacy of Héctor J. Campora and Vicente Solano Lima—under the banner Frente Justicialista de Liberación or FREJULI (Peronist Liberation Front)—won with 49.59 percent of the votes. Since Perón did not live in Argentina in 1972, he had been disqualified as a possible candidate. After he returned in 1973, and as a result of misintelligence within Peronism and the power struggle unleashed between its adherents on the right and the left,[81] Cámpora who, in the election, had the support of the youth movements—governed for only forty-nine days until he was forced to resign under pressure from Perón and the union bureaucracy. Thus, Peronists on the right, who were linked to Perón's private secretary López Rega, remained in control during the interim government of Raúl Lastiri, while the Peronist left lost ground (Torres, 1978).

Perón was elected president for the third time, with 61.85 percent of the votes, and was sworn in on October 12, 1973—just as an upsurge of political violence was beginning to claim well-known victims[82] and a further outbreak occurred in the guerrilla activities of Ejército Revolucionario del Pueblo (Revolutionary Party of the People), a Trotskyite group in origin that had already in the sixties been moving towards Che Guevara's theory concerning the focus of guerrilla activity.[83] Perón governed till his death on July 1, 1974, and was succeeded by his third wife Isabel, who had been vice-president. By that time, the Peronist left wing had broken away entirely and gone into opposition—even armed opposition, when the violence in Argentina took on a new character.[84]

The murder of Carlos Mugica in May 1974 dramatically uncovered (especially for Christians) the scope of the violence that was taking its toll on countless numbers of victims, even from among the clergy and people linked to the Church.[85] The policy of an eye for an eye predominated in all aspects of public life, and even the Catholic integralist right lost one of its most visible leaders when Carlos Sacheri was assassinated in December 1974. Political violence in Argentina finally reached a climax in the "dirty war" introduced by the military dictatorship on March 24, 1976.[86] As for the Argentine Church, beginning in 1955 and throughout the period leading up to this date it had been "polarized around two antagonistic positions: one position sought a solution to the crisis in a military regime tied to the dominant classes, and the other looked for a socialist type of solution, tied to the popular classes. Between these two clearly defined positions was to be found a *hesitant majority*" (Richard, 1987: 102; original emphasis).

## THE THEOLOGY OF DOMINATION: THE CHURCH UNDER DICTATORSHIP AND THE RETURN TO DEMOCRACY

The dictatorship that toppled Peronism on March 24, 1976, and installed Jorge Videla as president called itself "El Proceso Militar de Reorganización Nacional" (The Military Process of National Reorganization), distinguishing itself through careful labeling from the self-styled Revolución Libertadora and Revolución Argentina, the terms with which the two previous governments established through military intervention had described themselves. Alleging the existence of a power vacuum and the possibility of national disintegration through guerrilla movements and Marxist subversion, the armed forces saw themselves obliged to wage what became known as the "dirty war," based on a systematic repression that would culminate in the slaughter of any trace of virtual or potential opponents, all of whom could be classified under the term *subversives*. However, this dirty war was pure myth as Daniel Frontalini and Maria Cristina Caiati (1984) argue. The two authors analyze the 1976 militarization of the Argentine State—which gave rise to the most ferocious clandestine repression ever unleashed in the country— and compare it with the Italian experience during the confrontation with the Red Brigades.[87] They expose the dirty war rationale to be a subterfuge that allowed for the application of a new model of socioeconomic development—a model that would require the violent disciplining of civil society: "the project of obtaining objectives without delay requires a social peace that cannot be achieved among a conscientized people without appealing to State Terrorism. In order to guarantee the necessary social order, the peace of the cemetery must be imposed" (Frontalini & Caiati, 1984: 99).

The fall of the government of Isabel Perón was accepted with relief by many sectors of the population.[88] The Church greeted the military movement with its traditional complacency, looking for a strategic reaccommodation in relation to the new events and hoping that the new military government would impose order on the social chaos and would defend their interests. The bishops received the junta with a renewed desire to fraternize with the military corporation. However, within a year, the Permanent Commission of the Argentine Episcopal Conference had written to the junta an early—and, as it turned out, the only public institutional—display of reservations about the conduct of the armed forces. The bishops stated in their letter that they were pressured by

the situation of not a few citizens whose family and friends claim they have been kidnapped or have disappeared through the action of groups of people claiming to be from the Armed Forces or the police, without it being possible for them to be so in the vast majority of cases, and without their relatives or the ecclesiastical authorities even being able to obtain any information on the matter. (Documentos del Episcapado Argentino, 1982: 307)

However, the bishops also wound up condoning what had occurred when they stated,

Indeed, we recognize the exceptional situation through which the country is passing. We are aware of the threat to national life that subversion has meant and continues to mean. We understand that those who are responsible for the welfare of the country have found it necessary to take extraordinary measures. (Documentos del Episcopado Argentino, 1982: 308)

The Protestant activist Julio Barreiro, writing from Argentina, anticipated early on that the themes of human rights and ecumenism could lend new dimensions to the Latin American Church's mission. He suggested that its new role was to confront the increasing economic marginalization of a broad segment of the population, the practice of torture, the abuses of social justice, and the lack of liberty (Barreiro, 1977). But this kind of argument evoked few responses within the Argentine hierarchy at the time, especially in view of the close connections to be found between authoritarianism and culture and the attempts made to promote a Catholic neocorporativism by certain ecclesiastical dignitaries linked to the military process. The vicar to the forces, Monsignor Victorio Bonamin stated, "We may aspire to a Catholic State, yes, Catholic, not just Christian, with a Christian inspiration derived from the Gospels to illuminate political and cultural life and the economy itself" (cited by Avellaneda, 1986: 193).[89] While Emilio Mignone has argued that the Argentine Church sought to establish a model based on neo-Constantinianism (Mignone, 1988), another Catholic commentator described it more emphatically as a theology of domination (Dri, 1987).

The repression reached into every aspect of culture. The lyrics (but not the music) of the tango "Cambalache" were prohibited, along with the books of Freud, Freire, Marx, and even Einstein on account of his theory of relativity (Avellaneda, 1986; Massera, 1979: 86). The junta that governed Argentina between 1976 and 1983, following the dictates of the national security doctrine, pursued a practice of State terrorism through kidnap and torture that (although there is no precise count) caused between 20,000 and 30,000 persons to "disappear." In 1983 when President Raúl Alfonsín assumed office, he appointed a national commission to investigate the disappearance of persons, headed by the celebrated novelist Ernesto Sábato. The commission's findings are documented in the book *Nunca más* (CONADEP, 1984). It is stated there that the repression showed no respect for age, but concentrated especially on those who were sixteen to thirty-five years old, since 71 percent of the 9,000 cases documented were from that group. It was established that a number of children born in clandestine detention centers (and the book suggests that there were between 200 and 300 such children, of whom only 13 had been identified by 1984) were placed in "decent families," and the majority of their parents were eliminated. All sectors of society were affected, although workers and students represented more than 50 percent of all those kidnapped and eventually murdered. The following figures are cited in *Nunca más*:

| | |
|---|---|
| Workers: | 30.2% |
| Students: | 21.0% |
| Service-sector employees: | 17.9% |
| Professionals: | 10.7% |
| Teachers: | 5.7% |
| Housewives: | 3.8% |
| Members of the armed forces: | 2.5% |
| Journalists: | 1.6% |
| Actors: | 1.3% |
| Members of religious orders: | 0.3% |

At the same time, a great number of persons were kidnapped or arrested and held at the disposition of the executive authority—a legal category used to describe the handling of political detainees to whom the right to trial was denied. In spite of their number and the deprivation to which they were submitted, they were the lucky ones since, by being legally classified as political prisoners, they survived the policy of extermination. The following list of the number of such prisoners and the term of imprisonment is also taken from *Nunca más*:

| | |
|---|---|
| 4,029: | less than a year |
| 2,296: | 1–3 years |
| 1,172: | 3–5 years |

668:                                    5–7 years
431:                                    7–9 years

There is also evidence that the period under investigation was marked by the activation of secret detention and torture centers (CONADEP, 1984: 62–63) and by international coordination among the armed forces and police of Uruguay, Brazil, Argentina, and Chile—all countries under military government—and that there was pillaging by military task forces (units composed of various branches of the services, including the police and the gendarmerie), which had considerable autonomy and, in fact, constituted death squads who were at the service of what Guillermo O'Donnell has called the "sociology of fear" instilled in the country. O'Donnell argues, however, that such an extensive and detailed domination required something more than despotic control. For it to occur,

there was a society that policed itself: more precisely, there were numerous persons—I don't know how many, but certainly not a few—who, without any official obligation, simply because they wanted to, because it seemed right to them, because they accepted the promise of the order that the triumphant regime put to them as the only alternative to the constantly evoked image of pre-1976 chaos, actively and zealously occupied themselves with exercising their own authoritarian "pathos." (cited by Boron, 1990: 100)

One element within the Church—described by Rubén Dri as the right wing of the Church of Christendom (1987: 225), which held the upper hand until 1979 during the first phase of this period—not only encompassed the objective of the Military Process of National Reorganization (Dri, 1987: 171) and supported the genocide,[90] but justified it and provided theological legitimation. In June 1976 the apostolic nuncio Pio Laghi proposed that there be a total adherence on the part of the Church to the process conducted by the armed forces, arguing that

Christian values are threatened by the aggression of an ideology that is rejected by the people. For this reason, the Church and the Armed Forces, each must accept a share of responsibility; the former because it is part of the process and accompanies the latter, not only with its prayers, but with actions in defense and promotion of human rights and the fatherland. (cited by Dri, 1987: 184)

Rubén Dri and Emilio Mignone document extensively how a group of bishops and military chaplains gave religious legitimacy to the task forces, the disappearance of citizens, the invasion of property, and even torture and murder. Dri writes,

[Monsignor Antonio José Plaza, chaplain of police for Buenos Aires] and several chaplains, such as the priest Gallardo, maintained that torture was ethically legal if it was done only for a certain period of time. . . . Monsignor Plaza thought that you could torture for 4 hours without committing a sin. . . . Chaplain Gallardo allowed a period of 48 hours. (Dri, 1987: 306–7)

The theological legitimation expressly resorted to Biblical figures, including the Beast of the Book of Revelation, the forces of evil, and the Devil, to describe foreign ideologies such as Marxism and the subversion fought by the armed forces (Dri, 1987: 273–326). There are documented cases of priests cooperating with authorities at the secret detention centers, and military chaplains were used to exert psychological influence on detainees in order to make them reveal what they knew (Dri, 1987: 347–90; Mignone, 1988: 14 and 55). The repression also profoundly affected the elements of opposition within the Church, referred to by Dri (1987: 391–429) as the Popular Church, by Dussel (1979b: 356–65) as the Prophetic Church, and by Mignone (1988: 128–50) as the Persecuted Church. The list of those who were murdered subsequent to the establishment of the dictatorship in 1976 is long.[91] It includes the bishops who perished in automobile accidents that were apparently deliberate (e.g., Monsignor Enrique Angel Angelelli and Monsignor Carlos Ponce de León of San Nicolás de los Arroyos), the murder of three priests and two seminarians in the Church of San Patricio in the elegant Belgrano district of Buenos Aires, and the disappearance of two French nuns, apparently kidnapped by units of the navy. The frightening testimony of those who survived the torture sessions and the secret prisons shows the close relationship between the cross and the sword (Dri, 1987: 107). Only a small group of bishops (just four among eighty prelates active as cardinals, archbishops, and bishops, according to Mignone, 1988: 19) raised their voices to condemn the military junta and the violation of human rights. These were the bishop of Neuquén, Jaime de Nevares, a tireless fighter for human rights; the bishop of Viedma, Miguel Hesayne; the bishop of Quilmes, Jorge Novak; and the bishop of la Rioja, Enrique Angelelli.

During the period 1976–83, the executive power within the military dictatorship changed hands four times, the composition of the cabinet was modified on several occasions, and some very surprising decisions were made—including the decision to invade the Malvinas Islands (known by the British as the Falklands) in 1982, which led to war with England and subsequent defeat for Argentina, while also paving the way for democratic constitutional rule with the election of Raúl Alfonsín in 1983. During the dictatorship, the economy deteriorated considerably through accelerated deindustrialization and an enormous foreign debt, which grew from US $7.8 billion to 43.7 billion between 1976 and 1983, and had reached US $54.5 billion by 1987.[92]

The Argentine hierarchy, both by commission of action and by omission of action, was clearly linked to the military dictatorship. It disregarded the human rights organizations (many of them made up of practicing Catholics, such as the Mothers and Grandmothers of May Square) who systematically appealed to the bishops and were received by some of them on a personal basis, although never officially by the Episcopal Commission (Dri, 1987: 379). Even during the meeting of Latin American bishops held in Puebla, Mexico, in 1979, the Argentine bishops refused to receive a delegation of the Mothers of May Square who had traveled there to denounce the situation at home and to seek the solidarity of this distinguished gathering of ecclesiastical dignitaries. Furthermore, when Pope John Paul II—concerned over the problem of the disappeared persons in Argentina—first pronounced these concerns during his weekly audience of October 23, 1978, the effect on the Argentine hierarchy was practically nil: "When Cardinal Primatesta returned from Rome on November 13, he tried to downplay the importance of the statement, stating that the Pope's observations 'have been taken one-sidely' " (Mignone, 1988: 53).

All in all, during 1976–83 the Church sought to consolidate the alliance with the military power that it had developed since the thirties and strengthened under the military dictatorship of Onganía, and to obtain a preferential treatment for itself. As Mignone argues, the decision of the military dictatorship to grant a salary and pension to bishops and priests exemplifies the kind of benefits that has generated a historical pattern of dependence by the Church on the State. Referring to this relationship as part of the Church's neo-Constantinian model in Argentina, Mignone describes an alliance based on ideological congruity with military regimes that defended the interests and privileges of the Church. He asks how the bishops could possibly be expected to confront a regime that to their eyes was a Catholic State prepared to protect Church property and eliminate heresies and the enemies of the faith (Mignone, 1988).

Yet, while the hierarchy turned a blind eye to the abuses under the military regime, civil opposition did not disappear entirely, since a number of organizations in defense of human rights were founded or strengthened. These included the Permanent Assembly for Human Rights, the Ecumenical Movement for Human Rights, the Mothers of May Square, the Center for Legal and Social Studies, and a wide range of institutions that argued for human rights and an end to the practice of secret detention, murder, and torture. Among their leaders were Catholics such as the lawyer Emilio Fermín Mignone and the layman Adolfo Pérez Esquivel, winner of the Nobel Peace Prize in 1980, the coordinator of the Peace and Justice Service, who argued for nonviolence in defense of the dispossessed and who was himself kidnapped in 1976 and then released.

With the return of democracy in 1983, military personnel connected with the dictatorship's atrocities were brought to trial—a trial that revealed the sordid web of agreements made with elements of the Church, and the repression of opposition. The caustic assessment of Father Rubén Capitanio is symptomatic of what many Christians were thinking when the facts of the repression became clear:

The church is responsible for millions of lives lost, not for having killed them, but because it did not save them. When the Bishops realized they might be accused of omissions, they brought out a book recounting all the efforts they made. But this book that tried to justify them is nothing but a proof of guilt, for it shows that they knew what was happening. . . . I wonder what would have happened if, in April 1977, when their first letter was sent to the military junta, there had been a threat to excommunicate the junta, and that the military vicariate was going to resign, that all the military chaplains would resign, and there would have been a complete break with the government. (cited by Mignone, 1988: 101)

However, it was not only bishops, priests and chaplains who were linked to the military dictatorship, but also a great number of lay organic intellectuals of the Church, including three of four ministers of culture and education, members of the Supreme Court of Argentina, and members of several committees of the National Commission on Scientific and Technical Research, Education, and Technology (CONICET), all of whom are considered by Mignone to have been Catholic integralists (Mignone, 1988: 126).

The return of democracy in 1983 entailed a complicated process of adjustment to the new social conditions, on the part of the Church—

not only because of the exposure of its conduct during the military dictatorship, but above all because it had to deal with radicalism, which symbolized the same secularizing liberalism fought by the Church for more than one hundred fifty years. The confrontation with radicalism over a new divorce law in 1986 gave rise to demonstrations supported by several Catholic institutions in June and July of that year—with a rally held in Buenos Aires on July 5 for which the dioceses mobilized all its forces, but was only able to get forty thousand persons out into May Square in front of Government House. This clearly showed the inability of the Church to mobilize people in the period after the dictatorship.

The pope visited Argentina on April 6–12, 1987. The outcome of his visit was positive according to Ana María Ezcurra (1988: 190–91), because John Paul II did not see the transition to democracy as a risk for the Church and did not endorse the positions of Catholic integralist nationalism, although he did outline the idea of a Catholic nation—following the Polish model, perhaps—and did appeal for national reconciliation, while refusing to discuss the country's experience of repression under the previous military government.

The links of the Church with Peronism, which returned to power in 1989, are better than the links it had with Alfonsín's government. The Church is guaranteed control of the ministry of education; and the proximity to the Church of some important Peronist union leaders, such as Saúl Ubaldini,[93] Secretary-general of the Confederación General del Trabajo, is well known. But these improved connections do not accommodate it once and for all to the new demands of democracy. In part, the problem is that the application of the Peronist social model of a market economy does not ease relations between the poor Christian bases of society and a supposedly popular government, with the result that the Church finds itself in the middle but without the ability to mediate.

One progressive sector of the Church—symbolized by Friar Antonio Puigjané—is associated with guerrilla activities and the shady events of Holy Week 1988, when a group of poorly trained and ill-equipped guerrilleros attacked a barracks but were repulsed and wiped out. Later inquiries showed that some of them were linked to a social movement called "Todos por La Patria" (All for the Fatherland), which contained a considerable number of militant Christians—including Antonio Puigjané, who was imprisoned.

The Church of the postdictatorship period has not broken its authoritarian alliance with the military corporation. As one commentator has concluded, the leadership of the Church in Argentina maintains a "neo-conservatism, lukewarmly reformist, traditionalist and given to spiritual renewal. . . . It is a nationalism whose links with the directions of political liberalism are becoming taut, and this is a serious threat to the institutional stability of the country" (Ezcurra, 1988: 100).

## THE CATHOLIC CHURCH, RELIGION, AND HEGEMONY IN ARGENTINA

As an institution of religious mediation and a historical bloc, the Church in Argentina has gone through the same conflicts as the political sector: the conflicts of civil society and a conditioned State. That is to say, the state was effectively subdued by the pressures of civil society once the oligarchical pact had been exhausted, and has since been unable to reconstitute knowledge, the use of law, and the power and authority of the State and thereby create a stable pact of government within the context of Argentine capitalism.[94]

The history of division within the Church is paralleled in the vicissitudes of political life, as expressed through a number of well-known historical antinomies: independence versus regalism, liberals versus conservatives, unitarians versus federalists, positivism versus the spiritual, social integralists versus nationalist integralists, Peronists versus anti-Peronists, defenders of human rights versus defenders of the doctrine of national security. As Pablo Richard (1987: 102) points out there has probably always been a silent ("hesitant") majority of Catholics between the antinomic poles that allows itself to be drawn along by the course of events.

Since the early seventies, there have been two dividing lines in the Argentine Church, although the groups on either side of them are significantly interrelated. One of the fundamental divisions is that between pre- and postconciliar Catholics—between those who propose a redefinition of the Christian State in Argentina by arguing for neo-Christendom (Ezcurra, 1988), and those who are opposed to it, often brandishing the banners of Liberation Theology and the Popular Church. A second dividing line separates those who remained silent or supported the deadly military project of disciplining the country by a dirty war, from those who—even at risk to their own lives—defended human rights and the legitimacy of political dissent against a despotic regime that subjugated individual rights and imposed an official discourse.

The dependence of the Church as a result of its endeavor throughout the course of history to defend and perfect its rights with respect to the

State still continues. However, its moral authority, especially in the more politically conscious sectors of the population, has been profoundly eroded by its complicity with the military dictatorship. We can also reasonably assume that, had Argentina after the dictatorship been marked by an economic boom and a model of development characterized by political stability and the distribution of real income among the population, then popular Catholicism would likely have persisted in its ceremonial symbology but, at the same time, there would very probably have been an upsurge in anticlericalism at the level of popular common sense. However, the harsh social and economic conditions of the country leave us few glimmers of hope that there will soon occur any serious reevaluating or realigning of the people's affections. Popular religiosity, as well as the liturgy and various groups within the ecclesiastical institution, offer a spiritual symbolism—a refuge—that may play a psychological and eventually social role by making it possible to confront, or at least endure, the overwhelming burden of the everyday struggle.[95]

Two questions continue to be important. The first question involves to what extent, in any of its theological or pastoral variants, the Popular Church—which has been systematically beaten down by a hierarchy that supports a neo-Christian ideology—can emerge in the nineties as a political and social alternative, comparable to its Brazilian counterpart that is so active within the base communities. Alternatively, to what extent can the Popular Church, Tercermundismo, Catholic socialism, and the emergent Peronism of the seventies regain the social presence they once had, even if that had only been for a short period of time? Will the Church find institutional forms that, even under liberal regimes, will enhance both substantive and formal democracy? That is to say, will the Popular Church be able to offer an alternative to neo-Christendom, or is it irremediably condemned to remain within the confines of the institution?

The second question concerns the connections between cultural insertion (e.g., popular Catholicism) and the cultural and political hegemony of the Church. In this chapter we have argued that, for historical reasons, the Church is deeply rooted in the cultural experience of Catholicism, in the common sense of the Argentine people. However, we have also argued that this does not necessarily translate into political-cultural hegemony. The hierarchy's flirtations with the military corporation have not contributed to the maintenance of a cultural and political hegemony, but have only reinforced the alliances between the two corporations to the extent that it has allowed them both to pursue the restoration of order and to block progressive alternatives. If its cultural influence cannot be turned into hegemony, the Argentine Church will not be able to develop its links with the democratic state into a model in the style of the Polish Church—with an influence on social policy—and will probably be restricted to a relation with the state similar to the current experience of the Church in Spain, namely, continuous negotiation. Given its connections with the military corporation and the elective affinity of institutional principles between the two of them, the Church would likely be a deinstitutionalizing factor in the democratic experience. However, these are empirical questions that cannot be resolved at present.

Nevertheless, this inquiry into the links among religion, the Church, and hegemony in Argentina does permit certain conclusions. Historical analysis shows that religious unity hides a real multiplicity of conceptions of the world, as in those that manifest themselves most emphatically in the divisions between a conservative hierarchy seeking to found a new Christendom and the perspectives associated with Liberation Theology and the Popular and Democratic Church, which emerged very explicitly in Argentina in the different coalitions formed around the defense of human rights.

Gramsci's hypothesis discussed in Chapter 4 shows us that Christian integralism in Argentina was an attempt to create a hegemony that would supersede cultural insertion (expressed through popular Catholicism) in a context where political pluralism was restricted. It was in the thirties that the alliance between the armed forces and the hierarchy of the Church was formed—two corporations whose organizational routines and political philosophies (whose common sense, to express it in Gramscian terms) was more inclined toward authoritarianism than toward democratic pluralism. Moreover, it should be noted that, when the Argentine Church evolved toward a more liberal position in the sixties, this did not affect Church unity or substantially modify religious unity, especially where the link between popular Catholicism and the institutional Church was concerned. In fact, a certain religious unity was maintained while there was an increasing diversification in the institutions of political representation (such as the political parties) and in the social movements (such as the groups of young Peronists, or the connections between the Sacerdotes para el Tercer Mundo and the villero movement of the seventies).

Gramsci's hypothesis that religion is ideology—not understood merely as false consciousness, but as politics, as praxis, as conscious action in the quest for a common objective—is clearly borne out by analysis of the praxis of the Argentine Church. This praxis involves progressive and conservative elements, combined in a complex amalgam. However, there were moments in history when the domination of one ideology—neo-Christendom—and one style of politics seemed to hold sway within the Church, as was the case from 1976 to the beginning of the eighties, when the most corporatist and integralist sector of the Catholic right accepted politically, legitimized theologically, and collaborated pastorally with state terrorism, especially through the conduct of military chaplains.

The Church is a traditional intellectual and perhaps, as Dussel maintains, may occasionally behave as an ideological apparatus of the State, as part of political society in the exercise of political power. On other occasions, it may enjoy a degree of relative autonomy with respect to the State, as in the case of a Church that unites the political opposition. As Dussel observes, basing himself on the history of the Church in Latin America, the Luso-Hispanic heritage "converted the Church into an apparatus essential to the Spanish and Portuguese system of domination" (Dussel 1979b: 39). Alternatively, as we have seen in our study of the Church in Argentina, this heritage was also used by liberal governments to discipline a Church that could always count on a certain cultural influence.

As Gramsci points out, religion—part of a comprehensive cultural process—draws the masses closer to the intellectuals through the construction of a social and individual discipline, and it may use the everyday experience of men and women to create a hegemonic consensus. In Argentina, this consensus did not weaken the bases of operation of the dependent capitalist mode of production, but on the contrary strengthened it. And this occurred in spite of the fact that the Church always sought to maintain an uncomfortable third option, criticizing the excesses of capitalism and the materialistic luxury of a consumer society, while trying to protect the country from the atheistic materialism associated with socialism.

Religion as part of a common sense in Argentina administered by a specific institution such as the Catholic Church is able to maintain unity between the highest levels of the philosophy produced by its intellectuals and the common sense of the ordinary man and woman—a unity that can only be achieved in politics. However, it was precisely as a result of the Peronist experience that political unity became more difficult after 1955, because the common sense of the popular classes were identified with Peronism, while the official position of the Argentine Church was considered anti-Peronist. Likewise, this antinomy affected the unity of the traditional intellectuals of the Argentine Church, most of whom belonged to the petite bourgeoisie, and the popular classes with their distaste for the clergy and petite bourgeoisie preference for Peronism. Political unity will possibly be weakened substantially by the end of the fourth Peronist government under the administration of Carlos Menem (1989 to 1994), which advocates a market economy of popular capitalism (that is to say, a neoliberal model) contrary to the expectations of large elements within the Peronist movement. And this is in spite of the fact that Peronism will continue to court the Church, which will probably consider it to be a reliable ally to the extent that it effectively links the institutional Church to the majority of workers' unions.

Following Gramsci, we have also argued in Chapter 4 that religion may have a unified rational nucleus, which, given the right conditions of intellectual reflexivity, may evolve into a philosophy and a critical political praxis. This is to say that religion may be conceived as part of the good sense in common sense.

The Popular Church in Argentina since the sixties and seventies—especially the brief chaotic experience of the Sacerdotes para el Tercer Mundo, which attempted to link the institutional Church with both Peronism and Liberation Theology by means of a national popular socialism—has been an attempt to exploit the possibilities of religion as a mobilizing force for liberation. In the nineties, through a change of language and issues, the Popular Church is seeking to deflect the good sense of religion into a more comprehensive project entailing respect for human rights, a pluralist society, and a substantive democracy. The connection in meaning and history between the two tendencies (i.e., religion as liberation and as democracy) is evident, and their symbolic appeal has the same character. That is to say, religion is interpreted as a constituent element of a historical bloc, as part of a process of contradiction and correspondence between material relations and symbolic representations.[96]

Although Gramsci's analysis of good sense within common sense is derived from a cosmic view of religion, he concludes in his writings on popular religion that the popular classes are ideologically conservative and that it will be as difficult to convince the subaltern classes on any intellectual or moral reform as it will be to persuade the ruling classes. The persistence of the link between the institutional Church in Argentina and a popular Catholicism that is formalistic, culturalistic, and perhaps even anticlerical would seem to confirm Gramsci's suspicions. The Argentine experience shows that, as the Catholic Church adapts the transformations of the modern capitalist world in Latin America, it still retains the power and the practice of traditional intellectuals.

The political future of a traditionalist and neoconservative Catholic Church will probably reside in its capacity to control a significant portion of education in Argentina. This would give it an important political presence, since its struggle to confront State "secularism" (divorce laws, policy on birth control, etc.) has not yielded the desired results. If the State were at any time to revise its policy of giving subsidies to Catholic education, one of the principal mechanisms of the Church for mobilization of the population and for recruitment would be profoundly affected. Given current conditions of educational planning, the official Church will have to fight more daringly to maintain its position. There is no doubt that education as a way of forming human capital is being questioned in the last decade of this century—especially the value of private and social rates of return of secondary and higher education. As a result, overall investment by the State at these levels has tended to drop. In a system of publicly subsidized private education, a shrinking of the role of the State—as advocated by models of structural adjustment that imply a reduction in subsidies and a subsequent increase in user fee— is not necessarily good news. Without State subsidies, the elite schools will continue to function, but the incidence of Catholic education among sectors of the middle class and the marginalized urban population will decline perceptibly.

Of course, there remains the logical possibility that the Popular Church will regain its institutional status and become "the voice of the voiceless" in the context of the dramatic situation of poverty, unemployment, lack of public services, and violence that affects large sectors of the population in Argentina in the nineties. However, the realignment of the World System, the crisis in socialism and Marxism, and the systematic campaign unleashed by the Vatican and the Commission for the Defense of the Faith against the "militant ecclesiology"[97] of Liberation Theology places the Popular Church in a difficult position from which to formulate a postmodern project that will fire the imagination of a portion of the population into a viable social and political undertaking—and even more so since the fourth Peronist government.

In the absence of an alternative of this type, the Church will continue to be an important traditional intellectual rooted in Argentine politics, although its authoritarian practices, its links to the armed forces, and (for some sectors of the population) its ambiguous position on the question of human rights has eroded its power of convocation. In spite of this, its ubiquitousness and its participation in an authoritarian alliance with the armed forces make the institutional Church an important actor in either the consolidation or—its opposite—the destabilization of Argentina's fragile democracy.

## NOTES

1. "My definition of Christendom covers the relationship encompassing the terms 'church,' 'state,' and 'civil society.' Within Christendom the relationship of church and civil society is mediated by the Church–State relationship" (Richard, 1987: 15).

2. The emphasis on corporatism as an ideology is quite common in the literature. The *Diccionario de política* defines it as "a doctrine that proposes the organization of the collectivity on the basis of associations that represent professional interests and activities (corporations). Thanks to the organic solidarity of concrete interests and the formulae for collaboration that derive from them, corporatism proposes the removal or neutralization of conflictive elements, namely, competition in economics, the class struggle in society, ideological differences in politics" (Bobbio & Matteucci, 1981: 431). Several types of corporatism may be identified, including Catholic, directed (e.g., fascism or national socialism), technocratic, democratic, and participationist, all of which are studied as doctrines or forms of organization of a concrete policy (see Bobbio & Mateucci, 1981: 431–38). Regarding Latin America, Alfred Stepan has drawn attention to what he sees as the ideological substratum or normative approach to politics that can also be formulated as an abstract model of governance: the organic statist tradition. He correctly distinguishes this ideology, political philosophy, doctrine, or normative approach from corporatism as "a particular set of policies and institutional arrangements for structuring interest representation" (Stepan, 1978: 46). Thus, it is important not to confuse what might be considered a guide or rationale (organic statism) with a concrete corporatist policy that may or may not be totally founded on such a rationale. For an analysis of corporatist policies, see, for example, Torres (1989) and Morales-Gómez & Torres (1990).

3. Historian Claudio Veliz has emphasized that there are four principal factors related to the centralist character of social and political arrangements in Latin America: (1) absence of a genuinely feudal experience; (2) absence of religious nonconformity and the resulting latitudinarian centralism of the dominant religion; (3) absence of any circumstance over time that could conceivably be taken as the counterpart of the European industrial revolution (allowing that some sort of industrial development could occur in Latin American without an industrial revolution, just as the process of urbanization has preceded rather than accompanied or succeeded industrial expansion); and (4) absence of those ideological, social, and political traits usually associated with liberal thought. In Veliz's analysis, there is no liberal past in Latin America. Even the

liberal experiments of the late nineteenth century and first decades of the twentieth century are only a "historical pause" in the development of a historical and secular heritage: the centralist tradition with Spanish roots (Veliz, 1980).

4. Mayol and his colleagues, from whom the figures are taken, add the following comments: "The numerous priests who yield to the revolutionary cause and play a major role in several countries often do so at the cost of the irregular situation of breaking with the ecclesiastical authorities, who continue to identify the religious order with the political order" (Mayol, Habegger, & Armada, 1970: 18).

5. The dispute between unitarians and federalists hinged, in the end, on political control of the country being centralized in Buenos Aires (as favored by the unitarian faction) or on a regime of provincial autonomy (as argued by the federalists), some of the key issues being the sharing with the provinces of the customs levied centrally in Buenos Aires and the creation of provincial customs. See Ernesto Palacio (1979); Romero Carranza, Rodríguez Varela & Ventura Flores Pirán (1975); Félix Luna (1980). For a detailed analysis of the conflict between Catholics and liberals, see the work of Catholic historians such as Néstor Tomás Auza (1981) and John J. Kennedy (1958).

6. Emilio Mignone argues

The Argentine Church was yoked to the state by reason of the *patronato* (patronage) of the Indies, and it remains both legally and ideologically under the conception that originally inspired it. The basic elements of *patronato* can be found in Alexander VI's famous bull of May 4, 1493, which gave to the Catholic kings of Spain and Portugal newly discovered lands in other parts of the world, and those yet to be discovered. A similar document, *Universalis Ecclesiae*, published by Julius II on July 28, 1508, further developed the legislation and was incorporated into the Laws of the Indies. Of course *patronato* was not a new institution in the history of the Catholic Church. It had existed in Europe, in various forms, since the Middle Ages, and its concession to temporal power were broadened with the consolidation of absolute monarchies during the Renaissance. In most Latin American countries it ended with the separation of Church and State. . . .

[In the case of the United Provinces of the River Plate:] Faced with the conflict over how to replace the seat vacated by Magistral in the cathedral church of Buenos Aires, the junta decided to consult two famous canonists in Córdoba, Gregario Funes and Juan Luis de Aguirre. Their separate opinions, signed September 15, 1810, agreed that *patronato* was a prerogative attached to the sovereignty of kings, not their persons. Hence it should be regarded as having passed on to the independent national government. Since then, all constitutions, both proposed and accepted, including the one in 1853, and the present one (excepting only the provisional statute of 1815) have maintained *patronato*, and its counterpart, the maintenance of Catholic worship by the State. *Patronato* is present in the constitutional initiatives of 1813, in the provisional rule of 1817, in the constitutions of 1819 and 1826. Successive legal opinions, and especially the well-known *Memorial Ajustado* of 1834, develop the doctrine in the direction that favors its maintenance. The central issue was appointing bishops and other ecclesiastic officials, a right claimed by the state. (Mignone, 1988: 72–74)

7. History shows that the Argentine Congress sent Canon Valentín Gómez to the Holy See in order to agree upon a concordat. The Franciscan Pedro Pacheco, former professor of canon law at the University of Córdoba, had also traveled there on his own initiative and convinced the Vatican curia to send to Argentina, *in partibus infidelium*, an apostolic vicar with the rank of bishop.

8. The contemporaneous Argentine social scientist José Ingenieros accused Funes of having been bought by Rivadavia (Kennedy, 1958: 128).

9. In its disputes with the newly born liberal State, the Catholic Church in Argentina reflected aspects of the traditional Iberian culture of Latin America as well as the more militant activity of the papacy, which was trying to win political ground and spiritual leadership in a world profoundly altered by social, political, and economic change. Atilio Boron offers an intelligent summary of the problem that afflicted the Church:

Instead of "the lights of reason," our continent inherited the Tribunal of the Holy Inquisition, and instead of translating the Bible into vernacular languages, as Luther did 500 years ago, our culture was in the grip of the Syllabus and the Index. What did the Syllabus propose? In its pages, the most widespread "errors" of the time were condemned without exceptions: civil marriage, the submission of the Church to the State, Socialism, Communism, secret societies, Masonry, liberalism, the principle of popular sovereignty, laicism, freedom of worship, freedom of the press, rationalism, materialism, and many other things besides. (Boron, 1990: 32)

10. The Argentine economist Federico Pinedo points out that, during the presidency of Avellaneda, "agricultural production intensifies notoriously. . . . [F]rom 1876 and after there begins the export of produce that is to become one of the firmest bases of wealth in Argentina and that by the year '84 has reached more than 1,000,000 tons of wheat and corn" (cited by Carranza, Rodríguez Varela & Ventura Flores Pirán, 1975: 257). This extraordinary production must not only be attributed to the expansion of the agricultural frontier and the arrival of foreign labor (250,000 immigrants supported by Avellaneda's Colonization Law arrived between 1875 and 1880), but also to the fact that the railway network doubled its extension during his presidency.

11. It should be noted that, during the debate on the law providing for civil marriage (see below in the text), the Catholic daily *La Unión* pointed out that of the 280,000 immigrants who landed in the country between 1880 and 1886 only 22,000 declared they were not Catholic (Carranza, Rodríguez Varela & Ventura Fores Pirán, 1975: 347).

12. *El Nacional*, December 13, 1855.

13. The belligerent attitude among Catholics was in accord with the militant policy of Pope Leo XIII, who based himself on the notion of "just resistance" elaborated by Saint Thomas Aquinas, and argued in the encyclical *Libertas* that "if the laws of States are in open opposition to natural or divine law, or if they offend the Church, or contradict religious

duties, or violate the authority of Christ vested in the Supreme Pontiff, then resistance is a duty and obedience a crime" (cited by Carranza, Rodríguez Varela & Ventura Flores Pirán, 1975: 306).

14. As Atilio Boron points out, this was a decisive period of social confrontation: "The strikes by workers went from 80 in 1916 to 128, 196 and 367 in the three following years, while the number of strikers, barely 24,321 in 1916—the first year of the radical government—went up to 136,062 in the following year, 133,042 in 1918, and 308,967 in 1919, the year of the Semana Trágica" (Boron, 1976: 418).

15. The fall of radicalism has been the subject of broad historical scrutiny. Traditional explanations attribute its immediate causes to the advanced age of the leader Hipólito Yrigoyen, government corruption, fights within the party, or the ineptitude of Yrigoyen. In fact, it was when Yrigoyen became ill on September 5, and power remained in the hands of the vice-president (who declared a state of emergency), that the conspiracy headed by Uriburu evolved from an idea to a coup. Another possible analysis is to ignore these facts (which doubtless had some impact) and to assert that the forces of the traditional conservative oligarchy—which sought to restore a conservative government by uniting economic hegemony and political leadership—and the emerging force of an integral and aggressive Catholicism found an appropriate ally in the military institution to support their antiliberal, anti-Masonic and antisocialist conspiracy. The uprising of General Uriburu occurred on September 6, 1930, with the connivance of a number of young men opposed to their officers and to "antipersonalist" intellectuals (including the Catholic intelligentsia united around the recently created periodical *Criterio*), and with the war cry of the nationalist poet Leopoldo Lugones who, in the words of an influential Catholic conservative historian, declared that "it was 'the hour of the sword.' With this call for the army to intervene in politics, [Lugones] intended to indicate the need to restore the moral values of honor and patriotism that utilitarian politics had more than forgotten and of which that institution [the army] appeared as the traditional guardian" (Palacio, 1979: 654). It should also be stated that the struggle for control of Yacimientos Petrolíferos Argentinos (Argentinean Petroleum Resources), headed at that time by General Enrique Mosconi, is a factor to keep in mind, since nationalist historians have subsequently attributed the influence of American petroleum interests to the September Revolution (Palacio, 1979: 659).

16. Boron offers a stimulating argument to explain how the Church began to come out of isolation during the second government of General

Julio Argentino Roca (from 1898 to 1904), who had been the champion of laicization:

The new winds that began to blow with the new century began to modify this situation: on the one hand, the oligarchy, still proud, but historically exahusted, was losing its energy and its leaders strove to restore relations with the Church. The danger of a war with Chile [the border conflict having reached one of its decisive points toward the end of the century, but being resolved with the May Pacts of May 28, 1902] caused General Roca's second government to attempt to alleviate external pressures by renewing diplomatic relations with the Vatican, broken since 1894 and his previous government. The result was a kind of sincere repentance for the lay past of the regime and a renewed hostility against foreigners who taunted Argentina with being a bucolic country of "cows and grain". . . . On the other hand, what contributed to the solid recovery of the Church, which would then materialize in the thirties and forties, was something else: the failure of the classes tied to the oligarchical alliance in their plant to establish a liberal mass order. (Boron, 1990: 83–84)

17. Cited by Ana María Ezcurra (1988). The relation between Church and culture was broached by J. C. Scannone more than fifteen years ago in an article in which he argued, "I believe that there are two pitfalls to avoid: both conservative integralism, which confuses things, and absolute autonomism (whether of neoliberal or Marxist coloration), which separates them" (Scannone, 1975: 254). He concludes his contribution to Liberation Theology by stating,

The evangelization of culture (and of cultures), when understood in this way, presupposes respect both for the autonomy of the temporal and the transcendence and freedom of faith. More than a (thematic) synthesis between faith and culture, it is a *symbiosis* of the two. But it is a symbiosis that implies articulation of meaning (at least thematically); a symbiosis that also tends to present itself as a thematic object; and a symbiosis not only in the life and action of men, but also of peoples. (Scannone, 1975: 259)

The suggestion of a symbiosis between culture and faith that is both thematic (of tradition and hierarchy) and popular (of the people, the simple and the poor) anticipates one of the possible directions of Liberation Theology in a populist mode.

18. Ten years later would occur the creation of specialized movements (following the French and Belgian model), such as the JOC (Juventud Obrera Católica, or Young Catholic Workers), the JAC (Juventud Agraria Católica, or Agrarian Catholic Youth), the JUC (Juventud Universitaria Católica, or Catholic University Youth), and the JEC (Juventud de Educación Secundaria Católica, or Catholic Secondary School Youth), which were distinguished by class and social environment (Mallimaci, 1988: 10).

19. It should be recalled at this point that both modernism and integralism were projects that arose in Europe, were rooted in the Italian experience of the Roman Church, and were a concern in Antonio Gramsci's analyses of religion, science, and common sense (see our Chapter 4). In his *Prison Notebooks*, Gramsci affirms that "modernism has not created 'religious orders,' but a

political party—Christian Democracy" (Gramsci, 1980: 332). Integralism was a reaction to modernism associated with the papacy of Pius X; it sought, as a theological movement, to reaffirm the authority of the Church in relation to secularization.

20. On this question, see Fernando Martínez Paz (1966) and Ricardo G. Parera (1967). Based on a neo-Thomist interpretation, Maritain offered Catholic intellectuals in Argentina the bases for an integral Christian philosophy. His ground-breaking work *The Primacy of the Spiritual* (or *The Things That Are Not Caesar's*) supports the idea of a Christian humanism. In response to the antifascist struggles of World War II, Maritain adopted a decidedly democratic stance that, in the postwar period, was put forward as a democratic and pluralistic society on a world scale, reflecting a new Christianity. This kind of thought— the foundation of a Catholic politics (not of Catholics in politics, but of a political party with a clear Christian affiliation that would culminate in proposals for a Christian-Democratic party)—would eventually be in frank opposition to integralist neo-Christianity. Maritain visited Argentina for the first time in 1936, at the time of publication of his book *Humanisme Intégral* in France. Although well received by a large group of Catholic intellectuals, his thought was controversial and subject to many attacks; he was accused of heterodoxy by Christian nationalists, and especially by Father Julio Meinvielle, as Martínez Paz points out (1966: 162).

21. Considered one of the greatest exponents of Argentine integralism, Meinvielle's major works are cited in our bibliography (see Meinvielle, 1932, 1936, 1961 & 1970).

22. Boron writes as follows:

Since 1930, the Church changed progressively but methodically into the institution that provided the meanings and values which saturate society as a whole. Its domination is invisible, or scarcely perceivable to less informed spirits, but its predominance is practically irresistible at the level of the beliefs, opinions and values of the masses, and this is in spite of the fact that insofar as the encompassment and organization of the popular classes are concerned their results were less positive. (Boron 1990: 90)

23. One of the most suggestive analyses of this association, with its tragic consequences in the seventies, may be found in Emilio Mignone (1988).

24. John J. Kennedy, who describes the understanding and emotional approach apparent in Catholic thought of the time, argues that Monsignor De Andrea's model differed from the classical European corporatist State because he saw that the combination of corporativism (as a complex linked to different interest groups including labor, business, industry, agriculture, the professions, and the intellectuals) with democracy would result in the best possible form of government (Kennedy, 1958: 143).

25. His contribution for more than twenty years to the creation of Argentinean Catholic culture and his constant preaching for a Catholic social order, as opposed to the prevailing political alternatives, make Monsignor Franceschi

a controversial figure for historical assessment. Floreal Forni—writing from the perspective of Peronist criticism, and well informed through his past as a militant Catholic and student who fought in university movements—described Franceschi as the most moderate voice of the official Church (Forni, 1987a: 218). Other analysts, who mention the nazi-fascist tendencies attributed to him, also defend him (Kennedy, 1958: 172). A reading of some of Franceschi's editorials permits us to state that, if he was a moderate voice in Catholic integralism, then the description of the ideological position of the greater part of the Church hierarchy presents enormous difficulties for any analyst using a system of classification in which fascism represents the extreme right; the question to resolve is what lies further to the right of fascism.

26. The polemic between Meinvielle and Castellani over Maritain following the visit of the French philosopher to Argentina in 1936 may be found in the pages of *Criterio* (see Meinvielle, 1937, and Castellani, 1937). The simplicity of Meinvielle's analyses do not compare with Castellani's sophistication and versatility. In addition to being a political philosopher, Leonardo Castellani was also a novelist, short story writer, and literary critic and in 1963 was commentator and translator from the Greek of Saint John's Apocalypse.

27. The First Catholic Congress took place in 1884 in the midst of the debate over the new laicizing measures of the liberal government. The Second Catholic Congress was held 23 years later in 1907, and the Third in Córdoba in 1908 (Auza, 1968).

28. According to Auza, "The UDC was not a party and did not even attempt to be one; in accordance with forms then current in Europe, it was essentially a social and economic movement in character, constituted by citizens with an obligatory political vote, which in fact made it into a political force. It did not constitute a party or an electoral organization; it was limited to bringing its votes to the candidate or party that offered the best guarantees in relation to its program" (1984: 50).

29. Argentina managed to respond to this demand in spite of the stagnation in production by the rural sector after 1930.

30. Perón was president first during the period 1946–52, then after reelection in 1952 until the coup of 1955, and, finally, after being elected for a third time in 1973 until his death in June 1974.

31. John J. Kennedy's evaluation of Catholic thought during the period 1935–46 includes the following: "The charges of anti-democratic intent, especially in terms of a pro-fascist attitude, have been exaggerated. . . . A second conclusion is that there is probably a need for re-examination of much of the Catholic position between 1935 and 1946 when a great many of the criticisms leveled against it were colored by a view of Communism which most of the critics no longer hold" (1958: 185–86).

32. Father Pedro Bandanelli, for example, bitterly criticized the bishops during the second presidency of Perón for their support of the creation of the

Christian-Democratic Party. He was to exclaim in his characteristically blunt style, "I have never seen a bishop—and I have seen many—taking mate, for example, in a humble country home; but I have seen them, one and a thousand times, taking five o'clock tea in aristocratic houses" (Badanelli, 1960: 33).

33. It should be recalled that the *opposition* to Peronism was composed of a complex mix, including most radicals, the Communist Party, provincial conservative parties, and some sectors of the Catholic right, all of whom were encouraged by then Ambassador of the United States Spauille Braden, who characterized Perón as a fascist and argued tirelessly and publicly for the creation of an anti-Peronist front to block him from becoming the government in the elections of 1945.

34. Remembering the death of Marechal, Carlos Mugica commented to us in person in 1973 that Marechal was one of the first to understand the Christian values of Peronism on the basis of its effectiveness among the popular classes, not just its foundation on the social doctrine of the Church. An example of the link between Peronist thought, neo-Thomist philosophy, and the social doctrine of the Church may be found in Juan Domingo Perón, *La Comunidad Organizada* (1974). See also Carlos Mugica's "Los valores cristianos del peronismo" (in Mugica 1984: 63–81) and, on a more philosophical social level, the reflections of César Sánchez Aizcorbe (1973: 94–116).

35. The well-known pastoral letter of the Argentine bishops of November 15, 1945, on the duties of Catholics in the forthcoming elections, constituted a virtual endorsement of Perón's candidacy when it suggested that no Catholic could affiliate with or vote for parties that promoted the separation of Church and State (as did the opposition to Peronism), or for parties that proposed the "suppression of legal dispositions that recognized the rights of religion and particularly of the religious oath," or for parties that proposed laicism in the schools or a law for legal divorce. All this—in the context of a political campaign in which Perón had made his adherence to the social doctrine of the Church explicit, and against an opposition consolidated in the Unión Democrática (Democratic Union) that combined communists, Masons, and antilaicists, many of them radicals or members of socialist parties—doubtless contributed to the Catholic vote facilitating Perón's victory at the ballot box (Donini, 1985: 55). As Fortunato Mallimaci notes (1988: 77), medals appeared during the election campaign bearing the image of the Virgin of Luján (patroness of Argentina) and the face of Perón on the reverse. The socially and politically oriented Movimiento Cívico Católico (Catholic Civic Movement) spoke of the *"descamisados de Cristo"* (*descamisado* literally means "without a shirt," and figuratively "poor" or "down-and-out"), a clear reference to the suburban and farm workers who provoked a number of organized incidents on October 17 and whom the press described as the *"descamisados de Perón,"* given that they had taken off their shirts in the heat of the day during the demonstration in front of Government House—the Casa Rosada—in the Plaza de Mayo. The oligarchical right and

the virulently anti-Peronist elements used pejorative phrases to refer to Perón's partisans or the descamisados and spoke of them as "*el aluvión zoológico*" (the primeval slime) or "*cabecitas negras*" (niggers). At the same time, the periodical *Criterio*—particularly Monsignor Franceschi—adopted critical positions with respect to the future Peronist government, beginning by criticizing Perón's use of the social encyclicals in his speeches. In one of his articles, Franceschi wrote, "The encyclicals ask that society attend especially to the weakest and the unprotected, but not exclusively to them. It is not a question of justice for a single class, but for all classes. . . . And it will never be allowed for purely temporal—let alone partisan—purposes to use the word of so elevated an origin and so eminent an authority" (cited by Mallimaci, 1988: 78).

36. Gerardo Farrell, in *Iglesia y Pueblo en Argentina*, maintains that Peronism is an authentic national social-Christianity.

Finally Peronism comes on the scene with an explicit example of teaching that is a temporal concretion of the Gospels. . . . Perón himself, showing that his convictions were not only the product of a social accommodation, would, as Pope Pius XII would maintain, give the final blow to laicism through his teaching and his conduct. He undertook public acts of worship, his teaching is founded on Christian ethics and morals themselves, and he displayed the fact by citing the social encyclicals as the documents that inspired Justicialismo. At the same time, he established the instruction of religion in the schools. (Farrell, 1976; cited by Ezcurra, 1988: 53)

37. In spite of this, one of the most lucid analysts of the time—with a good dose of chauvinism, overconfidence in the revolutionary values of a national and popular movement such as Peronism, and a limited perception of the international context—saw Argentina as "one of the key places in the world, the link in the chain where Latin American dependence could be broken" (Hernández Arregui, 1957: 29).

38. A detailed discussion of the model of development in the region and of the social, political, and economic implications of U.S. intervention and monopolistic capitalism, as well as the reaccommodation of the dominant classes both in enclave societies and in societies that developed more autonomously, may be found in a number of classic texts, such as those by Fernando H. Cardoso & Enzo Faletto (1978), Helio Jaguaribe (1962), Celso Furtado (1974), and Helio Jaguaribe, Aldo Ferrer, Miguel S. Wionczek, et al. (1970). The most complete synthesis of this literature is still Aldo Solari, Rolando Franco & Joel Jutkowitz (1976).

39. The role in Peronist policy of Evita's confessor, the Jesuit Hernán Benítez; his activities as a mediator in conflictive circumstances, as in the National Eucharistic Congress of 1950; and the influence of his ideas on the Peronist movement while he was close to Evita, and therefore to Juan Perón, are briefly mentioned by Forni, who gives a positive assessment of his intellectual and political work: "On a religious level, [Benítez] is a legitimate precursor,

beyond his partisan passions, with the intellectual tools and the experiences of his time, of the Latin American movement of Liberation Theology" (Forni, 1987b: 202). See Benítez (1953).

40. Sebreli's words are quite unequivocal:

The relations between the Army and Evita expose the military mind: its class prejudice, its esprit de corps, its patriarchalism, its misogyny and typically petty bourgeois moral hypocrisy. Contempt for women is characteristic of religious and military groups because they are constituted on the basis of a desexualized friendship represented by comradeship among men alone; in which women act only as a disruptive force. But, in the case of Evita, the attack on her supposed immorality was, above all, an unconscious way of hiding the real social content that she implied: her identification with the working class. (Sebreli, 1990: 94–95)

A more critical view of Evita's role in promoting feminist thinking and polities in Argentina is Guivant (1986).

41. In 1952 the Movimiento Humanista Universitario (University Humanist Movement) was founded. It was Catholic in origin and sought to find a place in the National University, distinguishing itself from traditional conservatism, from Marxism as represented by the Federación Universitaria Argentina (University Federation of Argentina), and from the nationalism of official Peronism as represented by the Confederación General Universitaria (General University Confederation). Guido Di Tella, Guillermo O'Donnell, and Floreal Forni were some of its prominent members.

42. For some Catholic sociologists influenced by the analyses of Aldo Büntig, popular Catholicism—as the religion of the people—is "the normal result of the process of institutionalization and inculturation, proper to all universal religions that become a natural part of a particular socio-cultural world" (Soneira, 1982: 7). For this reason, it is one of the fundamental psychological, sociological, and axiological layers of popular Argentine culture.

43. Nevertheless, Forni notes to his dismay that, true to the orientation of the Vatican at the time, "Pope Pius XII, far from considering [Perón's government] a model of social democracy popularly applied, held it to be authoritarian and unreliable" (Forni, 1987b: 207).

44. The term *Forjista* is derived from the acronym FORJA, representing Fuerza Organizada de la Juventud Argentina (Organized Force of Argentinean Youth).

45. Forni's comment was written with regard to the bases of the interpretation proposed by Gerardo Farrell (Farrell, 1976).

46. Farrell's argument (1976) is that the tactical and tacit alliance between Peronism and the official Church that inspired their relation in the mid-forties would end when it became Peronism's new strategic initiative as representative of the Catholic people—therefore situating Perón much closer to the hierarchy than the hierarchy was prepared to accept.

47. Forni argues (1987b: 222) that Vatican policy during the Cold War was allied to that of the United States, so that relations between the nuncio and Perón were cool from the very beginning, thereby giving rise to the paradoxical situation in which a self-proclaimed Catholic country—a country that ostensibly applied the social teaching of the Church in public policy and endorsed its privileges entirely as an official institution—was treated with reservation by Rome, which kept its distance.

48. John William Cooke was a young Peronist deputy, and then Perón's personal representative in the country toward the end of the fifties after the fall of the president. Cooke is given credit as being one of the principal founders and ideologues of the "Peronist resistance" and of so-called revolutionary Peronism, as opposed to other tendencies (including the nationalist-fascist versions and the populist and/or negotiated "policies") that acquired a social-democratic and syndicalist political orientation, especially in the version of the metallurgical union leader Augusto Timoteo Vandor. Cooke's was an interpretation of Peronism as revolutionary nationalism—the only real alternative for constructing a national socialism. After the Cuban Revolution, he sought to persuade Perón to establish his residence in exile not in Madrid, but in Havana, thereby indicating that the position of his regime was both anti-imperialist and pro-socialist. Cooke's writings may rightly be considered among the first systematic theoretical works to use Marxism as a theory of revolution and the Peronist movement as the revolutionary party appropriate to the circumstances of Argentina. (See Cooke, 1970a, 1970b, 1972).

49. Law No. 12978, April 29, 1947. As Hernán Benítez remarked in 1953, "for these ten years, in the relations between the Church and the Peronist State, there was a basic understanding and a heartfelt cordiality between the supreme leaders" (Benítez, 1953: 377).

50. In a speech on November 10, 1954, Perón denounced certain clergymen linked to Acción Católica who engaged in anti-Peronist activities by trying to organize groups of professionals, university students, and workers. Perón insisted that this had nothing to do with the Church as an institution (Perón, 1964: 184) and even claimed that the hierarchy agreed with him in condemning these priests for departing from their specifically religious functions in order to devote themselves to activities that were clearly of a political character (Perón, 1964: 185). He was particularly irritated with a priest at the University of Córdoba "who says that we have to make a choice between Christ and Perón. I have never had a conflict with Christ. Precisely what I am trying to do is defend the doctrines of Christ, which for over two hundred years priests of this type in Argentina have sought unsuccessfully to destroy" (Perón, 1964: 187).

51. According to Ricardo Parera, "The weight of the Peronist regime, the impossibility of bringing about concrete civic action, and the lack of co-ordination among different groups caused these to relax their activities and

to fall back onto the task of enriching their knowledge" (Parera, 1967: 73).

52. Seen in historical perspective, however, it is clear that as Forni argues (1987a) Mounier was much more radical in his appreciation of this type of Catholic party than many others who came under the banner of Catholic personalism. In this regard, see Candide Moix:

Mounier was of the opinion that no political group should carry the adjective "Christian," unless it wished to expose itself to politico-religious interference. In his eyes, the development undergone by Christian democratic parties throughout Europe was not a sign of renovation, but "a cancer on the sick body of Christianity." Having said this, he did not doubt the value of certain Christian democrats, their good will and the undeniable service they rendered. But always and everywhere, what is important for Mounier is the struggle against confusion. In general, he reproached Christian democratic parties for their mediocre caution, their ignorance of historical realities, and the confusion they entertained between politics and religion: "Born to deliver the Christian world from its reactionary solidarities, the democratic parties, through a singular fate, risk becoming the ultimate refuge for them." (Moix, 1960: 269)

53. Cardinal Santiago Luis Copello's negotiating style and his conciliatory positions during the first administration and the first part of the second earned him tough criticism after the Revolución Libertadora, the coup that ousted Perón (Mallimaci, 1988). As Forni remarks, once Peronism was deposed "Copello was displaced on account of his excessively conciliatory spirit during the conflict, and after an interregnum under Monsignor Lafitte, a harsh anti-Peronist, Cardinal Antonio Caggiano became primate and Military Vicar (a newly instituted position that sealed an alliance between the two powers)" (Forni, 1988: 135).

54. Perón was reelected in 1952 for another six years, in the first election in Argentina in which women were able to vote, but was removed from power by the Revolución Libertadora in September 1955.

55. The priest from Santa Fé, Father Pedro Badanelli, reflects this view of reality in Argentina, believing that he can see a clear link between Peronism and popular Catholicism in clear opposition to the view of the hierarchy, whom he considers as having a pious vision of history totally lacking in realism. In order to document his analysis, Badanelli relates the story of how, after receiving instructions from the hierarchy to introduce Acción Católica in his rural parish, he invited a Jesuit priest to give a retreat for the young men and, when it was over, to say Mass. As a way of celebrating the consecration of these young men, Badanelli held a barbecue at which the Jesuit preached his last sermon, insisting on the virtues of perseverance and, especially, chastity. Badanelli relates that "at a certain time, already quite late, the boys made their farewells and left. . . . [O]n the following day, I found out—not without a little hilarity on my part, I confess—that to 'celebrate' their official admission to Acción Católica, the place they had gone to was a brothel" (Badanelli, 1960: 70).

56. Félix Luna (1980) argues that the Church had maintained a position for itself as the only independent institution refusing to associate itself in any substantial way with the Peronist State. Therefore, when in October 1954 Perón accused a group of prelates of being traitors and false Peronists, he began a process in which there was no turning back.

Even had he thought about it, he couldn't have committed a graver error. By attacking the one national institution that still held an independent position, he automatically converted it into the nucleus to which all the dispersed forces of opposition would adhere. The church hierarchy and the simple parish priests, out of a natural espirit de corps, stood shoulder to shoulder in defence of those who had been attacked. The Catholic faithful felt the winds of martyrdom striking them gloriously in the face. Lukewarm Catholics became fervent believers. And, in six months, that uniform and regimented country saw a formidable force appear that reacted to every one of the blows dealt by the government. (Luna, 1980: 248)

57. Mecham's analysis is that the same thing happened to the Argentine Church in relation to the "Peronist dictatorship" as in relation to the "Rosista dictatorship" of a hundred years before, when it ultimately succumbed to the power of the State, collaborated with it, and was "converted into a servile instrument of the tyranny [of Rosas]" (Mecham, 1966: 232). Something similar would have happened with Perón, but "fortunately, Perón's breaking of *entente* afforded Argentine clergy the opportunity to recover some dignity and prestige" (Mecham, 1966: 248).

58. Perón was exiled initially in Paraguay, then in Panama, and later accepted an invitation from General Franco to live in Madrid.

59. In fact, Argentina has shown a surprising political instability that has led to a profound breakdown of its democratic tradition over an extended period of time. Between 1916 and 1986 there was, on average, a new president every thirty-one months. During that period of 70 years, there have been twenty-nine presidents, although, constitutionally, there should have been only twelve or (or fourteen, if the two who resigned and one who died in office are taken into account). In the same period, seventeen presidents were army generals, only one of whom (Perón) was elected, the remainder having acquired the office after a coup or after a change of president during a military dictatorship.

60. Félix Luna described the situation very well when he remarked that the

[Revolución Libertadora] divided the country with bloodstains and tremendous arbitrariness that, as usually happens, gradually erased earlier memories. And the popular reply was similar to that of 1931: in the constituent elections of 1957, the overwhelming number of blank votes [the Peronist vote] was a decidedly eloquent pronouncement. From that moment, nobody could govern with the Peronists, but nobody could govern without them. Arturo Frondizi had to strike an agreement with them and fell because they won; Arturo Illia fell because they were about to win in 1967; Juan Carlos Onganía fell because the order and hierarchy of his structure crumbled amid the flames of the

Cordobazo; and Alejandro Agustín Lanusse had to yield to the triumph of the exiled leader. (Luna, 1980: 238)

61. The vote of July 28, 1957, had already shown the electoral strength of Peronism, since the blank vote ordered by Perón amounted to 2,115,861—a virtual majority over the party elected, the Unión Cívica Radical del Pueblo (People's Civic Radical Union), which obtained 2,106,524. However, when Frondizi was elected, only 836,658 cast blank ballots.

62. When on November 29, 1960, the Peronist Party was banned by decree throughout the entire country, the confrontation reached its most crucial point.

63. The references to the colors is taken from those used by the armed forces during military exercises to distinguish between contending units.

64. The Peronist blank votes amounted to 1,438,054.

65. The presence of the Church in Argentinean labor politics acquired a new dimension when Father José Ruperto and other priests placed themselves at the head of a march by unemployed members of the meat packers union who had been locked out by the closure of the refrigeration company Swift & Armour. The march was stopped by the police, but Father Ruperto was allowed to continue on as far as Government House (Dussel, 1983a: 244; Mayol, Habegger, & Armada, 1970: 140–144).

66. Referring to the policy of income redistribution proposed by the Radicals, Mónica Peralta Ramos remarks, "The re-appearance of the distributionist model represents the reaction of small and middle-sized business to the process of industrial concentration" (Peralta Ramos, 1972: 136).

67. The Cursillos de Cristiandad were spiritual retreats organized by Opus Dei as a means of converting Catholics to militant action.

68. Monsignor Podestá would be relieved of his duties on December 4, 1967, but remains in the history books as one of the few bishops able to approach the Peronist unions while he exercised his ministry in the heavily populated industrial area of Avellaneda.

69. See the history published by the movement itself (Movimiento, 1970b: 12).

70. The outlawing of Peronism in the 1962 elections and the nullification of the election of the governor of Buenos Aires won by the Peronist union leader Framini showed that, far from being an obsolete political force, Peronism had to be reckoned with as an important actor on the political scene. Parallel to the survival of historical Peronism and Peronist syndicalism, an entire new generation of Argentineans began to read writers such as Arturo Jauretche, Abelardo Ramos, Rodolfo Puiggrós, and J. J. Hernández Arregui who offered a view of Peronism that was not like fascism, but a nationalist, anti-imperialist, and national-socialist movement. This historical revisionism would have an impact on the Christian elements that joined the political struggle toward the end of the sixties. The new image of an intransigent Peronism—an image adhered to by grass-roots Christian-Democrats, the Sacerdotes para el Tercer Mundo, and

nationalists and socialists opposed to the neoliberal project of Onganía and the authoritarianism of the Revolución Argentina—was the key point for the formation of a new political alliance. These elements converged without any premeditated plan, militantly opposed to the regime whose social expression was the Cordobazo (see below in the text, and also note 73 below). At that time, the Colombian priest Camilo Torres symbolized the Christian revolutionary (see Torres, 1966), while, during its short life, the periodical *Cristianismo y Revolución*, edited from September 1966 until 1971 by García Elorrio, united these politically activated postconciliar elements for whom there must have been a clear separation between specific manifestations of faith (liturgical acts, the sacraments, reflection on the Gospels) and political practice that denounced the connivance of the institutional Church with the temporal power (Mayol, Habegger, & Armada, 1970).

71. The meeting brought one hundred forty-six prelates together, including cardinals, archbishops, and bishops; fourteen members of religious orders; six nuns; fifteen laypersons (four of them women); and various consultants, many of them linked to Liberation Theology (Dussel, 1979b: 74–75).

72. The economic policy of Krieger Vasena, the second minister for finance during the Revolución Argentina, was the most articulate and ambitious project developed in the postwar period for remodeling the structure of production and inserting Argentina into the World System in association with the policies of the United States and multinational, monopolistic capital. See Guillermo O'Donnell (1972, 1988) and Oscar Braun (1969, 1971) for a detailed analysis.

73. The Cordobazo has been the subject of countless interpretations as a feature of political struggle in an urban context. The least plausible is perhaps that which emphasizes the impoverishment of the working class and the deterioration of the economy. In structural terms, 1965–72 was one of the periods of most consistent growth, with an average annual increase in GNP of 4.2 percent, and only one year in which economic growth was less than the increase in the population. The creation of paid employment at an annual rate of 2.8 percent, as opposed to population growth of 1.8 percent, discredits any argument based on an increase in unemployment. Finally, in terms of real wages, it could be argued that the Córdoba workers who rebelled against state authoritarianism were among the best paid workers in the country (Torres, 1978).

74. The conflict between orthodox Peronists and the neo-Peronists who did not follow the dictates of Perón issued from Madrid had reached considerable proportions when the Congreso Normalizador (Congress to Re-Organize the Trade Union) was held on March 28–30, 1968. A more radicalized element headed by Ongaro (in alliance with orthodox Peronism) took control of the Congress but was not accepted by the neo-Peronist element headed by Vandor, with the result that the CGT broke in two: the CGT de los Argentinos, under the leadership of Raymundo Ongaro of the Graphics Workers Federation of

Buenos Aires; and the CGT de Azopardo, led by Augusto Timoteo Vandor, which elected Vicente Roqué as secretary-general.

75. The Montoneros were members of a Peronist guerrilla movement that constituted the greatest presence among the many young people who became politically active in the seventies. Many of the earliest Montoneros came from the right-wing nationalist movement Tacuara and others had been Acción Católica militants. Juan José Sebreli has argued that Marxism was grafted onto basic Christian principles, but that the influence of Catholicism would leave an indelible imprint on Montonero ideology, including "irrationalism, sectarianism, asceticism, the cult of individual sacrifice in honor of humanity, the yearning for absolutes, the adoration of death" (cited by Hilb & Lutzky, 1984: 106).

76. Carlos Mugica exemplified the new generation of Argentine priests who adopted a compromise with the people and an explicit political practice as a form of praxis and understanding of the Gospels. He was born on October 8, 1930, and was murdered by the Triple A (Alianza Anticommunista Argentina—Argentine Anticommunist Alliance—the Argentinean version of the death squads) on May 11, 1974, during the third Peronist government. He came from a comfortable, anti-Peronist, Catholic family, studied law, entered the diocesan seminary of Devoto in 1951 at the age of twenty-one, and was ordained in 1959. After his ordination, he worked in the North East Chaco-Santa Fé region, a highly depressed rural area with large native communities, in Argentina. When he returned to Buenos Aires, he was appointed vicar in the parish of Nuestra Señora del Socorro and also fulfilled duties in the secretariat of Cardinal Caggiano. He served as advisor to university students and, from 1963 until his death, taught as professor of theology in the Faculty of Political and Social Sciences and in the School of Medicine at the Universidad del Salvador. He studied for a year in France in 1968, an experience that marked his perception of world problems. When he returned to Argentina in 1969, he went to live in a poverty-stricken shantytown, following the tradition of the French and Belgian worker priests. Recognized as a *villero* (shantytown) leader, he was invited to accompany the two hundred personalities who went to Madrid to seek out Perón and accompany him back to Argentina; and on his return, he was offered a privileged place on the list of Peronist candidates for election of federal deputies. However, he did not accept this offer, declining even before the bishops decreed that priests could not accept political nominations (Mugica, 1984). During the early seventies, he worked with revolutionary Peronism, and especially with Juventud Peronista (Peronist Youth), until the organization was splintered on May 1, 1974, when Perón criticized the left-wing Peronista-Montoneros and thousands of young people withdrew from the massive demonstration in front of Government House where Perón was speaking. At that moment, Mugica closed ranks with the Juventud Peronista faction that remained loyal to Perón instead of attempting to create another alternative. At the same time, instead of

avidly pursuing the vicissitudes of politics, he renewed his political and religious work in the shantytowns.

I remember Mugica from his theology classes at the Universidad del Salvador. He was a charismatic and passionate man, with an extraordinary sensitivity and capacity to communicate with different sectors of society. His theology classes were a surprising experience in an Argentina that was in a state of profound social and political convulsion. With so many students registered in his courses and many more auditing them, people arrived very early to get a seat, like at some prestigious artistic function; and in classrooms that could squeeze in forty to fifty persons, there were more than eighty or ninety students, with people sitting in the corridor or peering in through the windows to catch his theological analyses.

77. The "villero" priests were termed thus not just because they lived in religious communities in a *villa* (shantytown)—Mugica lived in Retiro, a *villa* close to where the railway lines converged on Buenos Aires—but because they participated very actively in one of the most important social movements of the time, the Movimientos Villeros, which demanded municipal services such as water and electricity. The movements arose from the attempt by the municipality of Buenos Aires to eradicate the shantytowns on the outskirts of the capital at the end of the sixties.

78. In his analysis of foreign missionaries in Argentina, Ernest Sweeney argues that, although 90 percent of the population declares itself Catholic, only 10 percent practices—which results in very few vocations to the priesthood and religious orders and a need for priests and religious from abroad. Given the cultural connotations, the Church cannot accept that Argentina is "mission territory," but Sweeney's analysis of foreign missionaries between 1938 and 1962 shows nonetheless that, without the addition of the strength from outside the country, many of the works of the Church in Argentina could not be maintained (Sweeney, 1970). At present, there are a total of 2,284 parishes, 4,693 diocesan and religious priests, 14,245 members of religious orders, and 1,543 seminarians. At the same time, the Church controls 15,189 educational establishments, with 1,500,409 students (Cardinal Juan C. Aramburu, cited in Ezcurra, 1988: 190).

79. Showing a visceral anticommunism, and using an argument that combines sacristy gossip with data possibly derived from State information services, Carlos A. Sacheri (1970a) reviews the biographies of those whom he describes as precursors or leaders of the Sacerdotes para el Tercer Mundo, including the French worker priest Gilbert Rufenach; Father Miguel Ramondetti, the first secretary of the Argentine movement, who is accused of being a communist sympathizer; Father Arturo Paoli, an Italian member of the Hermanitos de Jesús (Little Brothers of Jesus), well known for his work in the quebracho forests of northern Santa Fé, and many others. The basis of his argument is the existence of a conspiracy of Jews, Masons, and communists seeking to use

the Church for their ends and exploiting the heresy of modernism, which, in contrast with other heresies, does not lead to separation from the Church, but to an attempt to change it from within.

80. Ferrer sought to expand the national market and exports at the same time. To this end, he used two instruments: the "buy Argentina" law (to expand the internal market), and a head tax on cattle in combination with a prohibition on the retail sale of meat (so that cattle producers would release their animals to the export market).

81. Political violence in Argentina reached unprecedented levels after the events at Ezeiza on June 20, 1973, when all the Peronist organizations marched in their thousands to the international airport of Ezeiza to receive their leader on his return. At what was expected to be a popular picnic, groups on the left and the right confronted each other militarily, causing a number of dead and wounded that has never been accurately confirmed (300 dead is one figure cited) and confirming that even the remarkable but always difficult coexistence of the different political elements within Peronism had come to an end. War had replaced politics (Latin American Studies Association, 1978: 19–24).

82. The number of newspaper reports that tell of kidnapping, public assassinations, terrorist acts, the increase in death squads such as the Triple A (see note 76 above), and the repression of political activists are overwhelming. Once the Peronist right began systematically to remove elements of the Peronist youth from the provincial governments, through federal intervention in the province of Buenos Aires, Córdoba, Formosa, Salta, and Santa Cruz, important members of the historical Peronist resistance—such as Atilio López, vice-governor of Córdoba and a well-known union leader—were murdered. Legal guarantees and public security were profoundly affected when such outstanding defenders of of political prisoners as the lawyers Rodolfo Ortega Peña and Silvio Frondizi, among others, were killed, adding their names to a long list of political victims never clarified by a Peronist government that succumbed to a whirlwind of confrontations among internal factions, erratic political decisions, corruption, administrative incompetence, and political favoritism. For a history of the period—especially its repression and violence—see Latin American Studies Association (1978). Miguel Bonasso (1988), and especially Richard Gillespie (1987).

83. The origins of the Ejército Revolucionario del Pueblo (ERP) go back to the mid-sixties when it was a faction within the Trotskyite group Palabra Obrera (Worker's Word), which was active from 1964 until the creation of the Partido Revolucionario de los Trabajadores (Revolutionary Party of the Workers), of which the ERP became the armed wing under the leadership of Luis Pujals and Mario Roberto Santucho. See Gillespie (1987: 87 and app. 1).

84. See the chronology in Hilb & Lutzky (1984: 109–26).

85. Enrique Dussel pauses in the course of his historical narrative to state categorically—and appealing to the Catholic symbolism of martyrdom—that "Carlos was a saint. His blood has made him holy. He is the sign and symbol

of every attempt at popular liberation at the end of the sixties and the beginning of the seventies. His testimony will not be forgotten" (1979b: 355).

86. On March 23–24, 1976, the armed forces brought about another coup that overthrew the government of Isabel Martínez de Perón and installed a military government, appointing General Jorge Videla as president and commander in chief of the army, seconded in the military junta by Air Force Brigadier Osvaldo Agosti and Admiral Emilio Massera. Declaring itself representative of Western and Christian values, and clearly inspired by the national security doctrine, the new government suspended all political and union activity, intervened in the Confederación General de Trabajadores, and suspended the right to strike indefinitely.

87. As documented by Frontalini and Caiati (1984), the military forces in Argentina consisted of some 200,000 members and opposed a group of guerrilla organizations that did not surpass 2,000 organized personnel, of which only a quarter were capable of combat. By contrast, the Red Brigades in Italy had approximately 2,000 armed militants and close to 100,000 sympathizers. However, the Italian government managed to dismember the organization in five years, from 1978 to 1983 by resorting to emergency laws and the use of intelligence services under the direct control of parliament. In Argentina the process was evidently one of systematic genocide, given that the offensive capability of the guerrillas was completely disrupted after a series of extensive setbacks in Tucumán and other provinces, as Frontalini and Caiti show. Their study provides the evidence that demonstrates a premeditated and systematic annihilation of opposition.

88. Economic conditions were difficult. Hyperinflation had reached an annual rate of 737.7 percent, investment was paralyzed, and exports were blocked—creating the conditions for a serious recession, especially in the industrial sector. The min-devaluations of the peso in relation to the dollar had increased the value of the latter ten times during the thirty-four months of the third Peronist government. In effect, the political economy of Argentina was a roller coaster, the drama of which was exceeded only by its political violence and the beginnings of a confrontation between the Peronist unions and the government. This situation offered the desolate landscape in public administration that the armed forces took advantage of to justify their intervention.

89. Rubén Dri points out that "the Military Vicariate, with its 250 priests and 130 chapels, played a fundamental role throughout the legitimizing activity of the Military Dictatorship" (1987: 357).

90. Dri qualifies this term and justifies using it: "It was not a race or a culture that was exterminated, but it was the generation of political, union, cultural, and religious leaders of the last decade" (1987: 159).

91. See, for example, the lists compiled by Enrique Dussel (1979b: 362–65) and Emilio Mignone (1988: 131–32) of priests and men and women religious who disappeared, were kidnapped, or were assassinated.

92. During the seven years of the dictatorship, Argentina paid US$14 billion in interest on its external debt. At the end of 1978 there was a severe conflict with Chile that could have ended in war had the pope not mediated between the two military dictatorships. In light of this conflict and the Malvinas War, the armed forces bought equipment worth an estimated US$8.6 billion including interest, although official figures are not available. For the same period, two items in the balance of payments (unidentified capital assets, and errors and omissions) account for US$28.9 billion that are thought to have been exported. It has been estimated that 44 percent of the funds received as loans were used to finance the export of capital, 33 percent to pay interest on the foreign debt, and 23 percent for arms and military equipment (Calcagno, 1988: 44–51).

93. However, Ubaldini has since become an opposition leader within Peronism against President Carlos Menem.

94. See the analyses of the conditioned State in Martin Carnoy and Joel Samoff (1990) and Carlos Alberto Torres (1991b).

95. The crowds drawn to festivities in honor of Saint Cayetano, the patron of labor—who is reputed to favor those seeking employment—are a case in point. They gather on the seventh of every month and become a massive demonstration on April 7, the feast day of the saint.

96. As a brief digression it may be mentioned that, given the peculiar context of Latin American Catholicism, the instrumentalization of symbols achieves its maximum expression during discussions of the position of the pope on the burning issues of the Continent, for which each sector of organic and traditional intellectuals gives a different reading. Evidently, the interpretation given by the bishops of the Latin American Episcopal Commission (CELAM) differs markedly from that of Catholic intellectuals on the left. For example, Enrique Dussel (1979a) saw nothing in the pope's speeches at Santo Domingo on January 27 and February 13, 1979 (just before the opening of the Third General Conference of the Latin American Episcopacy in Puebla, Mexico) that supported the model of Christendom. By contrast, countless bishops—with Monsignor Alfonso López Trujillo, secretary-general of CELAM at their head—jubilantly celebrated how the pope's speeches announced the end of Liberation Theology and closed the uncomfortable episode represented by the Medellín Documents. But when Ana María Ezcurra analyzed the pope's visit to Argentina in 1987, she drew the positive conclusion that, in spite of the pontiff's silences and omissions, his speech supported democracy and did not endorse the model of Christendom (Ezcurra, 1988: 149–92).

97. This is the subtitle of the book by the Brazilian Franciscan theologian Leonardo Boff, *Iglesia: carisma y poder* (1982), that was heavily censured by Rome.

# Bibliography

Adamson, Walter (1980). *Gramsci Hegemony and Revolution: A Study of Antonio Gramsci's Political and Cultural Theory*. Berkeley: University of California Press.

Alavi, Hamza, & Teodor Shanin, eds. (1982). *Introduction to the Sociology of Developing Societies*. New York: Monthly Review Press.

Altamira, A. (1975). "La pastoral popular. Documentos y Perspectivas (II)." *Stromata* 31, no. 3/4 (July–December): 221–35.

Althusser, Louis (1970). *Ideología y aparatos ideológicos del estado*. Buenos Aires: Nueva Visión.

———— (1971). *La filosofía como arma de la revolución*. Córdoba, Argentina: Pasado y Presente.

Alves, Ruben A. (1968). "Towards a Theology of Liberation." Th.D. dissertation, Princeton Theological Seminary.

Anderson, Perry (1978). *Las antinomias de Antonio Gramsci*. Barcelona, Spain: Fontanara.

Assmann, Hugo (1973). *Teología desde la praxis de la liberación*. Salamanca, Spain: Ediciones Sígueme.

———— (1975). *Theology for a Nomad Church*. Maryknoll, N.Y.: Orbis Books.

Auza, Néstor Tomás (1968). *Historia de los congresos católicos argentinos, 1884–1921*. Cuernavaca, México: CIDOC.

———— (1975). *Católicos y liberales en la generación del ochenta*. Buenos Aires: Ediciones Culturales Argentinas—Secretaría de Estado de Cultura, Ministerio de Cultura y Educación.

———— (1984). *Los católicos argentinos: su experiencia política y social*. Buenos

Aires: Editorial Claretiana.

Avellaneda, Andrés (1986). *Censura, autoritarismo y cultura: Argentina, 1960–1983*. Buenos Aires: Centro Editor de América Latina.

Badanelli, Pedro (1960). *Perón, la iglesia y un cura*. Buenos Aires: Editorial Tartesos.

Balve, Beba (1971). *Lucha de calles, lucha de clases*, Buenos Aires: La Rosa Blindada.

Barreiro, Julio (1977). "Nuevas dimensiones para la misión de la Iglesia en América Latina." *Cristianismo y sociedad* no. 52/53: 5–33.

Belo, Fernando (n.d.). "Una lectura materialista del Evangelio de San Marcos" Mimeograph.

Beltrán, María J. Lubertino (1987). *Perón y la Iglesia (1943–1955)*. Buenos Aires: Centro Editor de América Latina.

Bendix, Reinhard (1962). *Max Weber: An Intellectual Portrait*. New York: Doubleday/Anchor Books.

Benítez, Hernán (1953). *La aristocracia frente a la revolución*. Buenos Aires: Benítez de Aldama.

Berger, Peter (1967). *The Sacred Canopy: Elements of a Sociological Theory of Religion*. New York: Doubleday.

Bernstein, Richard (1985). *Habermas and Modernity*. Cambridge, Mass: MIT Press/Polity Press.

Berstein, Basil (1982). "Codes, modalities and the process of cultural reproductions: a model," in Michael W. Apple, ed. *Cultural and Economic Reproduction in Education*. Boston: Routledge & Kegan Paul.

Betto, Frei (1989). *Entrevista a Frei Betto. Debate sobre el marxismo: un aporte cristiano revolucionario*. Managua, Nicaragua: Universidad Centro Americana, Publicaciones del Departmento de Filosofía.

Block, Charles Y. (1972). "On the Study of Religious Commitment." in *Religious Education*, Research Supplement, "Religion and Society in Tension" (July/August).

Bobbio, Norberto, & Nicola Matteucci, eds. (1981). *Diccionario de Política*. Mexico City: Siglo XXI Editores.

Boff, Leonardo (1982). *Iglesia: carisma y poder. Ensayos de eclesiología militante*. Santander, Spain: Sal Terrae.

Bonasso, Miguel (1988). *Recuerdo de la muerte*. Buenos Aires: Punto Sur.

Bordin, Luigi (1987). *O Marxismo e a Teologia da Libertação*. Rio de Janeiro: Dois Pontos.

Boron, Atilio (1976). "The Formation and Crisis of the Liberal State in Argentina, 1880–1930." Ph.D. dissertation, Harvard University.

——— (1990). "Los legados de la cultura política del autoritarismo en la transición democrática de la Argentina." Mimeographed. Buenos Aires: EURAL.

——— et al. (1990). *La cultura autoritaria argentina en la transición a la democracia*. Buenos Aires: EURAL.

Borrat, Héctor & Aldo Büntig (1973). *El imperio y las iglesias*. Buenos Aires: Editorial Guadalupe.

Brandão, Carlos, ed. (1980). *A Questão Política de Educação Popular*. São Paulo: Brasilense.

Braun, Oscar (1969). *El capitalismo monopólico en Argentina*. Buenos Aires: Nueva Visión.

———, ed. (1971). *El capitalismo argentino en crisis*. Buenos Aires: Siglo XXI Editores.

Broccoli, Angelo (1972). *Antonio Gramsci e l'educazione come egemonia*. Florence: La Nueva Italia.

Brown, Cynthia (1978). *Literacy in 30 Hours: Paulo Freire's Process in North East Brazil*. Berkeley: California Center for Open Learning and Teaching.

Bruneau, Thomas (1974). *O Catolicismo brasileiro en época de transição*. São Paulo: Edições Loyola.

Brunner, J. J. (1978). "De las experiencias de control social." *Revista Mexicana de Sociología*. 40: 233–51.

Büntig, Aldo (1968). "Hipótesis para una interpretación del catolicismo en la Argentina." *CIAS* (Buenos Aires), no. 171: 7–39.

——— (1973). *Religión y enajenación en una sociedad dependiente*. Buenos Aires: Editorial Guadalupe.

Calcagno, Alfredo Eric (1988). *La perversa deuda*. Buenos Aires: Editorial Legasa.

Calvez, Jean-Ives (1966). *El pensamiento de Carlos Marx*. Madrid: Taurus.

Camara, Helder (1969). "Conversación con Helder Camara." *Revista Víspera* (Montevideo, Uruguay), 3, no. 10 (May).

Camargo, Cándido Procopio Ferreira de (1971). *Igreja e desenvolvimento*. São Paulo: Centro Brasileiro de Analise e Planejamento (CEBRAP).

Canitrot, Adolfo (1975). "La experiencia populista de redistribución de ingresos." *Desarrollo Económico*, 15, no. 59 (October–December): 331–51.

Cantero, E. (1975). "Paulo Freire y la educación liberadora." *Verbo*, Buenos Aires, 153: 39–58; 154: 19–44.

Cardoso, Fernando H., & Enzo Faletto (1978). *Dependency and Development in Latin America*. Berkeley & Los Angeles: University of California Press.

Carnoy, Martin, & Henry Levin (1985). *Schooling and Work in the Democratic State*. Stanford, Calif.: Stanford University Press.

Carnoy, Martin, & Joel Samoff, eds. (1990). *Education and Social Transition in the Third World: China, Cuba, Tanzania, Mozambique and Nicaragua*. Princeton, NJ: Princeton University Press.

Casiello, Juan (1948). *Iglesia y estado en la Argentina: regimen de sus relaciones*. Buenos Aires: Editorial Poblet.

Castellani, Leonardo (1937). "Maritain, hombre de acción." *Criterio*, no. 489.

Castro, Fidel (1974). *Fidel Castro habla a los cristianos revolucionarios*. Buenos Aires: Tierra Nueva.

Castro, Fidel, & Frei Betto (1987). *Fidel and Religion*. Introduction by Harvey Cox. New York: Touchstone Book.

Cavarozzi, Marcelo (1983). *Autoritarismo y democracia (1955–1983)*. Buenos Aires: Centro Editor de América Latina.

CEED (1970). *Dinámica de la población en México*. Mexico City: El Colegio de México.

CEHILA (1986). *Para uma historia da igreja na America Latina*. Petropolis, Brazil: Vozes.

Central Committee of the Socialist Party "Unificat," Cataluña, Spain (1977). "Declaración." *Contacto*, 14, no. 1 (February).

Central de Juventudes (1970). *Juventud, rebelión y nueva civilización*. Bogota: Editorial Paulina.

Chiesa, Carlos A. J., A. Jorge Soneira, Enrique H. Sosa, et al. (1982). *Comunión y participación: introducción a la enseñanza social de la Iglesia*. Buenos Aires: Editorial Guadalupe.

Chiesa, Carlos A. J. & Enrique H. Sosa (1983). *Iglesia y Justicialismo, 1943–1955*. Buenos Aires: Cuadernos de Iglesia y Sociedad, Centro de Investigación y Orientación Social.

Cleary, Edward L. (1985). *Crisis and Change: The Church in Latin America Today*. Maryknoll, N.Y.: Orbis Books.

Clévenot, M. (1980). *Lectura materialista de la Biblia*. Salamanca, Spain: Sígueme.

Comblin, J. (n.d.). *Iglesia y la ideología de la seguridad nacional*. Lima, Peru: Servicio de Documentación Miec-Jeci.

CONADEP (Comisión Nacional sobre la Desaparición de Personas) (1984). *Nunca más: Informe de la Comisión Nacional sobre la Desaparición de Personas*. Buenos Aires: EUDEBA.

Concatti, Rolando (1972). "Nuestra opción por el Peronismo." *Revista del Tercer Mundo*. 2 (January–June), 112–83.

——— (1975). "Profecía y política." *Revista Pueblo* (Buenos Aires), no. 1 (October).

Consejo Episcopal Latinoamericano (CELAM) (1985). *¿Otra Iglesia en la base?* Bogota: CELAM.

Cooke, John William (1970a). *Peronismo y liberación nacional*. Buenos Aires: Papiro.

——— (1970b). *Peronismo y revolución*. Buenos Aires: Papiro.

——— (1972). *Correspondencia Perón–Cooke*. Buenos Aires: Schapire Editor.

Cottier, Georges M-M. (1959). *L'athéisme du Jeune Marx*. Paris: Vrin.

Cristianos por el Socialismo (1972). *Primer encuentro latinoamericano de Cristianos por el Socialismo*. Lima: SEP.

De Ipola, Emilio (1982). *Ideología y discurso populista*. Mexico City: Folios Ediciones.

De Kadt, Emmanuel (1970). *Catholic Radicals in Brazil*. Oxford, England: Oxford University Press.

——— (1971). "Religião, Igreja e mutação social no Brasil." In Claudio Veliz (ed), *América Latina: Estructuras en Crise*. São Paulo, Brazil: Ibraja.

De la Cierva, Ricardo (1987). *Jesuitas, iglesia y marxismo 1965–1985: la teología de la liberación desenmascarada*. Barcelona, Spain: Plaza & Janes.

De Lella, Cayetano, comp. (1984). *Cristianismo y liberación en América Latina*. Mexico City: Ediciones Nuevomar.

D'Epinay, Christian Lalive (1975). "Sociedad dependiente, 'clases populares' y 'milenarismo.' " In *Dependencia y estructura de clases en América Latina*. Buenos Aires: Ediciones Megápolis: 271–91.

De Santa Ana, Julio, et al. (1974). *Conciencia y revolución*. Buenos Aires: Schapire.

Desroche, H. (1965). *Socialisme et sociologie religieuse*. Paris: Cujas.

Dias, Zwinglio M. (1978). "Institución y acontecimiento: Notas sobre las tensiones entre lo eclesiástico y lo eclesial en el interior de la comunidad cristiana." *Cristianismo y Sociedad*, no. 56.

Díaz Alejandro, Carlos F. (1970). *Essays on the Economic History of the Argentine Republic*. New Haven, Conn.: Yale University Press.

Díaz Murugarren, José (1977). "La religión como 'neurosis obsesiva.' " *Estudios Filosóficos*, Valladolid, Spain, no. 73 (September–December): 463–510.

Díaz-Salazar, Rafael (1991). *El Proyecto de Gramsci*. Barcelona, Spain: Ediciones HOAC-Anthropos.

Dillon Soares, Glaucio A., & José Luis Reyna (1962). "Status socioeconómico, religiosidad y dogmatismo." Mimeograph. Mexico City: N.D.

Documentos del Episcopado Argentino (1982). *Colección completa del magisterio postconciliar de la Conferencia Episcopal Argentina*. Buenos Aires: Editorial Claretiana.

Documentos Finales de Puebla (1979). *La evangelización en el presente y en el futuro de América Latina*. Mexico City: Paulinas.

Donini, Antonio (1985). *Religión y sociedad: reflexiones sociológicas sobre clericalismo, laicismo, laicidad*. Buenos Aires: Editorial Docencia.

Dos Santos, Theotonio (1976). "La crisis de la teoría del desarrollo y las relaciones de dependencia en América Latina." In various authors, *La dependencia político-económica de América Latina*. Mexico City: Siglo XXI Editores.

Drekonja, Gerhard (1971). "Religion and Social Change in Latin America." *Latin America Research Review* 6, no. 1 (Spring): 53–72.

Dri, Rubén (1950). *The Rules of Sociological Method*. Glencoe, Ill.: Free Press.

——— (1983). *La iglesia de los pobres. Para un reencuentro cristiano en Argentina*. Lima: CELADEC.

—— (1987). *Teología y dominación.* Buenos Aires: Roblanco.

Durkheim, Emile (1915). *The Elementary Forms of the Religious Life: A Study in Religious Sociology.* Trans. J. W. Swain. London: George Allen & Unwin.

—— (1965). *Las reglas del método sociológico.* Buenos Aires: Editorial Schapire.

Dussel, Enrique D. (1973). *América Latina: Dependencia y Liberación.* Buenos Aires: Fernando García Cambeiro Editor.

—— (1974a). "Cultura imperial, cultura ilustrada y liberación de la cultura popular." *Stromata,* 30 (January–June): 106–10.

—— (1974b). *El dualismo en la antropología de la cristiandad.* Buenos Aires: Editorial Guadalupe.

—— (1976). *History and the Theology of Liberation. A Latin American Perspective.* Maryknoll, N.Y.: Orbis Books.

—— (1977a). "Fetichización ontológica del sistema." *Revista Logos,* Mexico City, 5, no. 15 (September–December): 79–102.

—— (1977). *Religión.* Mexico City: Edicol.

—— (1979a). "Crítica al Documento de Consulta." Mimeograph. Mexico City: N.P.

—— (1979b). *De Medellín a Puebla. Una década de sangre y esperanza.* Mexico City: Edicol.

—— (1983a). *Historia de la Iglesia en América Latina. Coloniaje y Liberación (1492–1983).* Madrid: Mundo Negro-Esquila Misional.

—— (1983b). *Historia general de la Iglesia en América Latina.* Salamanca, Spain: CEHILA—Ediciones Sígueme.

—— (1986). *Los últimos 50 años (1930–1985) en la Historia de la Iglesia en América Latina.* Bogota, Colombia: Indo-American Press Service Editores.

Einaudi, L., et al. (1969). *Latin American Institutional Development: The Changing Catholic Church.* Santa Monica, Calif.: Rand Corporation.

Eisenstandt, S. N., ed. (1968). *The Protestant Ethic and Modernization: A Comparative View.* New York: Basic Books.

Eliade, Mircea (1968). *Myth and Reality.* New York: Harper Collins/Torchbook.

Ellis, Marc H., & Otto Maduro, eds. (1989). *The Future of Liberation Theology.* Maryknoll, N.Y.: Orbis Books.

Entwhistle, Harold (1979). *Antonio Gramsci: Conservative Schooling for Radical Politics.* Boston: Routledge & Kegan Paul.

Ezcurra, Ana María (1983). *Agresión ideológica contra la Revolución Sandinista.* Mexico City: Ediciones Neuvomar.

—— (1984). *El Vaticano y la administración Regan: convergencias en Centroamérica.* Mexico City: Ediciones Nuevomar.

—— (1988). *Iglesia y transición democrática: ofensiva del neoconservadurismo católico en América Latina.* Buenos Aires: Puntosur.

Farrell, Gerardo (1979). *Iglesia y pueblo en Argentina*. Buenos Aires: Editorial Patria Grande.

Ferrarotti, F. (1966). "Durkheim e M. Weber di fronte al fenómeno religioso." In *Cultorología del sacro e del profano*. Milan, Italy: Feltrinelli Editores.

Ferreira de Camargo, Cándido Antonio Procopio (1971). *Igreja y desenvolvimiento*. São Paulo: CEBRAP.

Fichter, J. (1972). *Sociología*. Barcelona, Spain: Herder.

Filippo, Virgilio (1948). *El plan quinquenal de Perón y los communistas*. Buenos Aires: Editorial Lista Blanca.

Fischoff, Ephraim (1944). "The Protestant Ethic and the Spirit of Capitalism: The History of a Controversy." *Social Research*, 11: 61–67.

Forni, Floreal (1987a). "Catolicismo y Peronismo (I)." *Unidos*, 14: 211–27.

———— (1987b). "Catolicismo y Peronismo (II)." *Unidos*, 17: 197–216.

———— (1988). "Catolicismo y Peronismo (III): del aggiornamento a las vísperas (1955–1969)." *Unidos*, 18: 121–44.

Framini, Andrés (1982). *Sindicalismo, el poder y la crisis: reportajes a Andrés Framini, Paulino Niembro y Miguel Unamuno*. Buenos Aires: Editorial de Belgrano.

Freire, Paulo (1972). "La misión educativa de las iglesias en América Latina." *Perspectivas de Diálogo*, Montevideo, Uruguay, 7, no. 66 (August): 172–79; no. 67 (September): 201–9.

Freire, Paulo, & Carlos Torres (1990). *Reading the World: Paulo Freire in Conversation with Carlos Alberto Torres*. Videotape. ACCESS Network, Edmonton, Alberta, Canada.

Freud, Sigmund (1950). *Totem and Taboo: Some Points of Agreement between the Mental Lives of Savages and Neurotics*. New York: W. W. Norton.

———— (1965). *The Psychopathology of Everyday Life*. New York: W. W. Norton.

Frontalini, Daniel, & Maria Cristina Caiati (1984). *El mito de la guerra sucia*. Buenos Aires: Centro de Estudios Legales y Sociales.

Furtado, Celso (1974). *O mito do desenvolvimento económico*. Rio de Janeiro: Paz e Terra.

Gabel, Joseph (1970). *Sociologie de l'aliénation*. Paris: Presses Universitaires de France.

Gajardo, Marcela (1983). "Evolución, situación actual y perspectivas de las estrategias de investigación participativa en América Latina." In M. Gajardo, comp., *Teoría y práctica de la educación popular*. Ottawa: International Development Research Center, IDRC-MR81s, August: 409–65.

Galasso, Norberto (1970). *Vida de Scalabrini Ortiz*. Buenos Aires: Ediciones del Mar Dulce.

———— (1985). *Jauretche y su época*. Buenos Aires: Peña Lillo Editor.

Galilea, Segundo (1974). "La liberazione come incontro fra politica e contemplazione." In various authors, "Prassi de Liberazione e fede cristiana." *Concilium* (Brescia, Italy), no. 6: 29–45.

Gandolfo, Mercedes (1969). *La iglesia factor de poder en la Argentina.* Montevideo, Uruguay: Ediciones Nuestro Tiempo.

Garaudy, Roger (1973). *Dios ha muerto, Estudio sobre Hegel.* Buenos Aires: Siglo XX Editores.

García Lupo, Rogelio (1971a). *Mercenarios y monopolios en la Argentina, de Onganía a Lanusse, 1966–1971.* Buenos Aires: Achaval Solo.

———. (1971b). *Contra la ocupación extranjera.* Buenos Aires: Editorial Centro.

Gera, Lucio, A. Büntig, & Osvaldo Catena (1974). *Teología, Pastoral y Dependencia.* Buenos Aires: Editorial Guadalupe.

Gera, Lucio & Guillermo Rodríguez Melgarejo (1970). "Hipótesis para una interpretación de la Iglesia argentina." Mimeograph. Buenos Aires: N.P.

Germani, Gino (1962). *Política y sociedad en una época de transición.* Buenos Aires: Editorial Paidós.

Gerth, H. & C. Wright-Mills (1971). *Carácter y estructura social.* Buenos Aires: Paidós.

Giddens, Anthony (1976). *New Rules of Sociological Method.* London: Hutchinson.

Gillespie, Richard (1987). *Soldados de Perón: los Montoneros.* Buenos Aires: Grijalbo.

Giménez, Gilberto (1975). "El golpe militar en Chile y la condenación de 'cristianos por el socialismo.' " *Contacto*, Mexico City, 12, nos. 1/2 (January–April): 12–116.

Giménez Zapiola, Marcos, ed. (1975). *El régimen oligárquico.* Buenos Aires: Amorrortu.

Girardi, Giulio (1977a). *Fé cristiana y materialismo histórico.* Salamanca, Spain: Sígueme.

——— (1977b). *Marxismo y cristianismo.* Barcelona & Madrid: Editorial Laia-Taurus.

Giroux, Henry (1983). "Theories of Reproduction and Resistance in the New Sociology of Education: A Critical Analysis." *Harvard Educational Review*, 53, no. 3 (August).

Giroux, Henry, & Peter McLaren, eds. (1989). *Critical Pedagogy, the State and Cultural Struggle.* Albany, N.Y.: State University of New York Press.

Gismondi, Michael (1988). "Conceptualizing Religion from Below. The Central American Experience." *Social Compass*, 35, nos. 2/3: 343–70.

Glock, Charles Y. (1972). "On the Study of Religious Commitment." *Religious Education*, Research Supplement (July/August).

———, comp. (1973). *Religion in Sociological Perspective; Essays in the Empirical Study of Religion.* Belmont, Calif.: Wadsworth.

Glock, Charles Y., & Rodney Stark (1965). *Religion and Society in Tension.* Chicago: Rand McNally.

Goddijn, H. & W. (1973). *Sociología de la religión y de la iglesia*. Buenos Aires: Ediciones Carlos Lohlé.

Goldenweiser, A. A. (1977). "Religion and Society: A Critique of Durkheim's Theory of the Origin and Nature of Religion." *Journal of Philosophy, Psychology and Scientific Method*, 4: 113–24.

Gómez de Souza, Luiz A. (1975). "Condicionamientos socio-políticos actuales de la teología de la liberación en América Latina." In *Liberación y Cautiverio*. Mexico City: Encuentro Latinoamericano de Teologia, August.

——— (1978). "Igreja y Sociedade: elementos para un marco teórico." *Revista Síntese*, Nova Fase, no. 13 (April–July): 15–29.

——— (1984). *JUC: os estudiantes católicos e a política*. Petrópolis, Brazil: Vozes.

Gouldner, Alvin W. (1970). *The Coming Crisis of Western Sociology*. New York: Basic Books.

Gramsci, Antonio (1975–77). *Obras de Antonio Gramsci*. 5 vols. Mexico City: Juan Pablos Editor.

——— (1980). *Selections from the Prison Notebooks of Antonio Gramsci*. Ed. & trans. Quintin Hoare & Geoffrey Nowell Smith. New York: International Publishers.

Guevara, Ernesto "Che" (1968). *The Diary of a Guerrilla*. New York: Bantam Books.

Guivant, Julia Silvia (1986). *La visible Eva Perón y el invisible rol político femenino del peronismo: 1946–1952*, Working Paper no. 60. Notre Dame: Kellogg Institute.

Gurvith, George (1970). *Los fundadores franceses de la sociología contemporánea*. Buenos Aires: Nueva Visión.

Gutiérrez, Gustavo (1970a). *Liberación: opción de la iglesia latinoamericana en la década del 70*. Bogota: Editorial Presencia.

——— (1970b). *Teología de la Liberación*. Lima: CEP.

——— (1973). *A Theology of Liberation, History, Politics and Salvation*. Maryknoll, N.Y.: Orbis Books.

——— (1978). "Sobre el documento de consulta." *Servir*, 14, no. 73.

Habermas, Jürgen (1975). *Problemas de legitimación en el capitalismo tardío*. Buenos Aires: Amorrortu Editores.

Halperin Donghi, Tulio (1975). *Historia Contemporánea de América Latina*. Madrid: Alianza Editorial.

Harris, Richard, & Carlos María Vilas, eds. (1985). *La revolución en Nicaragua. Liberación nacional, democracia popular y transformación económica*. Mexico City: Ediciones ERA.

Hegel, G.W.F. (1977). *Phenomenology of Spirit*. Trans. A. V. Miller, with analyses and foreword by J. N. Findlay. Oxford, England: Clarendon Press.

Hernández Arregui, J. J. (1957). *Imperialismo y cultura: la política en la inteligencia argentina*. Buenos Aires: Editorial Amerindia.

——— (1960). *La formación de la conciencia nacional*. Buenos Aires: Editorial Machea.

Hilb, Claudia & Daniel Lutzky (1984). *La nueva izquierda argentina: 1960–1980*. Buenos Aires: Centro Editor de América Latina.

Hinkelammert, Franz (1977). *Las armas ideológicas de la muerte: capitalismo y Cristianismo*. San José, Costa Rica: EDUCA—Colección DEI.

Horowitz, Irving L. (1969). *Historia y elementos de la sociología del conocimiento*. 2 vols. Buenos Aires: EUDEBA.

Ianni, Octavio (1975). *La formación del estado populista en América Latina*. Mexico City: Ediciones Era.

Instituto Latinoamericano de Doctrina y Estudios Sociales (ILADES) (1986). *Diálogo en torno a le Teología de la Liberación*. Santiago, Chile: ILADES—Editorial Salesiana.

Irarrázabal, Diego (1977). "Opciones para la tarea evangelizadora del pueblo." *Cristianismo y Sociedad* (Buenos Aires), 15, no. 51 (July–December): 15–29.

Jaguaribe, Helio (1962). *Desenvolvimento económico y desenvolvimento político*. Rio de Janeiro: Editora Fondo de Cultura.

Jaguaribe, Helio, Aldo Ferrer, Miguel S. Wionczek et al. (1970). *La dependencia político-económica de América Latina*. Mexico City: Siglo XXI Editores.

Jauretche, Arturo. (1973). *Los profetas del odio y la yapa*. Buenos Aires: A. Peña Lillo.

———. (1981). *Las polémicas de Jauretche*. Buenos Aires: Los Nacionales Editores.

——— (1984). *Barajar y dar de nuevo*. Buenos Aires: Los Nacionales Editores.

Jauretche, Arturo, J. Podestá, E. Sábato, et al. (1967). *El pensamiento nacional y la encíclica Populorum Progressio*. Buenos Aires: Plus Ultra.

Kardiner, Abram (1939). *The Individual and His Society: The Psychodynamics of Primitive Social Organization*. Foreword and two ethnological reports by Ralph Linton. New York: Columbia University Press.

Kennedy, John J. (1958). *Catholicism, Nationalism and Democracy in Argentina*. Notre Dame, Ind.: University of Notre Dame Press.

Ketteler, Wilhelm Emmanuel von (1981). *The Social Teachings of Wilhelm Emmanuel von Ketteler: Bishop of Mainz (1811–1877)*. Trans. Rupert J. Ederer. Washington, D.C.: University Press of America.

Kofler, Leo (1968). *La ciencia de la sociedad*. Madrid: Revista de Occidente.

Kropotkin, P. (1924). *Ethics: Origin and Development*. New York: Dial Press.

La Belle, Thomas J. (1986). *Nonformal Education in Latin America and the Caribbean: Stability, Reform or Revolution?* New York: Praeger.

Laclau, Ernesto (1979). *Política e ideologia na teoria Marxista: capitalismo, fascismo e populismo*. São Paulo: Paz e Terra.

Lafforgue, Edmundo (1980). *La escuela popular: su evolución y proyección*. Buenos Aires: Editorial Universitaria de Buenos Aires.

Laje, E. J. (1977a). "Análisis marxista y teología de la praxis en América Latina." *Strómata*, 33, nos. 1/2 (January–June): 41–47.

——— (1977b). "Magisterio de la iglesia y socialismo." *Strómata*, 33, nos. 3/4 (July–December): 159–94.

Lanusse, Alejandro A. (1977). *Mi testimonio*. Buenos Aires: Laserre Editores.

Latin American Studies Association (1978). *La represión en Argentina 1973–1974: documentos*. Mexico City: Facultad de Ciencias Políticas y Sociales, Universidad Nacional Autónoma de México.

Lavalli, J. (1968). *Max Weber: religione et società*. Bologna, Italy: II Mulino.

Le Bras, G. (1960). "Emile Durkheim et la sociologie des religions." *Annales de l'Université de Paris*.

Lenk, Kurt (1974). *El concepto de ideología*. Buenos Aires: Amorrortu Editores.

Lensk, Gregory (1961). *The Religious Factor*. New York: Basic Books.

Llorens, José M. (1972). *Opción fuera de la ley*. Mimeographed. Mendoza, Argentino: N.P.

Lukács, Georg (1980). *The Destruction of Reason*. Trans. Peter Palmer. London: Merlin Press.

Luna, Félix (1980). *Conflictos y armonías en la historia argentina*. Buenos Aires: Editorial de Belgrano.

Lunacharski, Anatoly V. (1976). *Religión y socialismo*. Salamanca, Spain: Sígueme.

Macciocchi, Maria Antonietta (1975). *Gramsci y la revolución de occidente*. Mexico City: Siglo XXI Editores.

Maduro, Otto (1979). *Religión y lucha de clases*. Caracas, Venezuela: Editorial Ateneo de Caracas.

——— (1981). *La cuestión religiosa en el Engels pre-marxista*. Caracas, Venezuela: Monte Avila Editores.

Mainwaring, Scott (1983). "The Catholic Youth Workers Movement (JOC) and the Emergence of the Popular Church in Brazil." Working Paper. Notre Dame, Ind.: University of Notre Dame, Helen Kellogg Institute for International Studies.

——— (1986). *The Catholic Church and Politics in Brazil, 1916–1985*. Stanford, Calif.: Stanford University Press.

Mainwaring, Scott, & Alexander Wilde, eds. (1989). *The Progressive Church in Latin America*. Notre Dame, Ind.: University of Notre Dame Press.

Mallimachi, Fortunato (1988). *El catolicismo integral de Argentina (1930–1946)*. From the Cuadernos Simón Rodríguez. Buenos Aires: Editorial Biblos/Fundación Simón Rodríguez.

Manacorda, Mario A. (1970). *Il principio educativo in Gramsci*. Cagliari, Italy: Armando Editore.

Marcuse, Herbert (1955). *Reason and Revolution*. 2nd ed. London: Routledge

& Kegan Paul.

———— (1973). *Studies in Critical Philosophy.* Trans. S. de Bres. Boston: Beacon Press.

Marins, José (1978). *La praxis de los Padres en América Latina.* Bogotá: Ediciones Paulinas.

Martínez Paz, Fernando (1966). *Maritain, politica, ideología: revolución cristiana en la Argentina.* Buenos Aires: Editorial Nahuel.

Marx, Karl (1968a). *Crítica de la filosofía del estado de Hegel.* Mexico City: Editorial Grijalbo.

———— (1968b). *Manuscritos económicos-filosóficos de 1844.* Mexico City: Editorial Grijalbo.

Marx, Karl, & Frederick Engels. *Anekdota.* February 13, Historisch-Kritische Gesamtausgabe (M.E.G.A.), Vol. I, 1/1. Frankfurt.

———— (1974). *La ideología alemana.* Trans. Wenceslao Roces. Barcelona, Spain: Ediciones Pueblos Unidos & Editorial Grijalbo.

———— (1982). "Pathways of Social Development: A Brief against Suprahistorical Theory." In Hamza Alavi & Teodor Shanin (eds.), *Introduction to the Sociology of "Developing Societies,"* pp. 109–11. New York & London: Monthly Review Press.

Massera, Emilio E. Alte (1979). *El camino de la democracia.* Buenos Aires: El Cid Editor.

Mate, Reyes & Hugo Assmann, eds. (1974). *Sobre la Religión.* 2 vols. Salamanca, Spain: Sígueme.

Matthes, Joachin (1971). *Introducción a la sociología de la religión.* 2 vols. Madrid: Alianza Universidad.

Mayntz, Robert (1967). *Sociología de la organización.* Madrid: Alianza Editorial.

Mayol, Alejandro, Norberto Habegger, & Arturo Armada (1970). *Los católicos posconciliares en la Argentina.* Buenos Aires: Ediciones Galerna.

Mecham, J. Lloyd (1966). *Church and State in Latin America: A History of Politico-ecclesiastical Relations.* Chapel Hill: University of North Carolina Press.

Meinvielle, Julio (1932). *Concepción católica de la política.* Buenos Aires: Cursos de Cultural Católica.

———— (1936). *El judío.* Buenos Aires: Editorial Antídoto.

———— (1937). "Los desvaríos de Maritain." *Criterio,* no. 488.

———— (1961). *El communismo en la revolución anti-cristiana.* Buenos Aires: Ediciones Teoría.

———— (1970). *La iglesia y el mundo moderno.* Buenos Aires: Ediciones Teoría.

Memoria y Esperanza (1980). *Iglesia argentina.* Buenos Aires: Grupo Memoria y Esperanza.

Mercader Martínez, Manuel (1974). *Cristianismo y revolución en América Latina.* Mexico City: Diógenes.

Meyer, Lorenzo (1977). "Historical Roots of the Authoritarian State in Mexico," in José Luis Reyna & Richard S. Weinert, eds., *Authoritarism in Mexico*, pp. 3–22. Philadelphia: Institute for the Study of Human Issues.

Méznaros, István (1978). *La teoría de la enajenación en Marx*. Mexico City: Ediciones Era.

Mignone, Emilio (1988). *Witness to the Truth: The Complicity of the Church and Dictatorship in Argentina, 1976–1983*. Maryknoll, N.Y.: Orbis Books.

Milanessi, J. (1974). *Sociología de la religión*. Madrid: Cuadernos de Pedagogía Catequística, CCS.

Milhau, Jacques (1974). "Ateísmo, ideología y religión." In Lucien Séve & Jacques Milhau, *Filosofía y religión*, pp. 82–118. Mexico City: Ediciones de Cultura Popular.

Miranda, Porfirio (1978). El cristianismo de Marx. Mexico City: Published by the author.

Moix, Candide (1960). *La Pensée d'Emmanuel Mounier*. Paris: Editions du Seuil.

Mondin, Battista (1973). *Teología Della Prassi*. Brescia, Italy: Queriana Editrice.

Morales-Gómez, Daniel & Carlos Alberto Torres (1990). *The State, Corporatist Politics and Education Policy Making in Mexico*. New York: Praeger.

Moreira, Alves, Márcio (1968). *O Cristo do Povo*. Rio de Janeiro: Editora Sabiá.

Morse, Richard (1981). "The Two Worlds of America: Intellectual Antecedents, Political Outcomes, Civilizational Prospects." Mimeograph. Stanford University.

———— (1982). *El espejo de Próspero*. Mexico: Siglo XXI Editores.

Mouffe, Chantal (1979). "Hegemony and Ideology in Gramsci." In Chantal Mouffe, ed., *Gramsci and Marxist Theory*. London: Routledge and Kegan Paul.

Movimiento de Sacerdotes para el Tercer Mundo (1970a, May). "Comunicado de Santa Fé." Mimeograph. Santa Fé, Argentina.

———— (1970b). *Nuestra Reflexión. Carta a los Obispos argentinos*. Buenos Aires: Publicaciones del Movimiento de Sacerdotes para el Tercer Mundo.

———— (1970c). *Sacerdotes para el Tercer Mundo: crónica—documentos—reflexión*. Documento no. 1. Buenos Aires: Publicaciones del Movimiento de Sacerdotes para el Tercer Mundo.

———— (1972). *Sacerdotes para el Tercer Mundo*. Buenos Aires: Publiciacónes del Movimiento de Sacerdotes para el Tercer Mundo.

———— (1973). *Los Sacerdotes para el Tercer Mundo y la actualidad nacional*. Buenos Aires: Ediciones La Rosa Blindada.

Mugica, Carlos (1973). *Peronismo y cristianismo*. Buenos Aires: Editorial Merlin.

———— (1984). *Carlos Mugica: una vida para el pueblo*. Buenos Aires: Pequén.

Murmis, Miguel & Juan Carlos Portantiero (1971). *Estudio sobre los orígenes del peronismo*. Buenos Aires: Siglo XXI Editores.

Najenson, José Luis (1979). "El Marxismo y la cuestión religiosa: tres tesis heterodoxas." Mimeograph. Mexico City: Facultad Latinoamericana de Ciencias Sociales (FLACSO).

Navarro, Marysa (1981). *Evita*. Buenos Aires: Corregidor.

Neyra, Juan Carlos et al. (1965). *Jauretche: una vida al servicio de la revolución nacional*. Buenos Aires: Grupo Editor de Buenos Aires.

Norman, Edward (1981). *Christianity in the Southern Hemisphere*. Oxford, England: Clarendon Press.

Novack, George (1979). *La teoría marxista de la alienación*. Barcelona, Spain: Editorial Fontamara.

O'Donnell, Guillermo (1972). *Modernización y Autoritarismo*. Buenos Aires: Paidós.

——— (1988). *Bureaucratic-Authoritarianism: Argentina 1966–73 in Comparative Perspective*. Berkeley: University of California Press.

Offe, Claus (1974). "Structural Problems of the Capitalist State: Class Rule and the Political System. On the Selectiveness of Political Institutions." In Klaus Von Beyme, ed. *German Political Studies*, 1, pp. 31–35. Beverly Hills, Calif.: Sage.

Oliveros Maqueo, Roberto (1977). *Liberación y teología: génesis y crecimiento de una reflexión, 1966–1976*. Lima: Centro de Estudios y Publicaciones (CEP).

Ortiz, Gustavo (1977). "La Teoría de la Dependencia, los cristianos radicalizados y el peronismo (apuntes para una discusión)." *Pucará* (Revista de la Facultad de Filosofía, Letras y Ciencias de la Educación, Universidad de Cuenca, Ecuador, no. 1 (January): 56–72.

Oszlak, Oscar (1982). *La formación del estado argentino*. Buenos Aires: Editorial de Belgrano.

Pagés, José (1956). *Orígenes y desarrollo de las democráticas cristianas en nuestro país*. Buenos Aires: edition of the author.

Paiva, Vanilda (1982). *Paulo Freire y el nacionalismo desarrollista*. Mexico City: Editorial Extemporáneos.

Palacio, Ernesto (1979). *Historia de la Argentina, 1515–1976*. Buenos Aires: Abeledo-Perrot.

Parera, Ricardo G. (1967). *Democracia cristiana en la argentina: los hechos y las ideas*. Buenos Aires: Editorial Nahuel.

Parsons, Talcott (1958). Prologue to M. Weber, *The Protestant Ethic and the Spirit of Capitalism*. New York: Scribners.

——— (1971). *The System of Modern Societies*. Englewood Cliffs, N.J.: Prentice-Hall.

Parsons, Talcott, R. Bales, & E. Shills (1970). *Apuntes sobre la teoría de la acción*. Buenos Aires: Amorrortu.

Paz, Néstor (1971). "Diario de un guerrillero." *Los Libros*, Buenos Aires.

Paz, Octavio (1961). *The Labyrinth of Solitude: Life and Thought in Mexico.* New York: Grove Press.

Peña, Milciades (1971). *Masas, caudillos y elites: la dependencia Argentina de Yrigoyen a Perón.* Buenos Aires: Ediciones Fichas.

Peralta Ramos, Mónica (1972). *Etapas de acumulación y alianzas de clase en Argentina.* Buenos Aires: Siglo XXI Editores.

Pereira Ramalho, J. (1977). "Algunas notas sobre dos perspectivas de pastoral popular." *Cristianismo y Sociedad* (Buenos Aires), 15, 51 (July–December): 3–15.

Perón, Eva (1987a). *Clases y escritos completos.* Buenos Aires: Editorial Megafón.

—— (1987a). *Historia del peronismo.* Buenos Aires: Editorial Volver.

Perón, Juan Domingo (1958). *La fuerza es el derecho de las bestias.* Montevideo, Uruguay: Editorial Cicerón.

—— (1964). "A Denunciation of Certain Argentine Churchmen" in Frederick B. Pike, ed., *The Conflict Between Church and State in Latin America*, pp. 183–187. New York: Alfred A. Knopf.

—— (1974). *La communidad organizada.* Buenos Aires: Secretaría Politica de la Presidencia de la Nacion.

Perón, Juan, Raúl A. Mende, Alberto Teisaire et al. (1954). *2° Plan quinquenal de la nación Argentina.* Buenos Aires: Hechos e Ideas.

Pike, Frederick B., ed. (1964). *The Conflict between Church and State in Latin America.* New York: Alfred A. Knopf.

Pike, Fredrick B. & Thomas Strich, eds. (1974). *The New Corporatism: Social-Political Structures in the Iberian World.* Notre Dame, Ind., & London: University of Notre Dame Press.

Pin, Emile (n.d.). "Apuntes sobre sociología de la religión y pastoral." Mimeograph. Cuernavaca, Mexico: CIDOC.

Portantiero, Juan Carlos (1973). "Clases dominantes y crisis política en Argentina." In O. Braun, *El capitalismo argentino en crisis.* Mexico City: Siglo XXI Editores.

—— (1980). "Gramsci para latinoamericanos." In C. Buci-Glucksmann, J. C. Portantiero, G. Vacca & M. A. Macciocchi, *Gramsci y la política.* Coord. C. Sirvent. Mexico City: Universidad Nacional Autónoma de México (UNAM).

—— (1981). *Los usos de Gramsci.* Mexico: Folios Ediciones.

Portelli, Hugues (1973). *Gramsci y el bloque histórico.* Buenos Aires: Siglo XXI Editores.

—— (1977). *Gramsci y la cuestión religiosa: una sociología marxista de la religión.* Madrid: Editorial Laia.

Potash, Robert (1971). *The Army and Politics in Argentina.* Stanford, Calif.: Stanford University Press.

Poulantzas, Nicos (1976). *Poder político y clases sociales en el estado capitalista*. Mexico City: Siglo XXI Editores.

———— (1977). "Introducción al estudio de la hegemonía en el estado." In *Hegemonía y dominación en el estado moderno*, 4th ed. Colección Cuadernos de Pasado y Presente no. 48. Mexico City: Siglo XXI Editores.

Puiggrós, Adriana (1983). "Discusiones y tendencias en la educación popular latinoamericana." *Nueva Antropología*, 5, no. 21 (June): 15–39.

———— (1984). *La educación popular en América Latina*. Mexico City: Nueva Imagen.

Puiggrós, Rodolfo (1965). *Historia crítica de los partidos políticos Argentinos*. Buenos Aires: Carlos Alvarez editor.

———— (1971a). *El Peronismo: sus causas*. Foreword by Juan Perón. Buenos Aires: Carlos Pérez editor.

———— (1971b). *Las izquierdas y el problema nacional*. Buenos Aires: Carlos Pérez Editor.

Ramos, Abelardo (1959). *Perón: historia de su triunfo y su derrota*. Buenos Aires: Amerindia.

———— (1961). *Revolución y contrarevolución en Argentina: las masas en nuestra historia*. Buenos Aires: La Reja.

———— (1981). *La era del peronismo*. Buenos Aires: Ediciones del Mar Dulce.

Raurich, Héctor (1976). *Hégel y la lógica de la Pasión*. Buenos Aires: Ediciones Marymar.

Recalde, Héctor (1985). *La Iglesia y la cuestión social*. Buenos Aires: Centro Editor de América Latina.

Richard, Pablo (1978). "América Latina: el rol político e histórico de la Iglesia." *Nueva Sociedad*, 36 (May/June).

———— (1980). *La iglesia latinoamericana entre el temor y la esperanza: apuntes teológicos para la década de los años 80*. San José, Costa Rica: DEI.

———— (1984). *Virada do século na América Latina*. São Paulo: Edições Paulinas.

———— (1985). *Raíces de la teología latinoamericana*. San José, Costa Rica: CEHILA-DEI.

———— (1987). *Death of Christendoms. Birth of the Church*. Maryknoll, N.Y.: Orbis Books.

Rodríguez, Jaime (1978). "Análisis crítico al marco teórico de la secularización en las relaciones religión y sociedad." *Revista Paraguaya de Sociología*, Asunción, 15, no. 41 (January–April): 35–56.

Rodríguez Zúñiga, L. (1978). *Para una lectura crítica de Durkheim*. Madrid: Akal Editor.

Romero, José Luis (1975). *Las ideas políticas en Argentina*. Buenos Aires: Fondo de Cultura Económica.

Romero Carranza, Ambrosio, Alberto Rodríguez Varela, & Eduardo Ventura

Flores Pirán (1975). *Historia Política de la Argentina*, 3 vols. Buenos Aires: Ediciones Pannedille.

Rositi, Franco (1979). "Ideología." In Paolo Farneti, ed., *Politica e societá*, pp. 447–62. Firenze: La Nuova Italia.

Roueanet, Sergio P. (1978). *Imaginario e Dominação*. Rio de Janeiro: Tempo Brasileiro.

Rude, George (1980). *Ideology and Popular Protest*. New York: Pantheon Books.

Russell, Bertrand (1973). *Religión y ciencia*. Mexico City: Fondo de Cultura Económica.

Sacheri, Carlos A. (1970). *La iglesia clandestina*. Buenos Aires: Ediciones del Cruzamante.

——— (1975). *El orden natural*. Lima: Instituto de Estudios y Promoción Social.

Sacerdotes para America Latina (SAL) (n.d.). *Un compromiso sacerdotal en la lucha de clases. Documentos 1972–1978*. Bogota.

Sacred Congregation for the Doctrine of the Faith (1984, August 6). "Instruction on Certain Aspects of the Theology of Liberation." Mimeograph. Vatican City.

Salvadori, Massimo L. (1970). *Gramsci e il problema storico della democrazia*. Turin: G. Einaudi.

Samuelson, Kurt (1957). *Religion and Economic Action*. Stockholm: Scandinavian University Books.

Sánchez Aizcorbe, C. (1973). "Reflexión crítica desde la filosofía sobre la socialización marxista, no-socialista y peronista." *Strómata*, 29, nos. 1/2 (January–June): 94–129.

Sánchez Gamarra, Alfredo (1949). *Vida del padre Grote: redentorista*. Buenos Aires: Editorial Stadium.

Sanders, Thomas (1967). "The Catholic Left in Brazil." In Kallman Silvert, ed., *Churches and States*. New York: American Universities Field Staff.

Scannone, J. C. (1973). "La Teología de la liberación." *CIAS* (Buenos Aires), no. 221: 5–10.

——— (1975). "Hacia una pastoral de la cultura." *Strómata*, 30, nos. 3/4 (July–December): 237–59.

——— (1976). "¿Vigencia de la sabiduría cristiana en el ethos popular de nuestro pueblo?" *Strómata*, 31, nos. 3/4 (July–December): 253–87.

Schaff, Adam (1980). Ideología y marxismo. Mexico City: Editorial Grijalbo.

Schmitter, Philipe C. (1975). *Corporatism and Public Policy in Authoritarian Portugal*. Contemporary Political Sociology Series, Vol. 1, no. 06-011. Beverly Hills, Calif.: Sage.

Sebreli, Juan José (1990). *Eva Perón: aventurera o militante*. Buenos Aires: Editorial La Pleyade.

Segunda Conferencia General del Episcopado Latinoamericano (1971). *Documentos finales de Medellín*. Buenos Aires: Ediciones Paulinas.

Segundo, Juan Luis, S. J. (1975). "Condicionamientos actuales de la reflexión teológica en Latinoamerica." In *Encuentro Latinoamericano de teología*, pp. 91–101. Mexico City.

——— (1985). *Theology and the Church: A Response to Cardinal Ratzinger and a Warning to the Whole Church*. Minneapolis, Minn.: Wiston Press.

Selser, Gregorio (1972). *El Onganiato: la espada y el hisopo*. Buenos Aires: Carlos Samonta Editor.

Seve, Lucien & Jacques Milhau (1974). *Filosofía y Religión*. Mexico City: Ediciones de Cultura Popular.

Sherover-Marcuse, Erica (1986). *Emancipation & Consciousness*. Oxford: Basil Blackwell.

Shoceck, H. (1973). *Diccionario de Sociología*. Barcelona, Spain: Herder.

Silva Gotay, Samuel (1981). *El pensamiento cristiano revolucionario en América Latina y el Caribe*. Salamanca, Spain: Ediciones Sígueme.

Solari, Aldo E., Rolando Franco, & Joel Jutkowitz (1976). *Teoría, acción social y desarrollo en América latina*. Mexico City: ILPES—Siglo XXI Editores.

Soneira, Abelardo Jorge (1981). *La inmigración y el proyecto liberal*. Buenos Aires: Centro Editor Argentino.

——— (1982). *La "religión del pueblo" y la identidad cultural argentina*, Vol. 2. Buenos Aires: Cuadernos de Iglesia y Sociedad, Centro de Investigación y Orientación Social.

Stepan, Alfred (1978). *The State and Society: Peru in Comparative Perspective*. Princeton, N.J.: Princeton University Press.

Sweeney, Ernest S. (1970). *Foreign Missionaries in Argentina, 1938–1962*. Cuernavaca, Mexico: CIDOC.

Teilhard de Chardin, Pierre (1965). *The Phenomenon of Man*, trans. Bernard Wall. Introduction by Julian Huxley. New York: Harper and Row.

——— (1969). *Human Energy*, trans. J. M. Cohen. London: Collins.

Texier, Jacques (1966). *Gramsci*. Paris: Segiers.

Therborn, Göran (1980). *The Ideology of Power and the Power of Ideology*. London: Verso.

Torres, Camilo (1966). *Camilo Torres*. Cuernavaca, Mexico: CIDOC.

Torres, Carlos Alberto (1978). "Análisis del proceso político y económico en la coyuntura argentina de 1973–74." Master's Thesis. Facultad Latinoamericana de Ciencias Sociales, Mexico City.

——— (1979a). "Religión y praxis social en América Latina." *Franciscanum*, 21, no. 61 (January–April): 89–104.

——— (1979b). "Teoría de la dependencia: nota crítica sobre su metodología histórico-estructural." *Nueva Sociedad* (Caracas) (May/June): 70–86.

——— (1982). "From the 'Pedagogy of the Oppressed' to a 'Luta Continua': Essay on the Political Pedagogy of Paulo Freire." *Education with Production Review*, Gaborone, Bostwana (November): 76–97.

——— (1985). *La praxis educativa de Paulo Freire*. 4th ed. Mexico City: Gernika.

——— (1989). "The Mexican State and Democracy: The Ambiguities of Corporatism." *International Journal of Politics, Culture and Society*, 2, no. 4 (Summer): 563–86.

——— (1990). *The Politics of Nonformal Education in Latin America*. New York: Praeger.

——— (1991a). "Argentina." In Philip Altbach, ed., *International Encyclopedia of Comparative Higher Education*, pp. 869–83. New York: Garland Publishing.

——— (1991b). "The State, Nonformal Education, and Socialism in Cuba, Nicaragua, and Grenada." *Comparative Education Review*, 35, no. 1 (February): 110–30.

Troeltsch, Ernest (1971). *The Absoluteness of Christianity and the History of Religions*, trans. David Reid. Introduction by James Luther Adams. Richmond, Va.: John Knox Press.

Universidad Católica Andres Bello (1977). *Iglesia latinoamericana, política y socialismo*. Caracas, Venezuela: Universidad Católica Andres Bello.

Universidad Católica de Santiago del Estero (1983). *La religiosidad popular en Santiago del Estero*. Santiago del Estero, Argentina: Ediciones de la Universidad Católica de Santiago del Estero.

Uricoechea, Fernando (1980). *The Patrimonial Foundations of the Brazilian Bureaucratic State*. Berkeley: University of California Press.

Vallier, Iván (1967). "Religious Elites: Differentiation and Development in Roman Catholicism." In Seymour M. Lipset & Aldo Solari, eds., *Elites in Latin America*. London: Oxford University Press.

——— (1971). *Catolicismo, control social y modernización en América Latina*. Buenos Aires: Amorrortu Editores.

——— (1972). *La iglesia latinoamericana y la política después de Medellín*. Bogota: CELAM-IPLA.

Various authors (1974). "Prassi di Liberazioni e fede cristiana." *Concilium*, Brescia, Italy, no. 6.

Various authors (1976). *Fe cristiana y cambio social en América Latina*. Salamanca, Spain: Ediciones Sígueme.

Various authors (1984). *Quince cristianos en la revolución*. Managua: Editorial Nueva Nicaragua.

Veliz, Claudio (1980). *The Centralist Tradition of Latin America*. Princeton, N.J.: Princeton University Press.

Vidales, Raúl (1978). *Cristianismo anti-burgués*. San José, Costa Rica: DEI.

Vilas, Carlos María (1984). *Perfiles de la revolución sandinista*. Buenos Aires: Legasa.

Wackenheim, Charles (1973). *La quiebra de la religión en Karl Marx*. Barcelona, Spain: Ediciones Península.

Weber, Max (1955). *La ética protestante y el espíritu del capitalismo*. Madrid: Revista de Derecho Privado.

———— (1964). *Economy and Society: An Outline of Interpretive Sociology*. Ed. G. Roth & C. Wittich. 3 vols. New York: Bedminster Press.

———— (1973). *Ensayos sobre metodología sociológica*. Buenos Aires: Amorrortu Editores.

Wiarda, Howard J. (1973). "Toward a Framework for the Study of Political Change in the Iberic-Latin Tradition: The Corporatist Model." *World Politics*, no. 25 (January): 206–35.

————, ed. (1974). *Politics and Social Change in Latin America: The Distinct Tradition*. Boston: University of Massachusetts Press.

Zachariah, Matthew (1985). *Revolution through Reform: A Comparison of Sarvodaya and Conscientization*. New York: Praeger.

Zeitlin, Irving (1968). *Ideology and the Development of Sociological Theory*. Englewood Cliffs, N.J.: Prentice-Hall.

# Index